# The Sparkle from the Coal

# The Sparkle from the Coal

*Rowan Williams' Theology of Imagination*

Barbara Howard

scm press

© Barbara Howard 2024

Published in 2024 by SCM Press
Editorial office
3rd Floor, Invicta House,
110 Golden Lane
London EC1Y 0TG, UK
www.scmpress.co.uk

SCM Press is an imprint of Hymns Ancient & Modern Ltd
(a registered charity)

Hymns Ancient & Modern® is a registered trademark of
Hymns Ancient & Modern Ltd
13A Hellesdon Park Road, Norwich,
Norfolk NR6 5DR, UK

All rights reserved. No part of this publication may be reproduced,
stored in a retrieval system, or transmitted,
in any form or by any means, electronic, mechanical,
photocopying or otherwise, without the prior permission of
the publisher, SCM Press.

Barbara Howard has asserted her right under the Copyright,
Designs and Patents Act 1988 to be identified as the Author of this Work

British Library Cataloguing in Publication data
A catalogue record for this book is available
from the British Library

Scripture quotations are from New Revised Standard Version Bible: Anglicized Edition, copyright © 1989, 1995 National Council of the Churches of Christ in the United States of America. Used by permission. All rights reserved worldwide.

ISBN: 978-0-334-06629-3

Typeset by Regent Typesetting

# Contents

| | |
|---|---|
| *Preface* | vii |
| Introduction | 1 |
| **Part One: Imagination: Its Nature and Operation** | 21 |
| 1 Imagination | 23 |
| 2 Symbolization: Meaning-making | 45 |
| 3 Analogy and the Structure of Reality | 62 |
| **Part Two: Desire in Williams' Theology** | 79 |
| 4 Divine Desire | 81 |
| 5 Human Desire | 99 |
| 6 The Church and the Transformation of Desire | 119 |
| **Part Three: Imagination in the Work of Rowan Williams** | 139 |
| 7 Language in a Communicative Universe | 141 |
| 8 *Poiesis* I: 'Making Other' | 157 |
| 9 *Poiesis* II: 'Making Strange' | 176 |
| 10 Rowan Williams' Theology of Imagination | 198 |
| Conclusion | 215 |
| Afterword: The Sparkle from the Coal | 220 |
| Felin Uchaf: Poetry in the Roundhouse | 220 |
| *Bibliography* | 223 |
| *Index* | 239 |

# Preface

This book had its distant genesis in a sermon delivered by Rowan Williams on the Feast of the Annunciation, 1992.[1] As I listened to that sermon, I heard theology presented in a form resembling poetry. It stirred my imagination and aroused in me the desire to explore the distinctive imaginative vision of this Anglican Church leader who is both Welsh bard and subtle theologian and whose works combine theological depth with the sensitive insights of a poet.

The theme of Williams' Annunciation sermon is the pregnancy of the girl called to 'bring God to birth in the world'.[2] Her pregnancy is the supreme expression of what Williams names as 'the strangeness of God that waits at the heart of [the] familiar'.[3] It is the guarantee that the world we inhabit is still 'pregnant with a different kind of life',[4] the life made known in Jesus, son of Mary, Son of God. Williams reminds us that it is through Jesus Christ that, with imaginations transfigured by grace, we may now glimpse the different kind of life of God present in the midst of the confusion and suffering of our world.

The image of a pregnant world is one of the many images illuminating Williams' writings, each capturing a key feature of his imaginative vision. Resonant with multiple allusions, the image of pregnancy alerts us to the mystery of generativity, divine and human, and to the presence of divine possibility within every aspect of earthly existence. It draws on human experience to point to the in-and-beyond relation of Creator and creation.

More recently Williams turned to the fifth-century ascetic Diadokos of Photike for the title of his study of Orthodox spirituality, *Looking East in Winter*. There he states that 'looking east in winter we feel the warmth of the sun on our faces, while still sensing an icy chill at our backs.'[5] Here the image confronts us with the ambiguity of human existence, experienced as unforeseen moments of grace-enabled joy in the midst of our confused daily struggles.

Selected for the title of this book, the image of the 'sparkle from the coal'[6] was borrowed by Williams to attest to his constant awareness of the lure of divine love, the 'magnet of all our hearts',[7] sparking a yearning within the dark recesses of the human spirit and drawing it upwards to the light of its Creator. Again, God is imaged as in-and-beyond the created order, active as the source towards whom we are allured by the power of divine love.

I have been teacher, welfare worker, parish priest and hospital chaplain. Three of those occupations brought me face to face with misery, poverty, violence and the abyss of tragic loss. I have stuttered to find words to console parents of stillborn twins, of teenage children killed in motor accidents, of a young man with kidney failure who, on turning 18, chose to disconnect from dialysis. While I couldn't find words, I somehow knew that I was held by grace as I sought to hold others in their grief. It was at times such as those that I experienced the 'sparkle from the coal' of human misery and found God present in and beyond my finite experience.

My intention in studying Williams' imagination was to discover the theological roots of his capacity to glimpse presence in absence, grace in darkness, and that sharp lifting of spirit that is 'the sparkle from the coal'.

*Barbara Howard*
*Trinity 2023*

## Notes

1 The text of the sermon is to be found in Rowan Williams, *A Ray of Darkness: Sermons and Reflections* (Lanham, MD: Cowley, 1995), pp. 13–15.
2 Williams, *A Ray of Darkness*, p. 13.
3 Rowan Williams, *Ponder These Things: Praying with Icons of the Virgin* (Mulgrave, Vic: John Garrett, 2002), p. xvii.
4 Williams, *Ponder These Things*, p. xvii.
5 Rowan Williams, *Looking East in Winter: Contemporary Thought and the Eastern Christian Tradition* (London: Bloomsbury Continuum, 2021), p. 8.
6 Rupert Shortt, *Rowan's Rule: The Biography of the Archbishop* (London: Hodder & Stoughton, 2008), p. 105. The reference is to the medieval text *The Cloud of Unknowing In the Which a Soul Is Oned with God*, 2nd edn with Introduction by Evelyn Underhill (London: Merchant Books, 2021), p. 22.
7 Shortt, *Rowan's Rule*, p. 106.

Unless otherwise stated, throughout the book all emphases/italics in quotations are original.

# Introduction

> If there is one thing I long for above all else, it's that the years to come may see Christianity in this country able again to capture the imagination of our culture, to draw the strongest energies of our thinking and feeling into the exploration of what our creeds put before us.[1]

## 'A distinctively Christian imagination'

'Imagination' was a key word in Rowan Williams' engagement with the public at the time of his election as Archbishop of Canterbury in 2002. His first press statement included the words quoted above, and his enthronement sermon in the following year concluded with a prayer that the Church be given 'an imagination set on fire by the vision of God the Holy Trinity'. Those statements highlight the importance he accords to human imagination in creating and communicating a vision of the Christian life that engages the energies and passions of a whole community. On his accession to the role of Archbishop of Canterbury, his stated primary concern was to share that powerful vision with the wider audience then made available to him.

A lecture delivered to the Hay-on-Wye Festival in June 2002 gives an insight into the urgency of Williams' concern to 'nourish' human imagination.[2] In that lecture, entitled 'Has Secularism Failed?', he laments the 'imaginative bereavement'[3] of 'programmatic' secularism with its instrumental and managerial focus.[4] Missing from that form of secularism is the sense that human existence is influenced by anything other than the 'tangible', the result being that both art and religion are thereby discounted. Williams' argument is that the imaginative resources of religion and art draw on dimensions of existence inaccessible to instrumental reason and raise questions about meaning unanswerable by a culture of consumerist materialism.

In somewhat more Wittgensteinian terms, he takes up a similar theme in the 2008 preface to his study of the work of Dostoevsky.[5] There he argues that 'no system of perceiving and receiving the world can fail to depend upon imagination, the capacity to see and speak into and out of a world that defies any final settlement as to how it shall be described.'[6]

Asserting that 'the forming of a corporate imagination is something that continues to be the more or less daily business of religious believers ... a process immeasurably more sophisticated than ... repetitive dogmatism', he concludes that 'some of the most decisive and innovative cultural currents of the history of the West' are to be attributed to the exercise by creative minds of a 'distinctively Christian imagination'.[7]

Imagination is thus seen by Williams as playing a critical role in the formation of personal and communal world views. He holds engagement with the creative potential of imagination to be essential in the development of a 'distinctively Christian' vision of human existence. As he has repeatedly stressed, the Christian faith is not a matter of a cognitive assent to dogma but the opening of imagination to a world 'immeasurably larger' and 'stranger' than is humanly conceivable.[8] This is the world revealed in the life, death and resurrection of Jesus of Nazareth, the world identified as the Kingdom of God.

Surprisingly, the emphasis Williams places on imagination is not matched by an extended theoretical and theological exploration of its nature and operation. The many references to imagination scattered among his voluminous writings lack precise definition, their significance deriving from their context and associations. It is primarily to his work on language, aesthetics and literature, as well as to his discussions of poetry, that we must look for an understanding of the importance he attributes to imagination for human development and community-formation.

The argument of this book is that those works on language and aesthetics are the fruit of a coherent and well-articulated metaphysical and theological vision, the vision referred to in the enthronement sermon, 'the vision of God the Holy Trinity'. For Rowan Williams, all Christian doctrine issues from belief in the divine life as an inexhaustible excess of 'ecstatic, kenotic' love. The vision of God as an eternally generating, responsive and overflowing relation of love is at the heart of Williams' understanding of the Christian faith, as it is expressed in the doctrines of creation, incarnation, redemption and sanctification.[9] That vision of the inexhaustible excess of divine love will be shown to be fundamental to his conception of imagination.

Any exploration of Williams' theology must, however, take account of the complexity of his concept of divine love, which is shown to encompass the reality of suffering and evil in an imperfect and 'fallen' world. As a theologian, Williams is alert not only to the many dangerously distorted expressions of imagination that result from human sin, but also to the difficulty of retaining a hope-filled perspective in the face of the tragedy and suffering that are undeniable features of contingent human existence.[10]

INTRODUCTION

A 1983 conference address offers insight into the tension experienced in maintaining the balance between trust in the sufficiency of divine grace and an Augustinian awareness of human sinfulness:

> Neither despair nor bland assurance, but faith is the mark of the Christian. [And] faith does depend on an ability to 'entertain' the Augustinian picture, an ability to see the world as unclear and the human spirit as confused and imprisoned in fantasies.[11]

The address goes on to probe the effort involved in discerning the presence of God amid the darkness of finite existence, an effort requiring from him 'the sparkle from the coal', that intense, persistent act of faithful love directed towards the 'cloud' veiling God from human vision.[12] What sustains him in that search is, he says, a constant awareness of 'the immeasurably more dreadful void of Jesus' prayer in Gethsemane and on the cross, that bloody crown of faith and love'.[13] As is evidenced by a perusal of Williams' writings, the frequent references to Jesus' very human anguish at those moments form a counterbalance to the somewhat idealistic tone of certain of this poet-theologian's declarations concerning 'the radiant beauty ... of the gospel ... [as] an endless gift of unconditional love'.[14]

The image of searching for the 'sparkle from the coal' also points to the significance accorded by Williams to apophasis, the *via negativa*. In line with the Orthodox theologian Vladimir Lossky,[15] Williams contends that apophasis is the 'attitude which should undergird *all* theological discourse and lead it towards the silence of contemplation and communion'.[16] It is this attitude that controls his whole approach to theology, alerting him to the danger of theological dogmatism and rendering him wary of all-inclusive attempts at systematization. For Williams, knowledge of God is never final. It is always open to further disclosure, and being relational, the result of personal encounter, is refined and enhanced by ongoing 'conversation' with others in and beyond the Christian Church.[17] Holding such a perspective, it is not surprising that he should be especially receptive to the transcendent dimension of imagination with its capacity to move beyond the actual to envisage alternative and hitherto unforeseen possibilities for human existence.

The argument I present in this study is that Rowan Williams attributes the human capacity for imagination to the 'energy' of divine love overflowing into creation. The corollary of that conclusion is that there is an inherent relation between imagination and human desire, and that both are subject to distortion in a 'fallen' world. Williams' position is that the renewal of human nature in Christ redirects desire and imagination towards their divine source, thereby initiating a lifelong process of grace-enabled transformation. Transformed in this way, imagination is both creative and eschatological and has an integral role in the realization of the divine purpose for creation.

I contend that these conclusions form the outline of a coherent theology of imagination, which is never formally articulated or systematized but which is nevertheless clearly discernible in the remarkably diverse writings of this Anglican priest who combines the skills of subtle theologian, incisive literary critic, sensitive spiritual director and perceptive poet.

My further contention is that the imaginative vision Williams holds up to a sceptical Western world derives its distinctiveness from the multiple sources from which he draws his inspiration: literature, art and music, aesthetics, Eastern and Western monastic practices, as well as a thorough grounding in patristic and contemporary theology. Accounting for the complexity of the vision is the tension maintained between the cataphatic and the apophatic, and the actual and the potential.

The position taken in this study is that the tension is to be attributed to Williams' grounding of the relation between God and creation in the *analogia entis*, as expounded by Erich Przywara.[18] Drawing on Przywara's insight into the 'structure' of reality as the analogical relation of 'in and beyond',[19] Williams' metaphysical theology maintains the analogical tension of 'non-dual, non-identity' between the infinite God, incommensurably Other than creation, and finite creation, ever dependent on its source in the 'excess' of divine love. That tension is conceived by both Przywara and Williams as characterizing the human condition.

The second source of tension for modern minds is Williams' insistence on both the inexhaustibility and the ultimate incomprehensibility of divine love. Such love, being infinite, is inexhaustible in its 'excess' of unfailing self-dispossession despite human rejection. To finite minds, it is incomprehensible in that it offers the freedom intrinsic to unconditional love, the freedom either to resist or to respond with a similar movement of self-dispossession. Incomprehensible too is the persistence of that love despite the human capacity for inflicting horrific harm on self and others. It is therefore not surprising that such a vision is labelled by many as impossibly unrealistic. It is a vision that Williams believes to be comprehensible only as a result of the transformation of imagination through a life-changing encounter with Jesus Christ.

# INTRODUCTION

## 'Emmaus'

Such an encounter is described in Williams' poem 'Emmaus',[20] a dense crystallization of the tension experienced by finite humanity in the presence of the divine.

> First the sun, then the shadow,
> so that I screw my eyes to see
> my friend's face, and its lines seem
> different, and the voice shakes in the hot air.
> Out of the rising white dust, feet
> tread a shape, and, out of step,
> another flat sound, stamped between voice
> and ears, dancing in the gaps, and dodging
> where words and feet do not fall.
>
> When our eyes meet, I see bewilderment
> (like mine): we cannot learn
> the rhythm we are asked to walk,
> and what we hear is not each other.
> Between us is filled up, the silence
> is filled up, lines of our hands
> and faces pushed into shape
> by the solid stranger, and the static
> breaks up our waves like dropped stones.
>
> So it is necessary to carry him with us,
> cupped between hands and profiles,
> so that the table is filled up, and as
> the food is set and the first wine splashes,
> a solid thumb and finger tear the thunderous
> grey bread. Now it is cold, even indoors,
> and the light falls sharply on our bones;
> the rain breathes out hard, dust blackens,
> and our released voices shine with water.

In the retelling of the Emmaus story, the poet presents us with the disconcerting shift of perspective effected by an encounter with the risen Jesus who comes as 'stranger' to all human preconceptions.[21] Told from the point of view of one of the two disciples on the Emmaus road, the experience of walking the familiar route home is suddenly made strange by the presence of the stranger who comes to join them. His presence seems to distort the usual landmarks, even effecting a subtle alteration to the other disciple's well-known features and voice. Creating still more discomfort is the pace set by the stranger. It is out of step with that of the two disciples, 'dancing' and 'dodging' in the gaps of their experience, obedient to a different, unexpected, unknown rhythm.

The two companions find themselves thrown off-kilter, 'bewildered' by the different rhythm of the stranger's steps, and by the silence that becomes a solid pressure, filling the gap between them, and pushing their faces 'into shape', into their true alignment. It is as though the stranger's disturbing presence creates a series of electric shocks, 'like dropped stones', jolting them out of the familiar rhythm of their former existence and transforming them. With the gap between their separate existences now filled by this mysterious companion, they find themselves bound together with him, such that they 'carry' him with them into their home, 'cupped between hands and profiles'.[22]

The climax comes in the sharing of the meal together where it is the stranger who takes the initiative. With a seemingly 'thunderous' roar, he tears apart the bread and their whole lives. Now, everything is seen and experienced differently. Illusions are dispersed. Comfortable, security-creating fantasies are shattered. The harsh reality of human existence, subject as it is to 'cold' and to the 'sharp' clarity of unshaded light and the misery of 'rain' and the transience of 'dust', is now revealed in all its starkness.

It is in the last line that new possibilities become evident. Released from the imprisonment of delusory fantasy by the 'water' (of baptism), the disciples are now enabled to speak with voices that 'shine' with the ever-renewed, and renewing, 'water' of the risen Christ's fathomless life.

The shock of the final lines of the poem dispels any illusion that Christian faith serves as a shelter from the stark realities of human existence. In that last stanza we find ourselves confronted with the disconcerting tension integral to Rowan Williams' imagination. The vision presented is the opposite of 'pie in the sky'. Far from being a comfortable retreat, Christian life is revealed as both demanding and liberating, as a challenge to maintain a realistic clarity of vision, while giving free expression to the glimpse of divine glory that 'shines' through the visible universe. It summons us to take account of the tragic dimension of life as well as of its beauty and wonder. Offering a divine perspective on events, it encourages the believer to proceed, like the Emmaus disciples, with confidence in the transforming, renewing presence of the risen Christ whatever the circumstance. It is that complex, multi-faceted conception of Christian imagination that I have set out to explore.

My aim of identifying Williams' theology of imagination defines the narrow focus of this study. In the role of acknowledged Christian leader, Williams continues to write and speak on a wide range of subjects, extending beyond academic theology to social and political commentary, history, education, ethics, economics, inter-faith dialogue, spirituality and the arts.[23] Commentary on those areas of concern is well outside the limits of my current project. I have confined my investigation to the significance accorded to imagination in Williams' theological account of the relation between God and creation, a relation that gives rise to the human capacity for 'making'.

Even within that specified limit, it will be impossible to give adequate attention to certain related contemporary directions in philosophical and aesthetic theology, namely, to developments in Augustinian studies[24] and in such movements as Neo-Thomism, Neo-Platonism and Radical Orthodoxy.[25] While there are commonalities of emphasis between Williams' thought and those lines of enquiry, there are also important differences that cannot be pursued by this study.

It should further be noted that the chapter on the role of the Christian Church in the formation of Christian imagination is not intended as a critically comprehensive examination of Williams' ecclesiology. Also limited by space is the attention given to sacramental theology, an area of particular importance for Williams and considered by him to play an essential role in the process of Christian formation.[26] Finally, it is necessary to note that the discussion of Williams' theological anthropology in Part Two focuses primarily on the significance of desire in human experience and is not to be regarded as a comprehensive account of his concept of human nature.

## Williams' methodology

When asked about his methodological starting point, Williams' response is that theology, like all human knowledge, always begins 'in the middle of things'.[27] In this reply we detect the significant influence of the Wittgenstein of the *Philosophical Investigations* whose observations of the working of language and culture serve as a reminder that we are 'always already' immersed in an immensely complex socio-linguistic context which influences interpretation and must be constantly revised through ongoing attention to other perspectives.[28] There is accordingly no final objective standpoint free of the impact of context. All thinking takes as its starting point the specific linguistic and cultural context in which it occurs and is always tentative, a matter of 'taking time' and remaining open to further development.[29]

Significant also for Williams' methodology is his exposure to monastic spirituality, especially within the Orthodox tradition with its emphasis on *apophasis*, 'the self-revelation of God in silence'.[30] Stating that 'theology begins as a celebratory phenomenon' in 'the preconscious ... "informal" theology of prayer, art and holy action',[31] he recognizes that, if such inchoate awareness is to communicate meaning, it must be developed as 'fully self-conscious reflection'.[32] He accordingly identifies three consecutive but interrelated theological modes: the *celebratory*, the *communicative* and the *critical*, each of which requires, and leads into, the others, in an unending cyclical process.

The celebratory mode in which God meets us in the middle of our daily experience is the genesis of all theology. God 'speaks' to us in our everyday existence within the finite world. As argued in his 2013 Gifford lectures,[33] Williams considers the universe itself to be communicative.[34] It is the communication of 'divine *Sophia*, the wisdom of the heart of things'.[35] 'What *is*, is because God addresses it, because God relates to it.'[36] In the lectures, he sets out to demonstrate that human knowledge functions against a 'hinterland of significance'[37] that is not directly accessible but is expressible in the unfinished, temporal character of human language.[38] It is this 'hinterland of significance' that gives meaning to existence itself, makes knowledge possible and is the primal address to which any communicative act constitutes a response.[39]

The substance of Williams' argument[40] is that the oddities and difficulties of human language bring us to the 'edge' of the literal; that is, to the limit of any straightforward 'parallel between what we say and what we perceive'.[41] At this limit, however, we do not cease to speak, since existence continues to 'interrogate' us, raising ever more questions.[42] Our sense of being interrogated by existence brings both the apprehension of 'dependent origination' and also the possibility of 'something ... that operates on another plane of awareness'.[43] Pursuing language to the 'edge' of pure description thus shifts speech to a different register, intended to point to, but not define, the context and possibility of all speaking: 'the framework within which this intelligible environment as a whole becomes intelligible at a different level'.[44] It is at this point that religious language is needed.[45] In Christian terms, this is the language of revelation, language which functions as representation rather than description.

The distinction between 'description' and 'representation' is critical to Williams' argument. As opposed to description, with its postulation of a direct unmediated relation between word and 'fact', representation operates 'within a schema of understanding, a complex of use and association or resonance and recognition patterns or habits'.[46] Both the thinking/

speaking subject and the object of speech and thought are encompassed within this schema. Genuine representation participates in what it perceives, in the attempt to 'embody, translate, make present or re-form' that perception.[47] In other words, to truly represent something in the outer world involves subjective participation in the thing represented, such participation both being affected by, and affecting, what is represented.

Representation thus has the character of metaphor, conveying both 'is' and 'is not'. Like a musical score, it is open to a range of interpretations.[48] The language of religion is necessarily representational since it functions in the context of a horizon of meaning in which the object of knowledge, God, is 'active "beyond" the grasp of the knower'.[49] The divine may be known only through participation, rather than detached objective observation. Participatory representation is thus the mode of the divine revelation imparted through the Hebrew and Christian scriptures.[50]

Williams argues that religious awareness begins when speech reaches the limits of its descriptive capacity and is obliged to continue in the register of participatory representation. We become conscious of responding to that to which our speech is ever gesturing but cannot define.[51] We recognize that we are first addressed by that 'hinterland of significance' to which we give the name 'God'. We recognize ourselves as beings who are addressed by God and who are accordingly dependent on divine address for our very existence and for knowledge of ourselves and our world.

Vehicles for such address are the natural world, other people, artistic expression, liturgy, ritual, sacrament and the sacred scriptures. All theological reflection must therefore begin with the awareness, however inchoate, of God's speaking to us in the situations of daily life, in the creative arts, in the more explicitly embodied language of religious ritual, and especially in the representational language of Holy Scripture. *Celebration*, as understood by Williams, is consequently the primary mode of theological speech.[52] Any other beginning risks the distortions of absolutizing the ineffable, of seeking unattainable certainty and claiming an impossible objectivity. We must begin from divine address communicated in the 'middle of things'.

Human response can, however, never be final as there is always more to be thought and said.[53] The *communicative* mode thus inevitably follows, as we seek to put words to the primal celebratory moment of address and try to *represent* the experience through the limitations of conceptual language and the varieties of imaginative expression. We do so for the purpose of sharing that experience with others and passing it on to subsequent generations. Williams demonstrates that such attempts are never final.[54] They invite further response in an ongoing, inevitably inconclusive dialogue which gives rise to differences of interpretation, additional understandings, contextual implications and ever new insights.[55] Further representation is always necessary.

The *critical* mode is the ethical consequence of the failure to give adequate expression to celebratory insights. How does one speak truthfully in attempting to articulate what is known through participation but which is always beyond adequate representation?[56] That is the issue with which Williams grapples repeatedly as he dialogues with a wide range of conversation partners drawn from various disciplines.[57] He concludes that it is the *difficulty* of speaking 'truly' that is itself an index of truthfulness. Truth lies in the continuing to question and to dialogue, and in the recognition that attempts to convey what is beyond language require the 'excessive' speech of metaphor, symbol, drama and paradox.[58]

The ultimate criterion of truthfulness is, however, what he calls 'achieved silence'; that is, the silence that results from this long-drawn-out struggle. It is the apophatic silence of utter dispossession, of knowing our displacement from the centre of existence.[59] It is truth conceived as ever greater openness to that which is beyond representation. Thus, we come again to the mode of *celebration*, but we come now changed, chastened, more deeply dependent, but also with firmer conviction and a fuller capacity for participation in the divine life.

The sequence followed by Williams in the process of theological reflection bears a marked resemblance to the hermeneutical arc proposed by Paul Ricoeur.[60] That arc is conceived by Ricoeur as movement from an initial grasp of a work's meaning (first naïveté), through a process of critical judgement (hermeneutic of suspicion), to an appreciation of the work considered as a whole in relation to its separate parts and its context (second naïveté). While Williams does not use the terms employed by Ricoeur, his methodology follows a similar arc.

Also similar is the beginning point adopted by Ricoeur in relation to poetry and scriptural revelation, that of 'participation-in or belonging-to an order of things that precedes our capacity to oppose ourselves to things taken as objects opposed to a subject'.[61] For the French philosopher, such participation is the result of God's initial invitation to us to respond through the 'opening' of the imagination.[62] From the similarity of the language of 'participation' and 'responsive opening' employed by the two thinkers, it may be argued that the insights earlier developed by Ricoeur are of significance for Williams' own conceptualization of religious language as the participatory representation of human responses to divine invitation.

Williams' methodology is decisive for the methodology to be followed in studying his theology of imagination. I also begin in the middle with Williams' experience of encounter with God as it is expressed in his poetry, his spiritual reflections and in the 'pondering' evoked as he 'pray[s] with icons'.[63] As evidenced by the 'Emmaus' poem, the most vivid expressions of Williams' imagination are to be found in these celebratory forms. Not the raw impressions of 'first naïveté', these forms are the product of the full cycle of critical reflection, and witness to a 'second naïveté' of mature theological insight. As such, they express the struggle to represent in language that which is known through both participation and critical reflection but which lies beyond mere description. Born out of the author's struggle, they oblige the listener/reader to undertake a similar struggle and thus share the participatory event that was the source of the poem.

An example is the first stanza of the 'Emmaus' poem. Here, by means of the staccato rhythm created by the rapid succession of short, one-syllable words, the listener/reader is exposed, with the disciples, to the disconcerting, disruptive presence of the stranger. With the appearance of the stranger, however, in the second half of the stanza, the abrupt monosyllabic rhythm is interspersed with longer continuous verbs: 'rising', 'dancing' and 'dodging'. Contrasting with the heavy downbeat of the monosyllables, the upward intonation of the verbal forms brings a sense of lightness, freedom and even joy. The stranger is the source of both disorientation and possibility. Complex layers of meaning are therefore communicated in the nine brief lines making up the first stanza.

Such meaning is the product not merely of the words themselves but also of various poetic devices: the rhythm created by word placement, the juxtaposition of downward and rising intonation patterns, the use of assonance ('shadow', 'shakes', 'shape'), and the multiple associations evoked by the words. The listener becomes a participant with the disciples in their encounter with the stranger, sharing their initial bewilderment and, in the final line of the poem, sharing also the 'shining' newness of life effected by the Christ who comes as stranger to our expectations. The complex theological 'truth' conveyed by the poem is thus participatory and experiential. As listeners and readers, we too experience the tension incurred by the presence in our finite world of the Incarnate One who, in Przywara's terms, is the analogical middle, the 'in-and-beyond' of human existence.

My argument is that Williams' imaginative vision is most clearly discernible when condensed as poetry and meditation. These forms are accordingly the primary source for my investigation into the significance accorded to imagination in his theology. His celebratory forms will therefore be placed into dialogue first with studies of imagination drawn from disciplines other than theology for the purpose of determining the possible distinctiveness of his contribution to that field. The principal dialogue will, however, be with his own communicative and critical theology, the aim being to draw out from those writings references to the operation and relevance of imagination so that these may be formulated as a coherent theology of imagination.[64]

Such a procedure is necessary in view of the fact that Williams himself does not offer an extended study of imagination and its relation to faith. While the word 'imagination' is included in the titles of *The Tragic Imagination*[65] and *Christian Imagination in Poetry and Polity*,[66] the primary subjects of those works are tragedy and poetry respectively. Only in *Grace and Necessity: Reflections on Art and Love*[67] do we find his most direct references to the operation of imagination and its implications for theology. Even there, however, the references, while illuminating, are sparse and are not developed into a more protracted analysis.

Account must also be taken of the insights into Williams' imagination provided by others. Although references to imagination are to be found in articles relating to Williams' conception of 'mystery',[68] spirituality[69] and holiness,[70] they do not constitute a consistent theological account. Michael Cox's thesis, 'Grammar and Glory', locates the sources of Williams' 'liturgical imagination' in the 'convergence' of Eastern Orthodox mystical spirituality and the philosophy of Wittgenstein but focuses on its importance in forming a 'liturgical humanity'.[71] This study is thus an enquiry into the workings of Williams' imagination, its theological underpinning and its contribution to current conceptions of imagination. Its conclusions will allow an assessment to be made of Williams' contribution to contemporary enquiries into imagination, and especially into the relation between imagination and Christian faith.

## Summary of chapters

The investigation into Rowan Williams' theology of imagination will follow three lines of enquiry. Part One lays the groundwork for an understanding of the nature and operation of imagination. Part Two explores the importance of divine desire in Williams' theology with a view to identifying the significance of desire for his conception of imagination. Part Three focuses on Williams' studies of language, aesthetics and literature since these writings offer the most direct evidence of the role of imagination in his theological vision. Drawing together conclusions from all three lines of enquiry, I develop a coherent account of Williams' theology of imagination.

In Part One I demonstrate that, in its capacity to connect different aspects of human experience, imagination is integral to symbolization and hence to language and modes of linguistic expression, including metaphor and analogy. I further demonstrate that the imaginative capacity to transcend the limits of the actual by means of analogy is the vehicle whereby divine reality may be apprehended by finite human beings.

Chapter 1 explores two main strands of philosophical enquiry into the nature and function of human imagination. The so-called epistemological tradition emphasizes its synthesizing capacity and its consequent importance for cognition, language and consciousness. The transcendent tradition focuses on the imaginative capacity to transcend the limitations of time and space and thus envisage alternative possibilities. Both traditions are evident in recent research into imagination and find expression in the 'trigger-resource-outcome' model developed by Zittoun and Gillespie.

Chapter 2 focuses on the synthesizing function of imagination as demonstrated in Williams' poem 'Deathship'.[72] It is argued that the capacity of imagination to connect perception, object and sign accounts for the development of language and the sharing of meaning. Particular attention is given to the significance of the figurative language of symbol, metaphor and myth for the expansion of knowledge. I conclude that critical symbolic realism is the mode of finite knowledge of both world and God as is evidenced in the work of Rowan Williams.

Chapter 3 explores the connective power of analogy exemplified by the poem 'Gethsemane'. The human ability to discern analogical relations across diverse areas of experience is considered for its significance for both cognitive science and Christian theology. The focus of the chapter is Erich Przywara's development of the Thomist concept of the *analogia entis* and its importance for Williams. It is argued that the *analogia entis*, as conceptualized by Przywara and Williams, is the explanatory principle which accounts for the capacity of the human imagination to transcend the limits of the finite.

Building on the foundation laid in Part One, Part Two is a detailed exploration of Williams' conception of divine love and the relation between divine *eros* and human imagination. Here I argue that, in Williams' thought, divine desire is the hermeneutical key explicating the finite/infinite analogical structure of reality. My conclusion is that the ecstatic, kenotic interrelations of the divine Trinity overflowing as *excess* in creation account for the otherness-oriented/synthesizing and self-transcending capacities of human imagination.

The focus of Chapter 4 is the centrality of divine desire in Williams' theology, as evidenced in his poem 'Our Lady of Vladimir'. I follow Williams' argument that the figure of the *crucified* Christ is the supreme revelation of the ecstatic, kenotic character of divine love, thereby opening the possibility of knowing God to be Trinity of inexhaustible love, ever desirous of our response. From an examination of Williams' analyses of divine desire in the works of Augustine, Aquinas, St John of the Cross and Hans Urs von Balthasar, I conclude that Williams sees finite reality to be permeated by the energy of otherness-oriented, self-dispossessive love. My further conclusion is that human imagination is the finite analogue of the energy of divine love.

In Chapter 5, Williams' meditation on the Orthodox Icon of the Transfiguration offers a diagnosis of finite humanity's response to the intensity of divine desire. Drawing on the work of Girard and Lacan, Williams points to the death-dealing fantasies of possessive violence and sacral fear that result when the imaginative energy of human desire is directed towards self-focused, finite goals. Only through renewal in Christ may human desire be oriented towards its true *end*, which is participation in the kenotic, ecstatic life of God. Likewise, imagination as the energy which impels desire, is refocused towards the realization of God's purpose for creation, the restoration of all things in Christ.

As exemplified by the poem 'The Outer Hermitage', Chapter 6 examines the process whereby Christ-renewed desire and imagination are gradually transformed by the Holy Spirit to become kenotically self-dispossessive and ecstatically otherness-oriented. In discussing the process of transformation, I outline Williams' argument concerning the centrality of the worship and practices of the Christian Church and draw attention to his emphasis on contemplative attentiveness to the otherness of creation in opening human imagination to the Otherness of God.

As the final building block for my argument, I turn, in Part Three, to Williams' discussions of language, aesthetics and literature with the aim of clarifying his use of the term 'imagination' and the significance of imagination for the realization of God's eschatological purpose.

The focus of Chapter 7 is Williams' notion of a 'communicative universe', as seen in the poem 'Invocation'. I show that Williams' analogical metaphysic of symbolic realism draws on Augustine's theory of language with its *res/signum* and *uti/frui* distinctions. Augustine argues that the created universe 'speaks' of divine *eros* but that the meaning of its 'speech' is correctly interpreted only by minds renewed by Christ who is the Sign from whom all finite signs gain meaning. In the second part of the chapter, I examine Williams' further insights into the theological significance of human language, as discussed in *The Edge of Words*, drawing attention to the implications of those insights for his conception of imagination.

Chapter 8 is an examination of Williams' reflections on the human capacity for *poiesis*. As implied in the poem 'Penrhys', art is shown to be the divinely bestowed gift of 'making other'. It creates the possibility of double vision and thus enables us to discern the presence of divine grace amid the tawdriness of daily life. Having noted the influence of Balthasar and Maritain in the development of Williams' aesthetic theology, I explore the key elements of his aesthetics. I argue that, for Williams, artistic creativity is impelled by the kenotic, ecstatic generativity of divine *eros* and is accordingly an imaginative movement of costly self-dispossessive love. It gives knowledge of dimensions of existence inaccessible to instrumental reason and participates in the realization of God's eschatological purpose.

In Chapter 9, the focus shifts to the ways in which the arts disrupt our conventional perception of reality, challenging us to question accepted patterns of belief and practice. A discussion of Williams' notion of 'excessive language' leads into an exploration of the excessive language of his poetry in which ordinary experience is 'made strange' for us, as evidenced by the poem 'Arabic Class'. The tension created by the excessive language of irony and paradox is explored through an examination of Williams' insights into Dostoevsky's literary method and into the European tragic tradition. I conclude that tension is central to Williams' theology of imagination, accounting for his conception of Christian imagination as essentially *tragic* in its ability to hold in ironic tension the contradictions of loss and hope, of past trauma and future possibility.

Chapter 10 is the culmination of my study of imagination in Williams' writings. His image of a 'world ... pregnant with a different kind of life'[73] draws together the various lines of thought that constitute his theology of imagination. Building on Przywara's conception of the in-and-beyond analogous relation between infinite divinity and finite creation, Williams develops a Trinitarian account of divine love as the source and animating energy of creation drawing it towards its consummation as response of love. The kenotic, ecstatic nature of that love is revealed in the crucified Christ who is the analogical middle between finite and infinite. I show that, for Williams, finite imagination is analogous to the energy of divine desire, impelling it towards the realization of God's ultimate purpose. Distorted in the conditions of finitude, imagination and desire must be renewed in Christ and transformed by the Spirit to become kenotically self-dispossessive and ecstatically oriented towards the flourishing of the whole created order. Significant for the process of transformation are the disciplines learned in the practice of religion and the arts. In an imperfect world, those disciplines teach us to hold the tension between pain and hope and thereby develop the capacity for what Williams calls 'tragic imagination'.

My conclusion draws on the poem 'Ceibr Cliff'. Written at the time of his father's death, the poem is a visceral expression of the wrenching anguish of our human experience of pain and loss even as we cling to the 'sparkle' of hope-filled love within the coal of finite existence.

## Notes

1 Reported by Andrew Goddard, *Rowan Williams: His Legacy* (Oxford: Lion Hudson, 2013), p. 45.

2 Rowan Williams, 'Has Secularism Failed? Notes on the Survival of the Spirit', Raymond Williams Lecture, June 2002, reproduced in Rowan Williams, *Faith in the Public Square* (London: Bloomsbury, 2012), pp. 11–22.

3 Williams, 'Has Secularism Failed?', p. 12.

4 'Programmatic' secularism is defined by Williams as the form of secularism in which the expression of religious conviction is banned from the public sphere. 'Introduction' in *Faith in the Public Square*, pp. 2–3.

5 Rowan Williams, *Dostoevsky: Language, Faith and Fiction* (London: Bloomsbury, 2008), p. ix.

6 Williams, *Dostoevsky*, p. x.

7 Williams, *Dostoevsky*, p. xi.

8 Rupert Shortt, *Rowan's Rule: The Biography of the Archbishop*, revised edition (London: Hodder and Stoughton, 2014), p. 520.

9 Justification for these claims is to be found in Part Two of this study.

10 Various commentators have noted what Mike Higton refers to as 'the unrelentingly *agonised*' tenor of Williams' writings. Mike Higton, *Difficult Gospel: The Theology of Rowan Williams* (London: SCM Press, 2004), p. 36. See also Brett Gray, *Jesus in the Theology of Rowan Williams* (London: Bloomsbury T&T Clark, 2016), ch. 6.

11 Address to the 1983 Loughborough Conference of Anglo-Catholics, reproduced in part in Shortt, *Rowan's Rule*, p. 104.

12 Shortt, *Rowan's Rule*, p. 105. The 'sparkle from the coal' image is a reference from the fourteenth-century work *Cloud of Unknowing*.

13 Shortt, *Rowan's Rule*, p. 105.

14 Conversation with Shortt, *Rowan's Rule*, p. 521. For a detailed account of the sources of Williams' 'tragic imagination' and its moderation over time, see Khegan Delport, 'Of Danger and Difficulty: Rowan Williams and "The Tragic Imagination"', *The Heythrop Journal* 61.3 (2017), pp. 505–20.

15 For his doctoral thesis, Williams studied the twentieth-century Russian theologian Vladimir Lossky, who argues that God, who is ultimately inaccessible to finite human minds, nevertheless acts in a movement of self-transcendence, ἐκστασις, to become known through personal encounter. See Rowan Williams, 'Lossky, the *via negativa* and the foundations of theology', in Mike Higton, ed., *Wrestling with Angels: Conversations in Modern Theology* (Grand Rapids, MI: William B. Eerdmans, 2007), pp. 1–24. See also his study of Eastern theology, *Looking East in Winter: Contemporary Thought and the Eastern Christian Tradition* (London: Bloomsbury Continuum, 2021).

16 Williams, 'Lossky', p. 2.

17 See, for example, Rowan Williams, 'Theological Integrity' in *On Christian Theology: Challenges in Contemporary Theology* (Malden, MA: Blackwell, 2000), pp. 4–5; 'Europe, Faith and Culture' in *Faith in the Public Square*, pp. 73–4; and 'Religious Diversity and Social Unity' in *Faith in the Public Square*, pp. 300–1.

18 Erich Przywara, *Analogia Entis: Metaphysics: Original Structure and Universal Rhythm*, trans. John R. Betz and David Bentley Hart (Grand Rapids, MI: William B. Eerdmans, 2014). According to Williams, Przywara's conclusions con-

cerning the analogical relation between finite and infinite were an 'appropriation' and further development of Nicholas of Cusa's *non aliud* principle, expressed by Williams as a relation of 'non-dual, non-identity'. Rowan Williams, *Christ the Heart of Creation* (London: Bloomsbury Continuum, 2018), pp. xiv–xv.

19 Williams, *Christ the Heart of Creation*, p. 223.

20 Rowan Williams, *Headwaters* (Oxford: Perpetua Press, 2008), p. 21.

21 Benjamin Myers, *Christ the Stranger: The Theology of Rowan Williams* (London: T&T Clark, 2012).

22 The image has eucharistic overtones.

23 Several of Williams' lectures and addresses on these subjects are to be found in *Faith in the Public Square*.

24 See, for example, Wayne J. Hankey, 'Self-Knowledge and God as Other in Augustine: Problems for a Postmodern Retrieval', *Bochumer Philosophisches Jahrbuch für Antike und Mittelalter* 4 (1999).

25 Williams acknowledges certain affinities between these movements and his own thinking in his 'Response to Kerr, Hedley, Pickstock, Ward and Soskice', *Modern Theology* 31.4 (2015), p. 634. For Williams' own account of his position in relation to Radical Orthodoxy, see David S. Cunningham, 'Living the Questions: The Converging Worlds of Rowan Williams', *The Christian Century* 119: 9 (2002), and Rupert Shortt, 'Rowan Williams on Belief and Theology – Some Basic Questions', *Fulcrum*, 14 December 2010, https://www.fulcrum-anglican.org.uk/articles/rowan-williams-on-belief-and-theology-some-basic-questions/17, accessed 20.06.2024. For a discussion of contemporary expressions of Christian Neoplatonism, see Wayne J. Hankey, '*Theoria versus Poesis*: Neoplatonism and Trinitarian Difference in Aquinas, John Milbank, Jean-Luc Marion and John Zizioulas', *Modern Theology* 15.4 (1999).

26 See, for example, Rowan Williams, 'Sacramental Living', *Trinity Papers* 32 (Parkville, Vic: University of Melbourne, 2002).

27 Williams, *On Christian Theology*, p. xii.

28 See, for example, Williams, 'The Suspicion of Suspicion', in Higton, ed., *Wrestling with Angels*, pp. 186–202.

29 Williams, 'The Suspicion of Suspicion', p. 199.

30 Williams, 'Lossky', p. 4. See also Rowan Williams, *Looking East in Winter: Contemporary Thought and the Eastern Christian Tradition* (London: Bloomsbury, 2021), p. 91.

31 Williams, *On Christian Theology*, p. xiii.

32 Williams, *On Christian Theology*, p. xiii.

33 Published as Rowan Williams, *The Edge of Words: God and the Habits of Language* (London: Bloomsbury, 2014).

34 Williams, *The Edge of Words*, p. xi.

35 Rowan Williams, *A Silent Action: Engagements with Thomas Merton* (London: SPCK, 2013), p. 72.

36 Williams, *A Silent Action*, p. 77.

37 Williams, *The Edge of Words*, pp. 32, 167, 170.

38 See Williams, *The Edge of Words*, ch. 4, 'Intelligent Bodies: Language as Material Practice'.

39 'Communicative' for Williams encompasses language, gesture and symbolization.

40 He draws support for his argument from recent reformulations of Aquinas's

'proofs' (*The Edge of Words*, pp. 5–10), Kant's Second Critique (pp. 10–14), and the Buddhist practice of *vipassana* (pp. 14–16).

41 Williams, *The Edge of Words*, p. 22.
42 Williams, *The Edge of Words*, p. 32.
43 Williams, *The Edge of Words*, p. 16.
44 Williams, *The Edge of Words*, p. 18.
45 See Williams, *The Edge of Words*, p. 34, where Williams endorses Michael Leunig's declaration that 'The word "God" cannot be grasped scientifically, rationally or even theologically without it exploding. It can only be held lightly and poetically.'
46 Williams, *The Edge of Words*, p. 23.
47 Williams, *The Edge of Words*, p. 22.
48 Williams, *The Edge of Words*, p. 195.
49 Williams, *The Edge of Words*, p. 31.
50 Rowan Williams, 'Trinity and Revelation' in *On Christian Theology*, pp. 136–42.
51 Williams, *The Edge of Words*, p. 33.
52 Williams, *The Edge of Words*, p. 33.
53 Williams, *The Edge of Words*, p. ix.
54 Williams, *The Edge of Words*, p. 165.
55 Williams, *The Edge of Words*, p. 115.
56 Williams, *The Edge of Words*, p. 167.
57 These include philosophy, psychology, neurology, aesthetics and literature. See references and bibliography for *The Edge of Words*.
58 Williams, *The Edge of Words*, ch. 5.
59 Williams, *The Edge of Words*, p. 177.
60 Paul Ricoeur, *From Text to Action: Essays in Hermeneutics, II*, trans. K. Blarney and J. B. Thompson (Evanston, IL: Northwestern University Press), p. 130.
61 Cited by Williams in *On Christian Theology*, p. 133. The reference is drawn from Paul Ricoeur, *Essays on Biblical Interpretation*, ed. L. S. Mudge (London: Fortress Press, 1980), p. 101.
62 Ricoeur, *From Text to Action*, p. 117.
63 Rowan Williams, *Ponder These Things: Praying with Icons of the Virgin* (Mulgrave, Vic: John Garrett, 2002), and *The Dwelling of the Light: Praying with Icons of Christ* (Mulgrave, Vic: John Garrett, 2003).
64 My methodology is similar to that employed by Austin Farrer in his 1948 Bampton Lectures, *The Glass of Vision*, in *Scripture, Metaphysics, and Poetry: Austin Farrer's* The Glass of Vision *with Critical Commentary*, ed. Robert MacSwain (Farnham: Ashgate, 2013), Preface, Kindle.
65 Rowan Williams, *The Tragic Imagination* (Oxford: Oxford University Press, 2016).
66 Rowan Williams, *Christian Imagination in Poetry and Polity: Some Anglican Voices from Temple to Herbert* (Oxford: SLG Press, 2004).
67 Rowan Williams, *Grace and Necessity: Reflections on Art and Love* (London: Morehouse, 2005).
68 Kent Eilers, 'Rowan Williams and Christian Language: Mystery, Disruption and Rebirth', *Christianity and Literature* 61.1 (2011).
69 Medi Volpe, '"Taking Time and Making Sense": Rowan Williams on the

Habits of Theological Imagination', *International Journal of Systematic Theology* 15.3 (2013).

70 Jonathan M. Platter, 'Holiness in Excess: Between Holiness and Metaphysics in the Wake of Rowan Williams', *The Heythrop Journal* 62.5 (2020).

71 D. Michael Cox, 'Grammar and glory: Eastern Orthodoxy, the "resolute" Wittgenstein, and the theology of Rowan Williams' (PhD Diss., University of Dayton, Dayton, OH, 2015), https://ecommons.udayton.edu/graduate_theses/799/.

72 Rowan Williams' poems are found in *The Poems of Rowan Williams* (Oxford: Perpetua Press, 2002); *Headwaters* (Oxford: Perpetua Press, 2003); *The Other Mountain* (Manchester: Carcanet, 2014).

73 Rowan Williams, *Ponder These Things: Praying with Icons of the Virgin* (Mulgrave, Vic: John Garrett, 2002), p. xvii.

PART ONE

# Imagination: Its Nature and Operation

## Introduction

Part One provides the theoretical foundation for my study of Rowan Williams' concept of imagination. In Chapter 1, an overview of traditional and contemporary theories concerning the nature and operation of imagination creates a framework against which Williams' usage of the term may be evaluated. Similarly, the discussion of symbolization in Chapter 2 serves as a reference point for Williams' epistemology of critical symbolic realism. The exploration of analogy in Chapter 3, with its focus on Przywara's treatment of the *analogia entis*, is the final structural element upon which I build my account of the role of imagination in Williams' theology.

# I

# Imagination

*The imagination is one of the highest prerogatives of man. By this faculty he unites former images and ideas, independently of the will, and thus creates brilliant and novel results.*
Charles Darwin[1]

*Our imaginative visions are central to our understanding of the world.*
Mary Midgley[2]

## Introduction

In *Real Presences*, George Steiner describes two contrasting depictions of the annunciation. The first, by Fra Angelico, portrays the in-breaking of the transcendent into human life, into what he calls 'the small house of our cautionary being'.[3] In this fresco, Mary is facing the angelic messenger, receptive both to his presence and his world-altering summons. The second depiction, painted almost a century later by Lorenzo Lotto, shows Mary turned away from 'the rushing radiance of the Messenger'.[4] In setting up this contrast, Steiner is reflecting on our human 'capacities for welcome or refusal' of the transcendent, as it is encountered in the arts and in religion.[5] It is a welcome or refusal of that which is 'other', the other that summons us out of egoistic self-enclosure into an engagement with a presence that transcends the self.

The two annunciation scenes represent, in Steiner's view, a significant shift within Western culture. It is a shift from a vision of reality where the presence of the divine permeates human existence to one in which 'God's presence is no longer a tenable supposition and ... his absence is no longer a felt ... weight.'[6] In modern culture, affirms Steiner, not only religion but also the artistic expressions of the human imagination risk becoming increasingly irrelevant, with a consequent diminishment of what it means to be human.

Steiner is not alone in this apprehension. It is a major concern of Rowan Williams, who repeatedly alerts us to the 'imaginative bereavement' of contemporary functional secularism and the threat it poses to our humanity.[7] Similar concerns have been expressed by thinkers drawn from different fields. The moral philosopher Mary Midgley decries the apparent hegemony in Western culture of the myth of the 'omnicompetence of science'[8] with its disregard of poetic and religious experience. The neurologist Iain McGilchrist points to the cultural prioritizing of the left brain function of analytic differentiation to the detriment of the right brain emphasis on holistic vision and understanding.[9] His concerns echo those of A. H. Whitehead, who distinguishes between 'immediacy perception', with its focus on detail, and 'causal efficacy', the preconscious perception of 'the pressure of the world of things' acting upon us, giving a sense of the larger picture.[10] The musician and writer Gary Lachman refers to the 'lost knowledge of the imagination',[11] downplayed as it is in the modern climate of scientific positivism. The philosopher of science Michael Polanyi advocates an appreciation of 'personal knowledge' and of the 'tacit' unspecifiable dimension of human experience, as opposed to so-called objective knowledge obtained by the scientific method.[12]

All decry the reduction of human experience to the purely immanent, to that which can be quantified, dissected and analysed. With Rowan Williams, they would agree that contemporary Western culture needs to be released from its 'anti-humanist closure'[13] so that it may again become imaginatively open to 'annunciations' of the transcendent. The claim of all these thinkers is that a fully human existence is one in which due place is given to the imagination, to the capacity to grasp realities that are not immediately present.[14] It is these realities, 'annunciations' that are glimpsed by the imagination, that give richness and depth to human existence, exposing the imaginative paucity of the supposedly 'scientific' vision and offering instead a vision of a world suffused with transcendent meaning.

These two visions of reality, with their contrasting valuations of the human capacity for imagination, are the point of departure for this book. In a culture that gives priority to the scientific, factual, quantifiable dimensions of existence while downplaying the creative, imaginative expressions of human experience, it is important to ascertain whether imagination serves a purpose other than that of fantasy and diversion.

To that question, both Western philosophy and Christian theology have responded with a certain ambivalence, treating imagination with suspicion and even opprobrium.[15] Despite such distrust, two 'great traditions' have continued to accord an important place to the study of imagination.[16] The first, chronologically prior, with its origins in prehistory, places the emphasis on imagination's creative, inspirational power. The second tradition, 'scientific' in intention,[17] is primarily concerned with the role played by imagination in cognition, language and consciousness. Both traditions are still evident in the current explosion of research into imagination, which is beginning to receive considerable attention not only from philosophy, aesthetics and religion but also from a range of other academic disciplines. In a culture dominated by functional instrumentalism, the current burgeoning interest in this area may be an indication that the human imagination is indeed irrepressible, a powerful force in human development.

Despite the increase in interest, a precise definition of imagination remains elusive. The philosopher Amy Kind comments that 'the question of what imagination is … has proved remarkably difficult to answer [and that] there is no single conception of imagination at play in philosophical discussions.'[18] While we have an intuitive understanding of what we mean when we employ the term, thinkers over the centuries have held very different conceptions of its nature and scope.[19] It has been variously defined as: the capacity to form mental images,[20] 'a basic image-schematic capacity for ordering our experience',[21] the mental construction of a possibility,[22] a power of seeing[23] and a mode of consciousness.[24] In their variety, such definitions highlight the wide range of theoretical positions concerning the functions attributed to human imagination.

In this chapter, I set out to sketch certain important landmarks in the development of the two philosophical traditions, culminating in a limited overview of some current thinking concerning the nature and scope of human imagination. The aim is to reach a more comprehensive understanding of the meaning and range of application of the term 'imagination', thereby providing a basis for comparison with my conclusions about the significance of human imagination for Rowan Williams' theology.

## The epistemological tradition

Dominant in Western philosophy over recent centuries, the epistemological tradition has focused on the importance of the synthesizing function of imagination for an understanding of human cognition. It has its origin in the thought of Aristotle, who conceived of imagination (*phantasia*) as the 'power' that mediates between perception and thought. According to Aristotle, human thought depends on images of particulars received through the senses and subsequently conceptualized by *phantasia* to become 'exemplifications of universals'.[25] Given that the images received by *phantasia* also evoke affective reactions such as desire or pain, *phantasia* is operative in provoking action and is therefore important for decision-making.[26]

Like Aristotle, Descartes accorded a mediating role to the '*phantasia*-organ' which, in his view, receives image impressions from the senses and conveys them to the memory or the intellect.[27] Similarly, the eighteenth-century Scottish philosopher David Hume conceived of imagination as 'our general mental faculty which operates with and upon the contents of our mind (ideas or images) with which we are furnished by impressions of the senses'.[28] He was a pioneer in acknowledging imagination to be a basic cognitive process and in recognizing its importance for modal knowledge, the consideration of possibility.[29] To him also is attributed the concept of 'imaginative resistance', which takes account of people's spontaneous revulsion against imagining certain phenomena and practices.

Immanuel Kant's theories occupy a watershed position in enquiry into imagination, being significant for both the epistemological and transcendent traditions.[30] A detailed account of the development of his discussion of imagination in the *Critique of Pure Reason*[31] and the *Critique of Judgement*[32] is beyond the scope of this study. My aim is to point to Kant's groundbreaking analysis of the role of imagination in contributing to every aspect of human functioning: cognitive, moral and aesthetic.[33]

Defining imagination as 'the faculty of representing an object even without its presence in intuition',[34] Kant held that it mediates between 'sensibility and understanding', such that perceptions received through the senses are synthesized into a 'manifold'[35] by the imagination, which assigns the object to a schema and thus to a concept. Perception involves the 'threefold synthesis' of sensory apprehension, imagination and conceptual recognition. Knowledge of the world is dependent on the mediating capacity of the imagination to transform sense perceptions into conceptual understanding.

In its mode of operation, the imagination is not only *reproductive* but also *productive*.[36] The *reproductive* function links a new sense perception with a previously established concept.[37] Mark Johnson describes it as 'the power to form unified images, and to recall in memory past images, so as to constitute a unified and coherent experience'.[38] In this respect, Kant is following his empiricist predecessors.[39] He moves beyond them, however, in his claim that experience cannot be solely explained by the imagination's reproductive function.[40] He argues that the human capacities for sensation and understanding contain 'pure concepts', which are a priori, and thus not derived from experience. The human capacity for categorization is a 'pure concept of the understanding',[41] while our intuitions of space and time are held to be 'pure forms of the sensibility'.[42] Such 'pure concepts' are considered to be evidence of the *productive* activity of the imagination.[43]

Linking sense experience and understanding is the schema, conceptualized by Kant as a 'general procedure of the imagination for providing a concept with its image'.[44] Through the exercise of the productive and reproductive imagination, objects are categorized according to schemata which are 'both sensible and intellectual'.[45] In accordance with these categorization 'rules', the imagination links images derived from the senses with abstract intellectual categories to form concepts. Johnson can therefore conclude that, for Kant, the imagination 'constitutes the temporal unity of our consciousness'.[46]

My cursory account of Kant's investigations into imagination in the *Critique of Pure Reason* has served to highlight the centrality of imagination in Kant's conception of cognition. The further discussion of imagination in the *Critique of Judgement* emphasizes its role in aesthetical judgement. In this respect, Kant's theory is also significant for the transcendent tradition and will be further discussed in that context.[47]

## The transcendent tradition

Originating in prehistory, and associated with divinity and creativity, the transcendent tradition is evidenced in the art, literature and philosophy of ancient Greece. For such pre-Socratic figures as Homer,[48] Heraclitus[49] and Aeschylus,[50] the source of creative inspiration was the invisible realm of the gods. This notion persists as an undercurrent in the work of Plato[51] who, despite considering the image-making power of imagination to be the lowest form of cognition,[52] nevertheless speaks of the poet 'as … a winged and holy thing' who creates by 'divine dispensation'.[53] In his exploration of imagination, Douglas Hedley refers to a 'Phaedran-imaginative-poetic Platonism' based in 'the experiential apprehension of the divine presence in the world'.[54] This sense of a divine 'surplus of ultimate meaning'[55] to be grasped experientially rather than conceptually, is the root of the transcendent imaginative tradition.

The 'experiential apprehension of divine presence' is at the heart of the philosophical method advocated, centuries later, by Giambattista Vico in his major work, *New Science*. In contrast to the Cartesian rationalism of eighteenth-century Europe, Vico accords an essential role to imagination as 'a mode of philosophical thought'.[56] His goal is the attainment of 'poetic wisdom' which, as depicted in the image that serves as frontispiece to *New Science*, relies on awareness of the interrelation between the divine source of existence (depicted as the all-seeing eye of God), philosophical enquiry (the figure of 'metaphysic') and poetic vision (represented by Homer).[57] Operative in generating poetic vision are the processes of *memoria* (memory), *fantasia* (the capacity to form mental images) and *ingegno* (the power of invention).[58] By means of these 'imaginative universals'[59] we are able to identify with other minds and earlier cultures.

Whereas the focus of Vico's imaginative vision is on the past as a source of wisdom, Immanuel Kant emphasizes the a priori *productive* function of imagination for its role in human creativity and moral judgement. In the *Critique of Judgement*, he argues that the purposiveness to be discerned in nature is the a priori transcendental principle governing aesthetic judgement.[60] He contends that such judgements are not open to proof but are both universal and subjective,[61] being 'a combination of the feeling of pleasure with the concept of the purposiveness of nature'.[62]

Aesthetical judgements are to be differentiated from teleological judgements: the latter are judgements of the Understanding and Reason since they relate to the purpose of the object, whereas aesthetical judgements issue from the pleasure or pain imparted by the formal properties of the object.[63] Unlike 'determinate' judgements derived from the empirical rules governing the development of concepts, aesthetic judgements are 'reflective', in that they can reflect on and combine various representations free from strict empirical control, and so can produce new concepts or a new organization of concepts. The creativity attributed to the 'genius' results from the free play of imagination and understanding.[64] Kant states:

> The imagination (as a productive cognitive faculty) is very powerful in creating another nature, as it were, out of the material that actual nature gives it. We entertain ourselves with it when experience becomes too commonplace, and by it we remould experience, always indeed in accordance with analogical laws, but yet also in accordance with principles which occupy a higher place in reason ... Thus we feel our freedom from the law of association (which attaches to the empirical employment of imagination), so that the material supplied to us by nature in accordance with this law can be worked up into something different which surpasses nature.[65]

The free play between understanding and the productive imagination produces new insights and meanings,[66] creating an 'aesthetic idea that simultaneously "presents" and "expands" th[e] original concept'[67] and thus points beyond the purely empirical.[68] Judgements of the aesthetic value of all forms of art are held to have universal validity only in respect of their formal properties, which inspire 'disinterested' pleasure in all beholders and thus enable them to reach a similar reflective conclusion.[69]

In the *Critique of Judgement*, Kant contends that aesthetic ideas, such as the idea of beauty, may also have moral significance. His argument here depends on the postulation that there are ideas such as 'freedom and the highest good' which involve 'pure concepts' not derived from sense experience.[70] Such ideas are purely rational. Certain aesthetic ideas are of this order, examples being the ideas of beauty and the sublime.[71] Endowed through art with 'the appearance of an objective reality', these aesthetic ideas become the visible expression of the highest purposes of humanity – 'goodness of soul, or purity, or strength, or repose'.[72] They 'make man more civilized, if not morally better, and win us in large measure from the tyranny of sense-proportions and thus prepare us for a Lordship in which Reason alone shall have authority'.[73]

In the breadth of his theory, Kant may be considered to bridge the epistemological/inspirational divide in his conceptualization of imagination. As the power of synthesis, imagination transforms sense impressions into conceptual categories and thus makes understanding possible. Working freely with understanding, it also becomes creative, offering new insights and meanings. It thus expands understanding and reveals something of the transcendent dimension of human existence.[74]

Kant's theory of imagination was a major influence on the nineteenth-century Romantic movement,[75] and especially on the thought of its principal English exponent, Samuel Taylor Coleridge.[76] Writing in reaction to the post-Cartesian disjunction between mind and matter, Coleridge sought to re-establish the connection that had prevailed in earlier centuries between the inner world of consciousness and the outer world of nature, both, for him, being intimations of the mind of God.[77]

Stating that imagination is 'a repetition in the finite mind of the eternal act of creation in the infinite I AM',[78] Coleridge attributed the source of human imagination to the creative power of the eternal Logos/Word, continuously at work within the natural world and within human minds. Correspondences thus exist between the outer world of nature and the inner world of the mind. Both are 'word-bearers', humanity through the gift of language, nature through its revelation of 'the lovely shapes and sounds intelligible/Of that eternal language which thy God/utters.'[79] For Coleridge, nature is therefore a network of symbols pointing beyond itself to God but also pointing within to the depths of human experience. Reality in his view is essentially symbolic.

This symbolic reality becomes accessible to human understanding through the medium of language. Distinguishing between the Primary and Secondary Imagination, Coleridge regards the first as the power of synthesis which, operating below the level of consciousness, not only enables us to perceive the external world but also brings coherence and meaning to those perceptions. The second is the conscious decision to 'dissolve' ordinary perception in order to 're-create', by means of symbol, a deepened perception of the hidden, inner mystery of the Divine Being immanent within the cosmos.

The differentiation between perception and imagination also preoccupied the twentieth-century French existentialist Jean-Paul Sartre, who argues that imagination is not merely one of the functions of consciousness but is rather 'a constitutive structure of [its] essence'.[80] Distinguishing imagination from other mental processes, he denies that, in its image-making capacity, it merely creates inner pictures.[81] Instead he asserts that the 'the image is a consciousness',[82] by which he means that the imagined image is the way consciousness relates to the object.[83] As a form of consciousness, imagining is distinguished from perception by the 'the phenomenon of quasi-observation'.[84] Whereas perception assumes that the object perceived is real, imagination 'posits its object as a nothingness'.[85] It therefore relates to the object imagined in one of four ways: as absent, as existing elsewhere, as not existing or as neutral in respect of the object's existence.[86] Finally, imagining is characterized by spontaneity as contrasted with the passivity of perception.[87] 'Imagining involves the generation of objects from within one's own mental resources'[88] and is a form of spontaneous creativity.

The objects/situations thus imagined are analogous to objects apprehended by perception but differ through their non-presence. Sartre concludes that they originate in our experiential knowledge of 'being-in-the-world', which is knowledge derived from our relationships, emotions, bodily sensations and beliefs.[89] It is the sort of knowledge designated by the French term *connaissance* (embodied personal knowledge) as contrasted with *savoir* (conceptual knowledge).

Sartre's emphasis on the non-presence, the 'nothingness', of what is imagined has been regarded as his most important contribution to an understanding of imagination.[90] The non-presence of the imaginary is evidence of the *freedom* of human consciousness to depart from the observable, thereby effecting a double feat of consciousness. Through the imaginative act of 'hold[ing] the real at a distance',[91] we not only become aware of 'the world as a synthetic totality' but are also free to stand back from, and thus escape immersion in, that totality.[92] Sartre concludes that the human ability to imagine the unreal on the basis of experience of the real is the source of our freedom to envisage future possibilities and thereby transcend the limits of actuality. Imagination is accordingly described by Sartre as 'transcendental consciousness'.[93]

Like Sartre, Paul Ricoeur distinguishes between imagination (seeing-as) and perception (mere seeing), insisting that they vary in their referential status in respect of reality.[94] While Ricoeur's extensive writings do not include a fully developed theory of imagination, his studies of metaphor,[95] narrative[96] and ideology[97] attest to the significance accorded to imagination as the metaphoric operation underpinning human thought, language and action. His conclusions are perhaps best summed up in the 1979 article 'The Function of Fiction in Shaping Reality', where he distinguishes between images as copies and images as fictions.[98]

Whereas a copied image designates the same object as the original, thus sharing its referent,[99] the fictional image has no referent in reality. Its reference is productive in that it represents something hitherto non-existent and is thus an augmentation of reality. Fictional imagery is not an act of perception but derives from the capacity of human language to produce an infinite number of novel expressions. By the operation of metaphor, language brings together and effects a relation between two different domains of experience, leading to 'semantic innovation',[100] a new meaning that is 'evoked and displayed'[101] rather than conceptually grasped.[102]

For Ricoeur, imagination is not mere rêverie, in the Bachelardian sense of free-floating imagery, but involves work.[103] It requires the labour of seeing-as so as to identify similarity in difference and new connections between experiences. In the externalization of the inner creative vision, there is also a process of condensation whereby the significant features are given prominence. Such an operation depends on the freedom to depart from the 'ordinary vision of reality'[104] in venturing into the unreal, into a 'state of non-engagement', in which 'new ideas, new values, new ways of being-in-the-world' may be tried.[105]

Ricoeur's theory is significant for its identification of the relation between imagination, language and praxis. In its potential for creating new meaning, the linguistic imagery produced by the imagination is capable of being developed into models, 'heuristic fictions for redescribing reality',[106] thereby offering 'an expanded vision of reality' and the possibility of developing new forms of social organization. The parallels between Ricoeur's thought and that of Rowan Williams will be discussed in Chapter 2.

## Contemporary theories

Contemporary research into imagination has raised awareness of the 'wide swath of everyday activities' that rely on imagination.[107] The range of research topics in the *Routledge Handbook of Philosophy of Imagination*[108] makes it clear that imagination is more than an 'image-making faculty', the distinction between sensory (including non-visual) and propositional imagination being an important area of exploration in current philosophical and psychological investigations.[109] While theories may differ as to the scope of imagination, there is general consensus that it is a form of consciousness integral to a range of mental processes. It may be concluded that, in its various modes, imagination is an essential function of human consciousness.

Of particular interest for the study of Rowan Williams are two current areas of enquiry which highlight the part played by imagination in human evolution and in the development of language and culture.[110] The first relates to the link between the human body and language, the second is concerned to explore the interrelationship between imagination and change, personal and social.

An example of embodiment theory is that of the anthropologist/philosopher Stephen Asma.[111] He contends that imagination is 'embodied *action*' rather than 'a kind of *cognition*'[112] and that it developed through the improvisation required to respond to the ever new and challenging situations posed by the external environment. Originating as an unconscious, 'emotionally driven' bodily process, the imagination, says Asma, is 'our early intellect [that] gave us the behavioral/mental scaffolding to organize and manage our experience long before words and concepts'.[113] Language and culture derive ultimately from the 'improvisational grammar' of sequenced motor activities, which led to image-schema manipulation, then to image narrative and finally to linguistic symbols.[114] Imagination as embodied action is, claims Asma, the basis of human cognition.

Support for Asma's theory is provided by the earlier seminal work of the cognitive scientists George Lakoff and Mark Johnson.[115] According to Johnson, 'any adequate account of meaning and rationality must give a central place to embodied and imaginative structures of understanding by which we grasp our world.'[116] His basic premise is that the constant impingement on the body of external physical forces, such as force, gravity, containment, has resulted in recurring patterns of experience that carry preconceptual meaning. These patterns develop into schemata, imaginative structures that organize actions, perception and conceptions;[117] schemata then become generalized to apply to both literal and figurative situations where the same relations are present.[118] Johnson argues that the transfer of meaning from the literal motor/perceptual to the abstract/figurative level occurs through metaphorical projection which is not arbitrary but is always constrained by the concrete bodily experience from which it arose.[119] Here metaphor, conceived as an 'irreducible, imaginative structure of human understanding',[120] is considered critical for the development of abstract meaning and therefore for human rationality.[121]

The centrality of metaphor for the generation of meaning is also argued by the psychiatrist Arnold Modell with his mind-body theory.[122] He contends that goal-directed bodily behaviour effects changes in the brain, creating an internal 'world' of meanings, the mind, which guides future action. In this way the mind becomes a 'self-contained system' which, while continuing to be impacted and modified by bodily sensations and the external environment, nevertheless develops as an unconscious autonomous process.[123] Metaphor serves to connect meanings held in the unconscious memory with conscious experience, thus creating meaning in the present and opening up future possibilities. Modell can therefore claim that 'matter becomes imagination'.[124]

The relationship between imagination and culture is of growing interest in the fields of cultural psychology, sociology and education.[125] Agustín Fuentes argues that human cognitive development was fuelled by a combination of social collaboration and creativity, the latter being the 'ability to move back and forth between, the "what is" and "what could be"'.[126] Together these two factors resulted in a capacity for 'semiosis – the use and creation of symbol',[127] giving rise to language, religion, art and science.

Glăveanu and Zittoun contend that 'the origin, tools and processes of our imagination unfold in the relational space *in between* minds, bodies, objects, traditions and institutions.'[128] Imagination thus has a social origin, being neither completely individually constructed nor totally culturally determined but occurring at the intersection between unique individual experience and the social and cultural environment. Embedded as we are in overlapping social and cultural contexts, humans are shaped both by the sociocultural environment and by the specific experiences unique to each individual, and any adequate account of imagination must take into account this interrelationship between a person's inner and outer worlds.

The sociocultural context acts as the primary resource for imaginative activity, its customs, values, assumptions, technological and cultural products being the material with which the imagination works.[129] It also serves to constrain the range of options open to the imaginer, since these depend on the possibilities available within a particular culture in any period. According to the anthropologist Vincent Crapanzano, 'each culture creates horizons for the imagination', which fix the limits of possibility within that culture.[130] Imagination can therefore be considered to operate against a '*hinterland* or an "arrière-pays"' of possibility, a 'symbolic universe' specific to a culture at a particular period.[131]

This is consistent with the concept of the social imaginary as suggested by the philosopher Cornelius Castoriadis[132] and employed by Charles Taylor to trace the Western transition from the medieval 'enchanted world' of unquestioned belief in God to the twenty-first-century 'secular age'.[133] According to Taylor, a social imaginary is 'the way ordinary people "imagine" their social surroundings ... a common understanding which makes possible common practices, and a widely shared sense of legitimacy'.[134] Essentially preconceptual, it is 'that largely unstructured and inarticulate understanding of our whole situation, within which particular features of our world [make sense]'.[135] 'Carried in images, stories, legends'[136] and, in the information age, in film, television, internet games and social media sites, social imaginaries are the taken-for-granted background against which human lives are lived; they therefore furnish, shape, colour and constrain an individual's imagination.[137]

A model which takes account of both the sociocultural and the individually embodied dimensions of imagination has been proposed by Zittoun and Gillespie.[138] Labelled as the 'trigger-resource-outcome' model, it depicts a loop connecting two modes of experience: the 'proximal', which is 'anchored in the experiencing body, in a given here-and-now moment', and the 'distal', which breaks with the present moment to move backward or forward in time or to consider abstract possibilities.[139] As shown in Figure 1 below, this imaginative loop follows a three-stage process, that of disengagement, exploration and reconnection.

The trigger for disengaging from present, proximal experience may be boredom, as in the case of daydreaming, or it may be a break with normal routine, such as an accident or a change in circumstances. The loop then follows a process of exploring the resources available within the distal realm: the memories and 'representations, discourses and ideas … available in [the] sociocultural environment'.[140] This distal realm is conceptualized as 'a three-dimensional space',[141] encompassing time, generalizability and plausibility. It is temporally oriented since imaginative activity may be directed towards the past, the future or to other present locations;[142] it is open to varying degrees of generalization from specific to highly abstract possibilities;[143] it may also produce more or less plausible speculations that have a greater or lesser likelihood or realization.[144] Imaginative exploration of the distal realm gives rise to the consideration of possible courses of action or to the picturing of a variety of situations as an escape from, or an alternative to, the present reality. The third stage of the model is the outcome produced upon conscious reconnection with the here-and-now, this outcome being potentially a new perspective, a change in emotional state or a decision about action.

Zittoun and Gillespie accordingly conceptualize imagination as being eminently practical, a means of accommodating to reality or of expanding proximal experience.[145] They hold it to be a process integral to every stage of an individual's life course,[146] as well as to cultural advancement and social change.[147] While it involves a temporary uncoupling from the actual in order to enter the 'distal', it serves to facilitate both adjustment to, and transformation of, the world in which we live.

Figure 1: Trigger-resource-outcome model

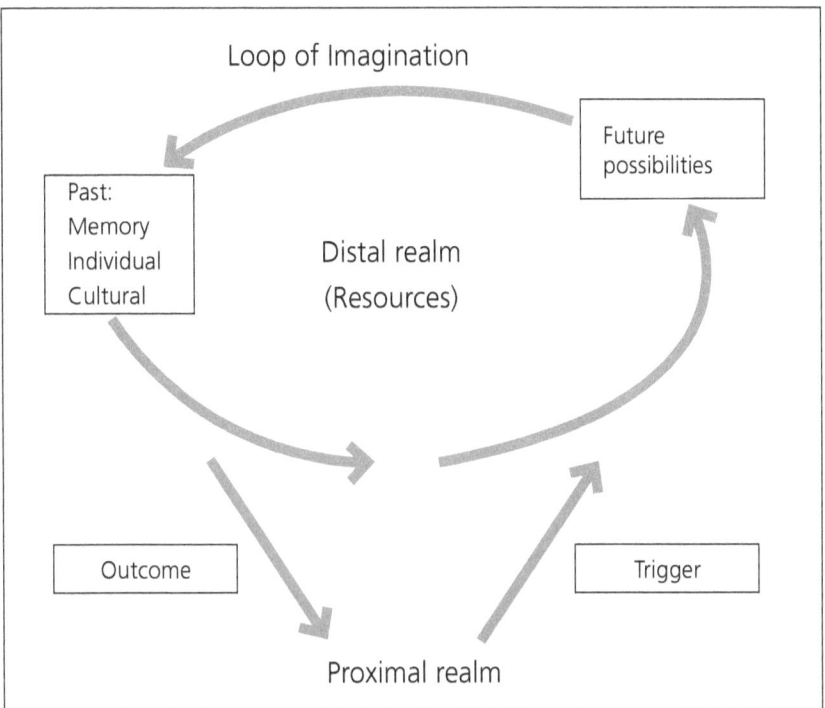

The trigger-resource-outcome model is a helpful way of conceptualizing the operation of the imagination as a mode of consciousness. Highlighting the freedom of imagination to uncouple from actuality, it connects present embodied experience with previous learning in the creation of a range of fictive futures for possible action. It also identifies the main constraint to which imagination is subject, namely the sociocultural context, which largely configures a person's imaginative horizon.

## Conclusion

Mysterious, evading precise definition and yet a pervasive mode of human consciousness, imagination has been shown to be operative in a wide range of mental processes and to be therefore essential for human functioning. The brief overview of imagination presented in this chapter serves to alert us to the two main functions of imagination: the human operations of synthesis and transcendence. Associated with these two functions are five interrelated and interdependent capacities.

## 1. The capacity to uncouple from the proximal realm (the power of freedom)

As Sartre observed, the basic human freedom to transcend the limits of actuality derives from the imagination's ability to uncouple from the immediate situation to contemplate alternative possibilities. In imagination, humans can stand back from the present context and, by so doing, are freed to view it from a distance and so gain a more holistic perspective. The freedom of imagination to depict and explore a range of possible futures is essential to everyday decision-making as well as to scientific discovery and social development.[148]

## 2. The capacity to connect disparate realms of experience (the power of synthesis)

Taken for granted within both traditions is the notion that the imagination functions to make connection: between the senses and understanding, between the actual and the possible, between the real and the unreal and, for some, between the finite and the infinite.[149] For Kant, Coleridge, Sartre and Ricoeur, such connection takes the form of synthesis, which not only bridges two forms of experience but also fuses them into something new – a concept, a possibility, an imaginary world. Of significance for the connectivity associated with imagination are the linguistic devices of metaphor and analogy, considered to be 'fundamental schema by which people conceptualize the world and their own activities'.[150]

## 3. The capacity for symbolization (the power of meaning-making)

Embodiment theories of language development accord a central place to the improvisational capacity of imagination to connect bodily sensation, mental schemata, and oral and written symbolic representations in the generation of linguistic meaning. The shared meanings rendered possible by linguistic symbolization are the source of human culture and the vehicle for its ongoing transformation.

## 4. The capacity to 'see beyond' the empirically verifiable (the power of transcendence)

The importance of imagination for human cognition is now generally acknowledged. The scope of the knowledge to be gained by imaginative cognitive processes remains a matter of dispute, some contending that it is limited to that which is observable and verifiable.[151] Others, however, emphasize the affective, interpersonal and transcendent dimensions of human knowing, differentiating, with Sartre, between *savoir* (factual and conceptual knowledge) and *connaissance* (experiential and relational knowledge). The latter form of knowledge relies on the leap of imagination to transcend individual consciousness and thereby enter into the experience of other persons. A similar leap is required to place oneself within other cultures and periods, to inhabit fictitious worlds or to postulate dimensions of existence beyond the empirical. Religion is dependent on the human capacity for such an imaginative leap.

## 5. The capacity to produce something new (the power of creativity)

To the imagination is attributed humanity's capacity for seemingly inexhaustible creative expression. The power of the *productive* imagination to produce newness is stressed by all within the transcendent tradition. As will be further discussed in the following chapters, such creative newness is related to the surplus of meaning in human language, which is perhaps an 'annunciation' of the transcendent surplus of meaning inherent within Divinity.

As will be developed in Parts Two and Three, my study of Rowan Williams' conception of imagination will take account of both the synthesizing and transcending functions of imagination. In the remaining chapters of Part One, I will examine in greater detail the synthesizing process of symbolization (Chapter 2) and the concept of analogy, which elucidates the relation between finite reality and the infinite (Chapter 3). I will argue that, for Williams, finite reality is essentially symbolic, and that his theological metaphysic is underpinned by the concept of the *analogia entis* (the analogy of being). My claim is that human imagination's capacity for both symbolization and transcendence is explicable in terms of the analogical structure of reality.

## Notes

1 Cited by Arnold H. Modell, *Imagination and the Meaningful Brain* (Cambridge, MA: MIT Press, 2006), p. 25.

2 Mary Midgley, *The Myths We Live By* (London: Routledge, 2011), Foreword.

3 George Steiner, *Real Presences* (Chicago, IL: University of Chicago Press, 1991), p. 143.

4 Steiner, *Real Presences*, p. 146.

5 Steiner, *Real Presences*, p. 147.

6 Steiner, *Real Presences*, p. 229.

7 Rowan Williams, *Faith in the Public Square* (London: Bloomsbury, 2012), p. 12. See also Rowan Williams, *The Truce of God: Peacemaking in Troubled Times*, 2nd edn (Norwich: Canterbury Press, 2005), p. viii; Rowan Williams, *Lost Icons* (Harrisburg, PA: Morehouse, 2000), p. 6.

8 Midgley, *The Myths We Live By*, chapter 1, section 4, Kindle. See also Mary Midgley, *Science and Poetry* (London: Routledge, 2001).

9 Iain McGilchrist, *The Master and His Emissary: The Divided Brain and the Making of the Western World* (New Haven, CT: Yale University Press, 2005). See also Paul Avis, *God and the Creative Imagination: Metaphor, Symbol and Myth in Religion and Theology* (London: Routledge, 1999), p. 25.

10 Steven Shaviro, 'Whitehead on Causality and Perception', *The Pinocchio Theory*, 6 June 2024, www.shaviro.com/Blog/?=1274, accessed 2.01.2019.

11 Gary Lachman, *Lost Knowledge of the Imagination* (Edinburgh: Floris Books, 2018).

12 Michael Polanyi, *Personal Knowledge: Towards a Post-Critical Philosophy* (London: Routledge, 1998) and *The Tacit Dimension* (Chicago, IL: University of Chicago Press, 1966).

13 Williams, *Faith in the Public Square*, p. 15.

14 Michael Martin, in *The Oxford Companion to Philosophy*, 2nd edn (Oxford: Oxford University Press, 2005), defines imagination as 'the power of the mind to consider things which are not present to the senses, and to consider that which is not taken to be real.' The philosopher Cornelius Castoriadis asserts that 'What is most human is not rationalism but the uncontrolled and uncontrollable continuous surge of creative radical imagination.' Cited by Modell, *Imagination and the Meaningful Brain*, Frontispiece.

15 See, for example, Richard Kearney, 'The Hebraic Imagination' and 'The Hellenic Imagination' in *The Wake of Imagination* (London: Hutchinson Education, 1988) where he notes that image-making has been regarded as idolatry (p. 43), rebellion against the gods (p. 86) and a 'mere plaything' (p. 97).

16 The notion of 'two traditions' in relation to imagination is discussed by Dorthe Jørgensen, 'The Philosophy of Imagination', in Tania Zittoun and Vlad Glăveanu, eds, *Handbook of Imagination and Culture* (New York: Oxford University Press, 2018), pp. 19–38; by Mark Johnson in *The Body in the Mind: The Bodily Basis of Meaning, Imagination and Reason* (Chicago, IL: University of Chicago Press, 1990), pp. 141–72; and by Amy Kind, *Knowledge Through Imagination*, ed. Amy Kind and Peter Kung (Oxford: Oxford University Press, 2016), p. 1.

17 'Scientific' here refers to *scientia*, demonstrable knowledge.

18 Amy Kind, ed., *The Routledge Handbook of Philosophy of Imagination* (London: Routledge, 2016), p. 1.

19 See also Amy Kind and Peter Kung, 'Introduction: The Puzzle of Imaginative Use' in *Knowledge Through Imagination*, p. 4.

20 Alan White argues that, until Sartre, Wittgenstein and Ryle, it was assumed that the term 'imagination' implied the existence of mental imagery. Alan R. White, *The Language of Imagination* (Oxford: Basil Blackwell, 1990), p. 3.

21 Johnson, *The Body in the Mind*, p. xx.

22 White, *The Language of Imagination*, p. 184.

23 Paul Ricoeur, reported by David J. Bryant, *Faith and the Play of Imagination: On the Role of Imagination in Religion* (Macon, GA: Mercer University Press, 1989), p. 92.

24 Jean-Paul Sartre, *The Imaginary: A Phenomenological Psychology of the Imagination*, trans. Jonathan Webber (New York: Routledge, 2003), p. 179.

25 Deborah K. W. Modrak, 'Aristotle on *Phantasia*', in Kind, *Routledge Handbook of Philosophy of Imagination*, p. 21.

26 Kind, *Routledge Handbook of Philosophy of Imagination*, pp. 22–4.

27 See Dennis L. Sepper, 'Descartes', in Kind, *Routledge Handbook of Philosophy of Imagination*, p. 31.

28 White, *Language of Imagination*, p. 38. Unlike his empiricist predecessors, Hume refutes the notion of a faculty of pure reason, holding instead that reason is one of the operations of the imagination.

29 Fabian Dorsch, 'Hume', in Kind, *Routledge Handbook of Philosophy of Imagination*, pp. 48–50.

30 See Samantha Matherne, 'Kant's Theory of the Imagination', in Kind, *Routledge Handbook of Philosophy of Imagination*, pp. 55, 66; Johnson, *The Body in the Mind*, p. 147. Jørgensen ('The Philosophy of Imagination', p. 20) agrees that Kant succeeds in bringing together the epistemological/Aristotelian and the inspirational/Platonic strands of imagination theory.

31 Immanuel Kant, *Critique of Pure Reason* (*CPR*). In this work Kant examines the role played by imagination in cognition. Originally published in 1781, it was revised in 1787, the two editions being differentiated by the letters A and B. My references are to the Penguin translation of the 1787 edition by J. M. D. Meiklejohn (London: George Bell & Sons, 1890), Digireads.com Publishing, 2018.

32 Immanuel Kant, *Critique of Judgement* (*CJ*). This work is an analysis of the human experience of beauty and the sublime. It explores the function of imagination in aesthetic judgement. The edition referenced is the translation by J. H. Bernard, 2nd rev. edn (London: Macmillan, 1892), Kindle.

33 Matherne, 'Kant's Theory of the Imagination', p. 55.

34 Kant, *Critique of Pure Reason*, Book 1, Ch. II, §20, Digireads.

35 The term 'manifold' refers to the complex of features (colour, shape etc.) constituting an object.

36 Kant, *CPR*, Book 1, Ch. II, §20, Digireads.

37 Matherne (p. 56) also cites the fuller account of Kant's differentiation between productive and reproductive imagination provided in Kant's 1798 *Anthropology from a Pragmatic Point of View*. Here Kant describes reproductive imagination as 'a faculty of the derivative exhibition of the object (*exhibition derivative*), which brings back to the mind an empirical observation that it had previously'.

38 Johnson, *The Body in the Mind*, p. 149.

39 Johnson, *The Body in the Mind*, p. 149.
40 See, for example, Rosefeldt's discussion of Kant's account of the role of imagination in cognition. Tobias Rosefeldt, 'Kant on the Epistemic Role of the Imagination', *Synthese* 198, suppl.13 (2019), pp. 3171–92.
41 Kant, *CPR*, Book I, Ch. II, §16.
42 Kant, *CPR*, Introduction, First Part, §1.
43 Kant, *CPR*, Introduction, First Part, 'Transcendental Aesthetic', §§1–10.
44 Kant, *CPR*, Book II, Ch. One.
45 Matherne, 'Kant's Theory of the Imagination', p. 60.
46 Johnson, *The Body in the Mind*, p. 143.
47 It should be noted that Kant's use of the term 'transcendental' refers specifically to the possibility of knowledge that is a priori and not derived from experience. It does not assume that such knowledge is of divine origin. Kant, *CPR*, Introduction VII.
48 Jørgensen, 'The Philosophy of Imagination', p. 20.
49 McGilchrist, *The Master and His Emissary*, p. 268.
50 McGilchrist, *The Master and His Emissary*, p. 273.
51 Douglas Hedley, *Living Forms of the Imagination* (London: T&T Clark International, 2008), p. 5; Jørgensen, 'The Philosophy of Imagination', pp. 21–2; Sepper, 'Descartes', p. 28.
52 Jørgensen, 'The Philosophy of Imagination', pp. 21–2.
53 Cited by Johnson, *The Body in the Mind*, p. 143.
54 Hedley, *Living Forms of the Imagination*, p. 6.
55 Hedley, *Living Forms of the Imagination*, p. 15.
56 See Emanuel Paparella, 'The Uniqueness of Vico's Poetic Philosophy', https://www.metanexus.net/uniqueness-giambattista-vicos-poetic-philosophy/, 5/7, accessed 27.04.2019.
57 Paparella, 'The Uniqueness of Vico's Poetic Philosophy', 1/7. See also Vico's claim that his metaphysics is 'consonant with Christian piety because it distinguishes divine from human truth and does not set up human knowledge as the rule for divine knowledge, but divine science as the rule for human knowledge'. Cited by Nancy du Bois Marcus, *Vico and Plato* (New York: Peter Lang, 2001), p. 2.
58 Donald Philip Verene, *Vico's Science of Imagination* (New York: Cornell University Press, 1991), p. 167.
59 Verene, *Vico's Science of Imagination*, p. 67.
60 Kant, *CJ*, p. 41. Kant insists (p. 42) that such judgements are not open to proof, but are both universal and subjective, being 'a combination of the feeling of pleasure with the concept of the purposiveness of nature' (pp. 45ff.). See also Kant, *CJ*, p. 213.
61 Kant, *CJ*, p. 42.
62 Kant, *CJ*, pp. 45ff.
63 Kant, *CJ*, p. 50.
64 Matherne, 'Kant's Theory of the Imagination', pp. 61–4; Johnson, *The Body in the Mind*, p. 158.
65 Kant, *CJ*, pp. 144–5.
66 Creativity for Kant results from the 'free' interplay of both understanding and imagination. This is contrasted with mere 'fantasy' as revealed in dreams and illusions, which, operating without rules, lacks input from understanding. Jørgensen, 'The Philosophy of Imagination', p. 30.

67 Matherne, 'Kant's Theory of the Imagination', p. 63.

68 There is continuing debate about whether Kant's account of imagination provides a source of modal knowledge. While implausible scenarios may readily be imagined, the possibility of their actual realization is open to dispute. See, for example, Kind and Kung, *Knowledge Through Imagination*, Part Three: Skeptical Approaches. Tobias Rosefeldt argues that modal knowledge is subject to certain conditions. He reports that Peter Kung's position is that the realization of an imagined possibility is dependent on the content of the imagined scenario. Scientifically and logically realizable content must be differentiated from that which is arbitrarily constructed by the imagination. Rosefeldt's own argument draws on Kant's demonstration of the a priori structures of time and space which are determinative for human perception. He concludes that imaginings in line with these structures 'can be a guide to what is metaphysically possible in the spatio-temporal world'. Rosefeldt, 'Kant and the Epistemic Role of the Imagination'.

69 Kant, *CJ*, pp. 84ff. See also Johnson, *The Body in the Mind*, pp. 159–60.

70 Matherne, 'Kant's Theory of Imagination', p. 64.

71 Kant, *CJ*, p. 84.

72 Kant, *Critique of Judgement*, cited by Matherne, 'Kant's Theory of Imagination', p. 64.

73 Kant, *CJ*, pp. 236–7.

74 It is interesting to note that Williams, in developing his theory of aesthetics, turns not to Kant but to the Thomist thinkers, Jacques Maritain and Hans Urs von Balthasar. See Chapter 8, '*Poiesis* 1: Making Other'. Williams' main reference to Kant is to be found in *The Edge of Words: God and the Habits of Language* (London: Bloomsbury, 2014), pp. 10–14, where he acknowledges the value of Kant's method in demonstrating what *cannot* be said about God but also points to the limits of Kant's methodology.

75 See John Macmurray, 'Kant and the Romantics' in *The Self as Agent* (London: Faber & Faber, 1957); Hedley, *Living Forms of the Imagination*, p. 6; J. Kneller, *Kant and the Power of the Imagination* (Cambridge: Cambridge University Press, 2007).

76 Richard Kearney, *The Wake of Imagination: Ideas of Creativity in Western Culture* (London: Faber & Faber, 1988), p. 182.

77 See J. Robert Berth, *The Symbolic Imagination: Coleridge and the Romantic Tradition* (New York: Fordham University Press, 2001), p. 46; Malcolm Guite, *Faith, Hope and Poetry: Theology and the Poetic Imagination* (London: Ashgate, 2012), p. 145.

78 Samuel Taylor Coleridge, *Biographia Literaria*, I, ed. J. Engell and W. Jackson Bate (Princeton, NJ: Princeton University Press, 1983), p. 304.

79 Coleridge, 'Frost at Midnight', cited by Guite, *Faith, Hope and Poetry*, p. 153.

80 Sartre, *The Imaginary*, p. 179.

81 Sartre, *The Imaginary*, p. 5.

82 Sartre, *The Imaginary*, p. 5.

83 Sartre, *The Imaginary*, p. 6.

84 Sartre, *The Imaginary*, p. 8. Perception sees from one perspective, 'quasi-observation intuits the object as a whole'.

85 Sartre, *The Imaginary*, p. 11.

86 Sartre, *The Imaginary*, p. 12.

87 Sartre, *The Imaginary*, p. 14.

88 Robert Hopkins, 'Sartre', in Kind, *Routledge Handbook of Philosophy of Imagination*, p. 83.
89 Sartre, *The Imaginary*, p. 186.
90 Hopkins, 'Sartre', p. 92.
91 Sartre, *The Imaginary*, p. 183.
92 Sartre, *The Imaginary*, p. 184.
93 Sartre, *The Imaginary*, p. 179.
94 Sartre, *The Imaginary*, p. 119.
95 Paul Ricoeur, *The Rule of Metaphor*, trans. Robert Czerny with Kathleen McLaughlin and John Costello (London: Routledge & Kegan Paul, 1978).
96 Paul Ricoeur, *Time and Narrative*, Vol. 1, trans. Kathleen McLaughlin and David Pellauer (Chicago: Chicago University Press, 1990).
97 Paul Ricoeur, *Lectures on Ideology and Utopia*, ed. and Introduction, G. H. Taylor (New York: Columbia University Press, 1986).
98 Paul Ricoeur, 'The Function of Fiction in Shaping Reality', in Mario J. Valdés, ed., *A Ricoeur Reader: Reflection and Imagination* (Hemel Hempstead: Harvester Wheatsheaf, 1991), pp. 117–36.
99 Ricoeur, 'The Function of Fiction', p. 120. He labels such reference a 'reproductive reference' in that it reproduces reality.
100 Ricoeur, 'The Function of Fiction', p. 135.
101 Ricoeur, 'The Function of Fiction', p. 127.
102 Ricoeur's theory of metaphor will be discussed in more detail in Part 2.
103 He notes that 'fiction' is derived from *facere*, 'to make', and is always a matter of labour. See Ricoeur, 'The Function of Fiction', p. 129.
104 Ricoeur, 'The Function of Fiction', p. 134.
105 Ricoeur, 'The Function of Fiction', p. 128.
106 Ricoeur, 'The Function of Fiction', p. 135. As discussed by Black and by Barbour, models are important heuristic devices in facilitating scientific discovery. Max Black, *Models and Metaphors* (Ithaca, NY: Cornell University Press, 1962); Ian Barbour, *Myths, Models and Paradigms* (London: SCM Press, 1974).
107 Amy Kind, 'Introduction', in Kind, *Routledge Handbook of Philosophy of Imagination*, p. 7.
108 The chapter headings in the *Handbook* cover such topics as memory, emotion, child development, modal epistemology, science and mathematics.
109 Neil Van Leeuwen, 'The Imaginative Agent', in Kind and Kung, *Knowledge Through Imagination*, pp. 86–7. Van Leeuwen here differentiates between three senses of imagination: constructive (propositional), attitude (including emotional) and imagistic imagining.
110 This has been the focus of study in such fields as anthropology, cognitive science, neurolinguistics and the philosophy of mind. See, for example, Stephen Mithin, *The Pre-History of the Mind: The Cognitive Origins of Art, Religion and Science* (London: Thames & Hudson, 1996); Daniel Dor, *The Instruction of Imagination: Language as Social Communication Technology* (Oxford: Oxford University Press, 2015); James R. Hurford, *The Origins of Language: A Slim Guide* (Oxford: Oxford University Press, 2014).
111 Stephen T. Asma, *The Evolution of Imagination* (Chicago, IL: University of Chicago Press, 2017).
112 Asma, *The Evolution of Imagination*, p. 4.
113 Asma, *The Evolution of Imagination*, pp. 8–9.

114 Asma, *The Evolution of Imagination*, p. 11.
115 George Lakoff and Mark Johnson, *Metaphors We Live By* (Chicago, IL: University of Chicago Press, 1980); *Philosophy in the Flesh: The Embodied Mind and its Challenge to Western Thought* (New York: Basic Books, 1999); Johnson, *The Body in the Mind* (1990).
116 Johnson, *The Body in the Mind*, p. xiii.
117 Johnson acknowledges his debt to Kant in his conceptualization of schemata and concept formation.
118 Examples are the 'in-out' structure of the containment schema used for both literal and figurative situations, and the 'from-to' structure of the path schema applicable to both change of location and change of state.
119 Johnson, *The Body in the Mind*, p. xv.
120 Johnson, *The Body in the Mind*, p. xiv.
121 Johnson contends that a complete theory of imagination must also take account of narrative as being central to the way 'humans experience and make sense of their world'. *The Body in the Mind*, pp. 171–2.
122 Modell, *Imagination and the Meaningful Brain*.
123 Modell, *Imagination and the Meaningful Brain*, p. 21.
124 Modell, *Imagination and the Meaningful Brain*, p. 1.
125 See, for example, the list of contributors to Zittoun and Glăveanu, *The Handbook of Imagination and Culture*.
126 Agustín Fuentes, *The Creative Spark: How Imagination Made Humans Exceptional* (New York: Penguin Random House, 2017), p. 2.
127 Fuentes, *The Creative Spark*, p. 213.
128 Vlad Petre Glăveanu and Tania Zittoun, 'The Future of Imagination in Sociocultural Research', in Zittoun and Glăveanu, *Handbook of Imagination and Culture*, p. 348.
129 Glăveanu and Zittoun, 'The Future of Imagination', p. 360. See also Zittoun and Gillespie, *Imagination in Human and Cultural Development* (London: Routledge, 2016), p. 64.
130 Zittoun and Gillespie, *Imagination in Human and Cultural Development*, p. 58.
131 Zittoun and Gillespie, *Imagination in Human and Cultural Development*, p. 57.
132 Castor Castoriadis, *L'Institution imaginaire de la société* (Paris: Editions du Seuil, 1975).
133 Charles Taylor, *A Secular Age* (Cambridge, MA: The Belknap Press, 2007), p. 25.
134 Taylor, *A Secular Age*, pp. 171–2.
135 Taylor, *A Secular Age*, p. 173.
136 Taylor, *A Secular Age*, p. 172.
137 Zittoun and Glăveanu, 'Imagination at the Frontiers of Psychology', in *Handbook of Imagination and Culture*.
138 Zittoun and Gillespie, *Imagination in Human and Cultural Development*, ch.3, pp. 38–54.
139 Zittoun and Gillespie, *Imagination in Human and Cultural Development*, p. 8.
140 Zittoun and Gillespie, *Imagination in Human and Cultural Development*, p. 45.

141 Zittoun and Gillespie, *Imagination in Human and Cultural Development*, p. 48.

142 Zittoun and Gillespie, *Imagination in Human and Cultural Development*, p. 49.

143 Zittoun and Gillespie, *Imagination in Human and Cultural Development*, pp. 49–50.

144 Zittoun and Gillespie, *Imagination in Human and Cultural Development*, p. 51.

145 See Tania Zittoun and Frédéric Cerchia, 'Imagination as Expansion of Experience', *Integrative Psychological and Behavioral Science* 47 (2013), pp. 305–24.

146 Zittoun and Gillespie, *Imagination in Human and Cultural Development*, pp. 90–110.

147 Zittoun and Gillespie, *Imagination in Human and Cultural Development*, pp. 111–24.

148 Questions concerning the operation and reliability of imagination in modal thinking feature prominently in current philosophical investigations. See, for example, Peter Kung, 'Imagination and Modal Epistemology', in Kind, *Routledge Handbook of Philosophy of Imagination*, pp. 437–50.

149 See, for example, White, *The Language of Imagination*, p. 46; Johnson, *The Body in the Mind*, p. 141.

150 Raymond W. Gibbs, Jr, 'Metaphor and Thought: The State of the Art', in *The Cambridge Handbook of Metaphor and Thought*, ed. Raymond W. Gibbs, Jr (New York: Cambridge University Press, 2008), p. 3.

151 Kind and Kung's collection of essays, *Knowledge Through Imagination*, includes a section on 'skeptical approaches' to the issue of the role of imagination in knowledge acquisition. In the essay 'Imagination Through Knowledge', Sharon Spaulding questions whether imagination '*directly* yields knowledge' but does grant that it 'plays an important epistemic role' (p. 224).

# 2

# Symbolization: Meaning-making

## Introduction

The brief overview in Chapter 1 of the two philosophical traditions associated with the study of imagination leads to the conclusion that, in human development, both cognition and creativity depend on the synthesizing and transcending operations of imagination. Imagination was identified with the human ability to detach from the actual to envisage possibility, to connect disparate realms of experience, to develop meaning through symbolization, to transcend the empirical and to produce hitherto unforeseen ways of modelling finite reality. It was asserted that it is the human capacity for imagination that makes change possible, bringing developments in all areas of human activity.

Chapter 2 is concerned with an exploration of the imaginative capacity for connecting perception, object and sign in the production of language and the communication of meaning. A study of the origin and development of language is well beyond the scope of this book. It is sufficient to conclude, as Rowan Williams has suggested, that 'the origin and acquisition of language … is associated with a particular moment in cultural evolution, made possible by a particular moment in the physical evolution of the cerebral cortex, at which *representation* became a shared human practice.'[1] 'Representation' in the sense employed by Williams signifies the presentation through another medium of an aspect of perception. Language as a conventional system of signs is the primary medium whereby perceptions are re-presented for the purpose of communication.

In this chapter the linguistic processes of symbolization, metaphor and myth will be examined with the intention of highlighting the ways in which imagination operates to connect bodily sensation and linguistic symbol, and thus establish relations among discrete objects, experiences, memories and events. I begin my exploration of the human imaginative capacity for making such connections with Rowan Williams' poem 'Deathship'.[2]

## 'Deathship'

Written in memory of the poet-priest R. S. Thomas, 'Deathship'[3] takes as its starting point the Welsh poet's lifelong fascination with the sea. Here, the sea is not merely the physical stretch of water visible from Thomas's house but is a symbol of the journey of death upon which the poet is about to embark. The background to the poem is Williams' awareness of Thomas's lifelong anguish at the impenetrability of divine darkness, an anguish softened in his later years by a sense of God's greater closeness and 'gentleness'.[4]

> The last years, words from a window
> smoothing the sea, the iron back and forth
> to probe the fugitive wrinkles
> carving a path down to the lost gate.
>
> What hid in the pale clefts till now
> feels for the light, a soft uncertain
> fingering as if through
> stone, through furrows of flint.
>
> The tides pressed neat as for an evening out:
> time to drag down a black boat from the shed,
> off through the gate, to balance
> on the slow sea at dark, ready to sail.
>
> The smoke will rise, the cloudy pillar
> wavering across the sky's long page.
> At dawn, somewhere westward,
> the boat flares in a blaze of crying birds.

At the end of his life, Thomas is no longer capable of venturing down to the sea through 'the lost gate' of physical access to the water and of spiritual access to God. Instead, he must probe the oceanic mystery of divine presence 'from a window', seeking uncertainly to feel his way towards God through 'clefts' in the flinty stone of divine Otherness. For him, however, the effort of seeking God has recently eased a little. Like a housewife's iron, 'smoothing' the 'fugitive wrinkles' of divine mystery, his words now more closely approximate to the truth of God.

Sensing God's nearness, he realizes that the time has come to launch the ship of his human body on to the sea of darkness and death. From the shore, others watch his departure, and it is they who glimpse the pillar of cloud leading him to the Promised Land, and who behold the blazing flare of consummation and hear the cries of the birds drawn towards the pole of God's eternal light.[5]

Williams' poem serves to introduce the linguistic devices employed by the imagination to bring together different aspects of human experience, thereby creating multiple resonances of meaning, such that our perception of reality is enhanced and deepened. The poem depends on the analogy of death as a voyage into unknown seas. The sea symbolizes not only death but also the mysterious depths of God; the window is that of physical and spiritual vision; the gate signifies both physical and spiritual access; poetic words become an iron smoothing the mysterious sea of divine truth; the pillar of cloud and the blazing boat are symbols drawn from biblical and mythical sources; and the crying birds are a reference to one of Thomas's poems. The mind seeking God is an analogy of fingers seeking crevices in rock faces. Words metaphorically 'carve a path' towards understanding.

Together these language forms communicate a sense of what it was like for R. S. Thomas, in his last years, to find himself edging closer to the God who, save for the occasional 'Bright Field',[6] had remained agonizingly hidden from him throughout his life. The sixteen lines of Williams' poem offer the listener/reader a more perceptive glimpse of the deceased poet than do most obituaries. They give support to the claim, enunciated by Williams and others, that the surplus of meaning inherent in an imaginative use of language enables us to apprehend the world more fully.[7]

## Symbolization

The imaginative capacity for symbolization is said to be distinctive to human beings.[8] The human ability to 'throw together', and thus connect, object, sign and meaning, has been considered to be the source of language, as well as of art and religion.[9] According to Paul Avis, it is 'through our symbol-making capacity [that] we make sense of the world and find meaning in life'.[10] Symbolization is so ubiquitous in human experience that its operation is generally unnoticed: the language system of symbolic signs is taken for granted, as is the fact that we are 'embedded in a world of dense symbolic landscapes'.[11] It is often only through the arts or religion that we become aware of the symbolic mediation of human consciousness.

## Symbol

Symbols arise from the power of the imagination to make connections between dissimilar entities or between disparate domains of experience and to link the concrete with the abstract. Avis defines symbol as 'imagining one thing in the form of another'.[12] In so doing he points to the two aspects he considers fundamental to a symbol, namely imaginative participation and form. By 'form' he is referring to the Aristotelian distinction between substance and accidents, the form being the 'essence' of the representative entity as opposed to its incidental features.

Avis goes on to cite Susanne Langer's assertion: 'The power of understanding symbols, i.e. of regarding everything about a sense-datum as irrelevant except a certain form that it embodies, is the most characteristic mental trait of mankind.'[13] The creation and processing of symbols requires an imaginative act, the capacity to enter into and indwell the representative phenomenon so as to discern its essential inner meaning. 'In symbolism,' says Avis, '*mimesis* (representation) leads to *methexis* (participation).'[14]

While Avis makes no attempt to analyse the phenomenological process involved in such indwelling, others such as Martin Heidegger[15] and Gaston Bachelard[16] have written extensively on the subject.[17] Dominic Griffiths makes reference to Heidegger's reflection on Van Gogh's 1886 painting of a pair of shoes. The depiction 'calls us to go beyond the mere thingness of the object' to discern the 'toilsome tread of the worker [and] the accumulated tenacity of her slow trudge'.[18] In this painting the old, worn boots serve as a symbol of a whole way of life: the arduous existence of Dutch peasant farmers and the qualities of character called for by this life.

It is this imaginative participatory aspect of the symbol which, in Avis's view, differentiates it from the sign. Purely arbitrary and conventional, signs make connections with *known* experience. Symbols, by contrast, are never arbitrary in that they convey something of the qualities of the phenomenon symbolized. They transcend existing meanings, pointing beyond themselves to that which is only partly or not yet known, and in so doing they convey new meaning. Avis can thus assert that symbols 'speak to us of things beyond our ken', having 'reference to transcendent reality and themselves participat[ing] in that reality'.[19] In this way, symbols are revelatory, bringing to awareness dimensions of existence inaccessible to empirical examination. They are essential for religious language as a means of referring to that which is beyond ordinary experience, becoming, as suggested by Coleridge, 'a bridge between God and the world'.[20]

## SYMBOLIZATION: MEANING-MAKING

The surplus of meaning produced by a symbol is the focus of Ricoeur's hermeneutical analysis of the power of the symbolic.[21] Defining the symbolic as 'any structure of signification in which a direct primary, literal meaning designates, in addition, another meaning which is indirect, secondary and figurative and which can be apprehended only through the first',[22] Ricoeur stresses the 'opaque', multilayered, 'inexhaustible depth' of the symbol,[23] which opens up a range of possible interpretations, creating a dynamic interplay of meanings. The symbol always conveys more than a single denotation since it carries a whole 'world' of associations derived from one's language and culture. It therefore 'invites thought' and critical reflection.[24] Whether verbal or non-verbal, it is inextricably tied to language, becoming meaningful only through the process of interpretation.

Significant in Ricoeur's account of symbolism is his differentiation between symbols-as-sign and symbols-as-representation. The latter type of symbol has a mediating function; it is not a substitute for something else but points towards, and gives expression to, a greater awareness of reality. It gives access to three different zones of experience – the cosmic, oneiric and poetic – and is thereby the means by which the 'expressivity' of the universe is mediated to human consciousness.[25]

Cosmic symbols attribute sacred meaning to natural phenomena. Oneiric symbols emerge from the unconscious human psyche, enabling self-expression and self-understanding. Poetic symbols, on the other hand, are 'language in a state of emergence'.[26] They reveal the capacity of language to bring to expression, and hence to awareness, new ways of seeing the world and new possibilities for human existence. Creative of newness, they expand human capability.

Ricoeur thus concurs with Bachelard's conclusion that 'The poetic image ... becomes a new being of our language, expressing us by making us what it expresses.'[27] It increases our knowledge of who we are but, as Ricoeur is adamant, it does so by the second critical movement of bringing awareness of the totality from which we have consciously uprooted ourselves and yet to which we continue to belong.[28] The surplus of meaning inherent in the symbol not only increases the gamut of language but also serves to make and remake us as human beings and to bring us to greater awareness of the reality of which we are a part.

Perhaps the most exalted theory of symbol is that of the Romantic poet Coleridge. For him, true symbols, unlike artificially contrived analogies, are 'the visible tips of an ontological iceberg',[29] and thus effect contact with the transcendent. This contact is possible because:

> A Symbol is characterized by ... the translucence of the Eternal through and in the Temporal. It always partakes of the Reality, which it renders intelligible; and while it enunciates the whole, abides itself as a living part in that Unity, of which it is representative.[30]

That 'Reality', according to Coleridge, is the divine Logos, the Word, both eternal and temporal, which brought creation into being as a temporal expression of the Eternal, and which continues to be glimpsed within the objects of nature by those who seek to see beyond the surface to discern the eternal source. Such see-ers are generally poets, open to glimpse the transcendent in the immanent.

As will be demonstrated in later chapters, the insights of both Coleridge and Ricoeur into the power of symbol to create new meaning, and to effect connection with the transcendent, are shared and further developed by Rowan Williams.[31]

## *Metaphor*

The titles of the books *Metaphors We Live By*[32] and *The Myths We Live By*[33] point to the pervasiveness in human thought, language and action of the phenomenon of metaphor and its narrative extension in the form of myth. Both titles also signal the increased attention paid to metaphor over recent years, not only by literary scholars but also by psychologists, philosophers and cognitive scientists. Summing up recent research developments for *The Cambridge Handbook of Metaphor and Thought*, Raymond Gibbs Jr asserts that metaphor is 'a fundamental scheme by which people conceptualise the world and their own activities'.[34] He concludes that metaphor structures our experience of the world.[35]

As in the case of imagination, 'metaphor' eludes ready definition. Derived from the Greek *meta*, meaning 'beyond', and *pherein*, to 'carry', it signifies the transfer of meaning from one domain of experience to another and thus points to the connective power of imagination. While some define it broadly, including non-verbal as well as verbal examples, Janet Martin Soskice restricts it to language. She asserts that 'metaphor is that figure of speech whereby we speak of one thing in terms which are seen to be suggestive of another.'[36] Her expansion of the last phrase is important in that it signals the allusive nature and power of metaphor. It is not a simple comparison but 'carries across' to the subject under consideration a whole complex set of associations belonging to a different domain of experience. Similarly, Avis refers to the 'stereoscopic function' of metaphor, asserting that it 'is not just naming one thing in terms of another, but seeing, experiencing and intellectualizing one thing in the light of another'.[37] Ricoeur argues that metaphor holds in tension similarity and difference, finding similarity within dissimilar semantic fields.[38]

From the above definitions it is clear that metaphors gain their effect not from the words but from the conceptual operation involved in their formulation and processing. Soskice's 'interanimation theory'[39] maintains that 'A metaphor is a form of language use with a unity of subject-matter and which yet draws upon two (or more) sets of associations, and does so, characteristically, by involving the consideration of a model or models.'[40] The reference to models is indicative of the structural character of metaphoric thought. Conveying a meaning that can be expressed in no other way, metaphors bring together the networks of associations evoked by both tenor (subject) and vehicle (descriptor). Understanding is made possible by the fact that such associative networks often take the form of models, complex conceptual systems designed to describe and explain phenomena. Metaphors are therefore not mere embellishments of an idea but, by means of the organizational coherence of their associative networks, serve to structure the way we perceive and experience the world.

In this respect the role of the reader is essential since the understanding of a metaphor depends on the reader's 'ability to see it as suggesting a model or models which enable him to go on extending the significance of what he has read or heard'.[41] It is up to the reader to discern the richness of associations elicited by a metaphorical description.

Avis's survey of metaphor stresses its event character[42] whereby two perceptions are 'fused together'[43] to create a new 'identity',[44] thus offering the reader a new way of seeing and experiencing the world. By 'joining ... different domains of experience which do not readily fit together', metaphors can generate insight, and thus be the source of new knowledge.[45] It is the capacity of metaphorical language to bring about new meaning that gives it 'ontological relevance' since 'with this new meaning new being is brought to speech'.[46] Rowan Williams argues that 'metaphor – seeing the familiar in and through the alien – is a means of discovery.'[47] His poem 'Deathship' is evidence of the associative complexity and new insight produced by metaphorical language.

Ricoeur's interest in metaphor lies precisely in this capacity for creating new possibilities for human existence from 'the interplay between sameness and difference'.[48] Unlike Avis, however, Ricoeur denies that the power of metaphor lies in the fusing together of differences. For him, it consists in the 'shock of contradiction' occasioned by the confrontation of different semantic networks.[49] His claim is that, far from becoming fused, the two networks are 'dismantled' by the process of metaphorization to generate 'semantic innovation'.[50] The creation of a 'new being in language'[51] has ontological significance in that it coincides with the discovery of a new conception of reality. He can therefore claim that 'The strategy of discourse implied in metaphorical languages is ... to shatter and to increase our sense of reality by shattering and increasing our language ... With metaphor we experience the metamorphosis of both language and reality.'[52] For Ricoeur, the possibilities for newness inhering in metaphorical language are a source of hope.[53] It is because language offers the freedom to 'increase our sense of reality' that hope is always possible, even in the face of death. The capacity of symbolic and metaphoric language to open on to hope leads to the study of myth.

## Myth

Myths have been described as 'the dreams of the human race',[54] 'the *imaginary nucleus* of any culture',[55] 'the earliest and ... the most vivid forms of reflection on the truth of existence'[56] and 'imaginative patterns, networks of powerful symbols that suggest particular ways of interpreting the world [and] shape its meaning'.[57] Often dismissed as mere fiction, myths are shown to be integral to all cultures, being the bearers of the implicit and unquestioned meanings that hold those cultures together.[58] According to both functionalist (Malinowski) and structural (Lévi-Strauss) theories, myth serves to 'ensure social stability and to perpetuate received ways of doing things'.[59]

Not confined to the early stages of cultural development, myths continue to 'form part of our mental furniture',[60] the power of these myths lying in the fact of their remaining generally unrecognized. Mary Midgley has drawn attention to the hold exercised over the Western mind of the modern myths of the social contract, the inevitability of progress and the omnicompetence of science. Iain McGilchrist points to the limitations of the popular conceptualization of the brain as a computer,[61] while Conrad Lodziak has sought to dismantle the myth of consumerism.[62] As is the case with all mythical world views, such myths, if left unexamined, serve to structure and delimit the conceptualization of experience, and so to restrict the range of imaginable possibilities for thought and action.

Paul Ricoeur's study of myth stresses both its capacity to provide meaning, integration and hope, and its tendency to 'perversion'.[63] Pointing to two twentieth-century examples of such perversion, the 'myth of absolute power' (fascism) and the 'myth of the sacrificial scapegoat' (anti-Semitism and racism), he argues for the necessity of a hermeneutical approach to the evaluation of myth. Such an approach not only acknowledges the positive function performed by myth in establishing social identity and cohesion but also requires a critical interrogation of the unstated value base evidenced in the power relations to which it gives rise. For Ricoeur, the 'critical criterion' by which the 'mythical foundation' of a society is to be assessed is whether such a myth has as its 'horizon the liberation of humanity *as a whole*'.[64] He concludes that the imaginative dimension, *mythos*, and the critical appraisal afforded by reason, *logos*, are both indispensable: 'every *mythos* harbors a *logos* which requires to be exhibited.'[65]

According to Ricoeur, it is the horizon opened by myth that makes it 'the bearer of possible worlds'.[66] In his view, myths have the capacity to function at both the particular and universal level and are to be distinguished by the dimension of existence to which they refer. Myths foundational for a particular culture point to the historical, 'chronicle' dimension of existence, whereas the 'wisdom dimension' is activated by myths that offer truths applicable to all.[67] It is this universal category of myth that harbours surplus meaning. Such myths are able to transcend national and cultural barriers and enlarge horizons of understanding, thereby becoming the 'bearer of other *possible* worlds'.[68] Escaping the captivity of past and present, they allow us to glimpse hitherto unforeseen forms of social existence and thus have a utopian purpose.

The indispensability of imagined utopias is the subject of Ricoeur's *Lectures on Ideology and Utopia*.[69] Here he links myth with the notion of the social imaginary. Asserting that 'every society possesses ... a socio-political *imaginaire*',[70] he describes the latter as 'an ensemble of symbolic discourses'[71] composed of the collective narratives and myths that shape the communal imagination of that society. At the heart of the social imaginary is an 'ideology'[72] that links a community to its origins in some foundational event and which serves to integrate and validate the social order over time. In doing so, it may become 'fixed and fetishized'[73] and therefore resistant to change. In such a circumstance, elements of the original vision may operate as a force of 'rupture', bringing judgment concerning what has been lost and a utopian vision of renewal, of a 'society that is not-yet'.[74]

His conclusion is that '*ideology* as a symbolic confirmation of the past and *utopia* as a symbolic opening towards the future are complementary; if cut off from each other they can lead to a form of political pathology.'[75] Critical awareness of the mythical substratum is imperative for the health of a society. This conclusion is in line with Rowan Williams' contention that the 'imaginative bereavement' of contemporary Western society is partly attributable to its loss of connection with its foundational Judeo-Christian myth.[76]

The dual orientation of myth towards both past (ideology) and future (utopia) derives from its character as narrative. Inherent in narrative is the dimension of time, expressed through language. Myths are stories about the past that provide meaning for the present and possibilities for the future. Like all stories, they are a way of structuring the human experience of time.[77] Our individual experience of time is the interplay between the life story we constantly construct for ourselves and the larger sociocultural narrative in which our lives are immersed, a narrative constantly in the process of reconstruction.[78]

Language is therefore essential to the phenomenon of 'human time'. Anticipation of the future depends on recollection of the past, since the future is generated out of the possible new interpretations contained within the narrative accounts of the past. History and fiction are two interrelated ways of living 'human time', history through its repeated reinterpretations (refigurations) of the past, fiction through its ordering (configuration) of time to create alternatives to the world of the present, and therefore the possibility of a future different from the past. In this way, narrative has the capacity to reconfigure and transform past experience. Significantly, it also opens up new possibilities for the future, thereby bringing hope.[79]

## Rowan Williams and Ricoeur

In a number of early essays, Williams draws on Ricoeur's observations about the surplus of meaning inherent in symbolic language and the relation between language and reality.[80] He follows Ricoeur in arguing that the phenomenon of human language attests 'to the truth that consciousness is not self-originated, and is called to response'.[81] As a consequence, language is potentially open to that which transcends the limits of finite existence. Human experience is especially enlarged by poetic language with its use of symbol and metaphor. The surplus of meaning embodied by these linguistic devices not only enables an immediacy of experiential contact with the phenomenon in question but also 'breaks open' a new and different perspective on the world, and thus a new and different way of being.

Particularly important for Williams is Ricoeur's conclusion that poetic language 'restores to us that participation-in or belonging-to an order of things which precedes our capacity to oppose ourselves to things taken as objects opposed to a subject'.[82] The subject-object perspective of modern humanity is thus reversed to make us the responsive recipient of a reality beyond ourselves and within which we belong. From such an experience, new insights are gained, and new possibilities revealed. Human creativity is accordingly conceived by both Ricoeur and Williams as a response to the invitation offered by the universe, and divine revelation is to be identified with both God's initial speaking of the world into being and the response of a human imagination open to the 'language' of the material world.[83]

The significance of imaginative response for both thinkers is highlighted by Ricoeur's observation that 'revelation is addressed not so much to a will called upon to submit as to an imagination called upon to "open itself".'[84] As the conclusion of the hermeneutical spiral, such receptivity to the excess of meaning intrinsic to symbolic language brings the realization that 'the symbol opens out on to the endless horizons of desire refining itself into the love of creation and creator.'[85] Noteworthy here is the association of imagination with desire, which will be shown in Part Two to be crucial to Williams' conception of imagination. While reference to Ricoeur is largely absent from Williams' later writings on language and aesthetics, we may conclude that the French philosopher's thinking helped to form the substratum of Williams' aesthetical theory and theology of imagination.

## Symbolism and the depiction of reality

The study of symbolism in its various forms makes a number of significant assertions about figurative language and the apperception of reality. Symbolic language demands that both the author and the receiver of the communication become 'see-ers' and 'participants', going beyond the surface meaning to explore a depth and richness of associations that must be processed not just cognitively but also affectively and imaginatively. For symbolic language to yield meaning, it requires active imaginative participation, and it is as a result of such participation that one's sense of the world, of other people and of oneself is renewed, expanded, enriched and deepened.

In this way, symbolic language is revelatory, bringing to awareness dimensions of existence inaccessible to empirical examination. In Ricoeur's terms, it serves to 'shatter' previous perceptions of reality in order to give access to new understandings of existence and increased possibilities for action. The dimension of temporality inherent in narrative and myth situates present experience within a framework that encompasses past and future, making it possible to reconceptualize the past and envisage alternative ways of living into the future. It is therefore claimed that figurative language, in all its expressions, generates the freedom both to think and act differently. It gives rise to the hope that the future is open to new ways of being and new forms of action.

Assertions such as the above assume a conception of reality extending beyond those aspects accessible to empirical verification. They attest to the possibility of transcendence glimpsed in and through the experience of the immanent; they point to the occurrence of 'annunciations' bringing transformation to the scope and meaning of everyday existence. Fundamental to such claims are three contentions concerning the nature of reality: first, that it exists independently of the human mind; second, that the real transcends the limits of finite experience and knowledge; and third, that language is the medium by which reality is accessed by finite minds.[86] The conclusion is that the various forms of symbolism operate from a position of 'figurative realism'. Such a position, according to Avis, asserts that:

> Creative, figurative language is significant, cognitive and unsubstitutable, though not veridical – that is to say, it is not a window into reality as it is, transparent and undistorted, but a reflection in human thought of the actual impact of objective reality, though refracted, dimmed and distorted by the psychological, sociological, political and cultural lenses through which we must inevitably look.[87]

Human cognitive processes are considered to offer authentic but non-comprehensive access to reality through the medium of language, both literal and figurative.[88] Whereas literal language can claim to both describe and refer to the phenomena alluded to, figurative language, by contrast, has a referential but not descriptive function.[89] It points to that which transcends the empirically verifiable, thus offering a glimpse of aspects of reality inaccessible to sense perception. Soskice contends that such language is 'reality-depicting', in that it offers a picture, image or model that is capable of providing truthful information about reality while not claiming to be exhaustive in its depiction.[90] The very vagueness of this language leaves it open to revision or further elaboration and, as a consequence, to ever new truth-conveying insights into reality.[91] Figurative language is therefore indispensable for referring to the ethical, aesthetic and religious dimensions of existence. It does not claim to capture the whole 'transparent and undistorted' truth about reality but rather to point to truth as it is experienced within the limitations of finite existence.

As will become increasingly evident in later chapters, Williams' conception of the relation between imagination and human knowledge is that of critical symbolic realism.[92] Such a position assumes that the human capacity for imagination offers access to previously unexplored and unforeseen dimensions of the 'real'. While the knowledge thus gained may be considered truthful but not exhaustive, he is careful to insist, with

Avis, that it must be subjected to repeated critical interrogation in view of inevitable cultural, psychological and political distortions. Williams' position will be further explicated in the chapters that follow.

## Conclusion

The ubiquity of figurative language leads into the realm of metaphysics. Evoked by such language is the dimension of the transcendent, which raises the question of the relation of finite existence to the realm of the infinite, absolute, eternal. As evidenced in philosophy, art and religion, the human imagination exhibits the freedom to disconnect from observable actuality in order to discern dimensions of existence beyond the empirically verifiable. What are the conditions that make such imaginative connection possible? That is the question to which Chapter 3 seeks to respond through a study of the phenomenon of analogy, taking into account its significance for both cognitive science and metaphysical theology. I argue that the answer provided by Erich Przywara's account of the *analogia entis* is the metaphysical underpinning of Rowan Williams' theology of imagination.

### Notes

1 Rowan Williams, *The Edge of Words: God and the Habits of Language* (London: Bloomsbury, 2014), p. 20.

2 Williams, *The Poems of Rowan Williams* (Oxford: Perpetua Press, 2002), p. 73.

3 Williams, *The Poems of Rowan Williams*, p. 73.

4 Rowan Williams, *Christian Imagination in Poetry and Polity: Some Anglican Voices from Temple to Herbert* (Oxford: SLG Press, 2004), p. 37.

5 The 'crying birds' are a reference to Thomas's poem 'Migrants' about migrating birds 'calling to one another' on their way to the 'climate of their conception' in the collection *Counterpoint* (Newcastle upon Tyne: Bloodaxe Books, 1990), p. 54.

6 R. S. Thomas, 'The Bright Field' in *Collected Poems* (London: Phoenix, 2000), p. 302.

7 Rowan Williams, *Grace and Necessity: Reflections on Art and Love* (London: Morehouse, 2005), p. 147. In his searching exploration of the poems in *A Century of Poetry*, Williams demonstrates how poetry has the capacity to expand and deepen our perception of reality. Rowan Williams, *A Century of Poetry: 100 Poems for Searching the Heart* (London: SPCK, 2022).

8 See, for example, Agustín Fuentes, *The Creative Spark: How Imagination Made Humans Exceptional* (New York: Penguin Random House, 2017), p. 213; Paul Avis, *God and the Creative Imagination: Metaphor, Symbol and Myth in Religion and Theology* (London: Routledge, 1999), p. 104.

9 Fuentes, *Creative Spark*, pp. 213–15; Trevor Hart, *Between the Image and the Word: Theological Engagements with Imagination, Language and Literature* (Farnham: Ashgate, 2013), p. 2; Malcolm Guite, *Faith, Hope and Poetry: Theology and the Poetic Imagination* (London: Routledge, 2016), p. 6.

10 Avis, *God and the Creative Imagination*, p. 104.

11 Fuentes, *Creative Spark*, p. 214.

12 Avis, *God and the Creative Imagination*, p. 103.

13 Avis, *God and the Creative Imagination*, p. 103.

14 Avis, *God and the Creative Imagination*, p. 108.

15 Martin Heidegger, *Basic Writings*, ed. David F. Krell (San Francisco, CA: HarperCollins, 1993).

16 Gaston Bachelard, *La Poétique de l'Espace* (Paris: Presses Universitaires de France, 1957).

17 Ricoeur identifies three stages of understanding symbol: 'living *in* symbols', 'personal involvement' in the symbol, and 'think[ing] *from* symbols'. See Paul Ricoeur, 'The Hermeneutics of Symbols' in *The Philosophy of Paul Ricoeur: An Anthology of His Work*, ed. Charles E. Reagan and David Stewart (Boston, MA: Beacon Press, 1978), pp. 44–5.

18 Dominic Griffiths, 'The Poet as "Worldmaker": T. S. Eliot and the Religious Imagination', in *Poetry and the Religious Imagination: The Power of the Word*, ed. Francesca Bugliani Knox and David Lonsdale (Farnham: Ashgate, 2015), p. 164.

19 Avis, *God and the Creative Imagination*, p. 106.

20 Avis, *God and the Creative Imagination*, p. 108.

21 See Ricoeur, 'The Hermeneutics of Symbols', pp. 36–8. See also Richard Kearney, 'Between Imagination and Language' in *On Paul Ricoeur: The Owl of Minerva* (Abingdon: Routledge, 2017), pp. 35–58.

22 Cited by Kearney, *On Paul Ricoeur*, p. 23.

23 Ricoeur, 'The Hermeneutics of Symbols', p. 38. For an analysis of the ontological significance of metaphorical and symbolic language in the work of Heidegger, Bachelard and Ricoeur inter alia, see Clive Cazeaux, *Metaphor and Continental Philosophy* (New York: Routledge, 2007).

24 Ricoeur, 'The Hermeneutics of Symbols', p. 37.

25 Paul Ricoeur, 'The Symbol Gives Rise to Thought' in *Philosophical Anthropology: Writings and Lectures*, Volume 3, ed. Johann Michel and Jérôme Porée (Cambridge: Polity Press, 2016), pp. 109–10.

26 Ricoeur, 'The Symbol Gives Rise to Thought', p. 110.

27 Ricoeur, 'The Symbol Gives Rise to Thought', p. 110.

28 Ricoeur, 'The Symbol Gives Rise to Thought', p. 123. Ricoeur states that 'the symbol gives rise to the thought that the *cogito* is inside being and not vice versa.'

29 The quotation is from M. J. Swiatecka and is cited by Avis, *God and the Creative Imagination*, p. 107.

30 Samuel Taylor Coleridge, *The Statesman's Manual or The Bible the Best Guide to Political Skill and Foresight: A Lay Sermon Addressed to the Higher Classes of Society, with an Appendix containing Comments and Essays connected with the Study of the Inspired Writings* (London: Gale & Fenner, 1816), p. 37.

31 In his reflection on the poem 'Neither' by R. S. Thomas, Williams writes that 'When language is suffused with [the unsuspected possibilities that belong to the life of God], it displays God.' Williams, *A Century of Poetry*, p. 332.

32 George Lakoff and Mark Johnson, *Metaphors We Live By* (Chicago, IL: University of Chicago Press, 1980).
33 Mary Midgley, *The Myths We Live By* (London: Routledge, 2011).
34 Raymond W. Gibbs, Jr, 'Metaphor and Thought: The State of the Art', in *The Cambridge Handbook of Metaphor and Thought*, ed. Raymond W. Gibbs, Jr (New York: Cambridge University Press, 2008), p. 3.
35 Gibbs, 'Metaphor and Thought', p. 13.
36 Janet Martin Soskice, *Metaphor and Religious Language* (Oxford: Clarendon Press, 1985), p. 15.
37 Avis, *God and the Creative Imagination*, p. 97.
38 Paul Ricoeur, 'Word, Polysemy, Metaphor: Creativity in Language' in *A Ricoeur Reader; Reflection and Imagination*, ed. Mario J. Valdés (Hemel Hempstead: Harvester Wheatsheaf, 1991), p. 83.
39 Soskice, *Metaphor and Religious Language*, p. 43.
40 Soskice, *Metaphor and Religious Language*, p. 49.
41 Soskice, *Metaphor and Religious Language*, p. 51.
42 Avis, *God and the Creative Imagination*, p. 96.
43 David J. Bryant, *Faith and the Play of Imagination: On the Role of Imagination in Religion* (Macon, GA: Mercer University Press, 1989), p. 100.
44 Bryant, *Faith and the Play of Imagination*, p. 98.
45 As Soskice has pointed out, the gaining of insight is dependent on the prior knowledge and reflective participation of the reader.
46 Avis, *God and the Creative Imagination*, p. 100. The quotation is from J. Webster, 'Eberhard Jüngel on the Language of Faith', *Modern Theology*, 1985, 1, pp. 253–76.
47 Rowan Williams, *A Century of Poetry*, p. 234.
48 Paul Ricoeur, 'Word, Polysemy, Metaphor' in Valdés, *Ricoeur Reader*, p. 82.
49 Bryant, *Faith and the Play of Imagination*, p. 94.
50 Kearney, *On Paul Ricoeur*, pp. 51–2.
51 Kearney, *On Paul Ricoeur*, p. 53.
52 Ricoeur, 'Word, Polysemy, Metaphor' in Valdés, *A Ricoeur Reader*, p. 85.
53 For the significance of hope and freedom in Ricoeur's philosophical anthropology, see Dominic Griffiths, 'The Poet as Worldmaker' in Knox and Lonsdale, *Poetry and the Religious Imagination*, pp. 167–70.
54 Reported by Avis, *God and the Creative Imagination*, p. 126.
55 Paul Ricoeur, 'Myth as the Bearer of Possible Worlds' in Kearney, *On Paul Ricoeur*, p. 117.
56 Avis, *God and the Creative Imagination*, p. 133.
57 Midgley, *The Myths We Live By*, p. 1.
58 Avis, *God and the Creative Imagination*, p. 128.
59 Avis, *God and the Creative Imagination*, p. 128.
60 Avis, *God and the Creative Imagination*, p. 115.
61 Iain McGilchrist, *The Master and His Emissary: The Divided Brain and the Making of the Western World* (New Haven, CT: Yale University Press, 2005).
62 Conrad Lodziak, *The Myth of Consumerism* (London: Pluto Press, 2002).
63 Ricoeur, 'Myth as the Bearer of Possible Worlds', p. 120.
64 Ricoeur, 'Myth as the Bearer of Possible Worlds', p. 120.
65 Ricoeur, 'Myth as the Bearer of Possible Worlds', p. 121.
66 Ricoeur, 'Myth as the Bearer of Possible Worlds', p. 120.

67 Ricoeur, 'Myth as the Bearer of Possible Worlds', p. 123.
68 Ricoeur, 'Myth as the Bearer of Possible Worlds', p. 123.
69 Paul Ricoeur, *Lectures on Ideology and Utopia*, ed. George Taylor (New York: Columbia University Press, 1986).
70 Paul Ricoeur, 'The Creativity of Language' in Kearney, *On Paul Ricoeur*, p. 138.
71 Ricoeur, 'The Creativity of Language', p. 138.
72 'Ideology' in Ricoeur's usage does not have a negative connotation but forms the imaginative kernel of all societies.
73 Ricoeur, 'The Creativity of Language', p. 138.
74 Ricoeur, 'The Creativity of Language', p. 138.
75 Ricoeur, 'The Creativity of Language', p. 138.
76 Williams, 'Changing the Myths We Live By' in *Faith in the Public Square* (London: Bloomsbury, 2012), pp. 175–84.
77 Williams, 'Changing the Myths We Live By', p. 127.
78 Williams, 'Changing the Myths We Live By', p. 133. 'Human action is never raw or immediate reality but an action that has been symbolized and resymbolized over and over again.'
79 The dual character of myths with their combination of 'honest harshness' and 'wishful hoping' is also stressed by Williams, who argues that the 'plot lines' of myths and fairy tales offer a realistic framework for human existence in their presentation of both challenge and possible ways through difficulty. 'No More Happy Endings: We need fairy tales now more than ever', *New Statesman*, 22 December 2014, updated 25 August 2015, https://www.newstatesman.com/long-reads/2014/12/rowan-williams-why-we-need-fairy-tales-now-more-ever, accessed 29.06.2024.
80 For Williams' early references to Ricoeur, see 'Balthasar, Rahner and the Apprehension of Being', in John Riches, ed., *The Analogy of Beauty* (Edinburgh: T&T Clark, 1982), and 'The Suspicion of Suspicion: Wittgenstein and Bonhoeffer', in Richard Bell, ed., *Grammar of the Heart: New Essays in Moral Philosophy and Theology* (San Francisco, CA: Harper & Row, 1988), both essays republished in Mike Higton, ed., *Wrestling with Angels: Conversations in Modern Theology* (Grand Rapids, MI: William B. Eerdmans, 2007). See also 'Trinity and Revelation', *Modern Theology* 2.3, 1986, republished in Williams, *On Christian Theology: Challenges in Contemporary Theology* (Malden, MA: Blackwell, 2000).
81 Williams, *Wrestling with Angels*, p. 97. In *The Edge of Words*, Williams takes as his starting point the notion, put forward by Ricoeur and others, that the fact of human language implies a prior initiative, the generative activity of divine Being.
82 Cited by Williams, *On Christian Theology*, p. 133.
83 This notion is further developed in *Looking East in Winter*, where Williams argues that the theological concept of the eternal Logos, incarnate in Jesus Christ, illuminates the relation between human language and the finite *logoi* of the material world. See ch. 3, 'The Embodied Logos: Reason, Knowledge and Relation', in *Looking East in Winter: Contemporary Thought and the Eastern Christian Tradition* (London: Bloomsbury, 2021), pp. 88–92.
84 Williams, *Looking East in Winter*, p. 147.
85 Williams, *Wrestling with Angels*, p. 196.
86 Used in the broad sense of a system of signs, language includes mathematical symbolic formulas.

87 Avis, *God and the Creative Imagination*, p. ix.

88 In view of the growing body of evidence attesting to the ubiquity of metaphor in human language, 'literal' here is used in the sense given by Ricoeur, namely 'usual', 'conventional', as contrasted with the creative novelty of the figurative.

89 See Soskice, *Metaphor and Religious Language*, p. 140: 'this separation of referring and defining is at the very heart of metaphorical speaking' and is necessary for any speech about a transcendent God. As discussed in the Introduction, the same distinction is made by Rowan Williams. See *The Edge of Words*, pp. 22–4.

90 Soskice, *Metaphor and Religious Language*, p. 148.

91 Soskice, *Metaphor and Religious Language*, p. 133.

92 For Williams' position on symbolic realism, see 'Trinity and Ontology', *On Christian Theology*, pp. 148–66; '"Religious realism": On not quite agreeing with Don Cupitt', *Wrestling with Angels*, pp. 228–54; and his discussion of the Orthodox classic, the *Philokalia*, in *Looking East in Winter*, pp. 29–30. See also Catherine Pickstock's analysis of Williams' 'modernist ... symbolist' metaphysics in 'Matter and Mattering: The Metaphysics of Rowan Williams', *Modern Theology* 31.4 (2015), pp. 599–617.

# 3

# Analogy and the Structure of Reality

## Introduction

In Chapter 2 it was argued that symbolization is the key cognitive process whereby experience is given meaning through the symbolic medium of language, thus making communication possible. By means of the figurative language of symbol, metaphor and myth, human consciousness is expanded to encompass hitherto unforeseen possibilities and thus transcend the limits of the actual.

Chapter 3 is an exploration of the cognitive process of analogy, commonly understood as 'a comparison between one thing and another, typically for the purpose of explanation or clarification'.[1] As with symbol and metaphor, analogy identifies similarities across different domains and, by establishing a relation between them, generates a new mental schema and thus an expansion of cognitive capacity. In scope and function, however, analogy has a broader range of application, as will be demonstrated in this chapter.

Described by Roger White as 'highly slippery', the word 'analogy' eludes a single definition, being used by various theorists in different ways.[2] While the Greek word ἀναλογία was originally employed in the field of mathematics with the meaning of 'ratio',[3] in contemporary cognitive science it signifies the human capacity for categorization. As a metaphysical term it was used by Plato and Aristotle to express the relation between finite entities and eternal Forms.[4] Its usage in Christian theology is generally attributed to St Thomas Aquinas, the term *analogia entis* being subsequently coined to refer to the relation of God to creation.[5] It is that analogical relation that is particularly significant for this study. It will be argued that the human capacity to make the leap of imagination to establish connection between known and unknown, finite and infinite, created being and uncreated Being, is to be understood in terms of the analogical structure of reality, a structure of similarity-in-greater-difference.

I use Rowan Williams' poem 'Gethsemane' to introduce and illustrate the argument of this chapter. In the poem, the bright, penetrating light of a Middle Eastern summer becomes an analogy of the insistent presence of God pressing down on the city regarded as holy by three religions. The ability to make such an analogical leap is considered by certain cognitive theorists to be basic to the human thought process of conceptualization. A brief discussion of the increasing interest in analogy in contemporary studies of cognition will lead into an account of its metaphysical significance for the thought of Aristotle and Aquinas. The main thrust of the chapter will be the development by Erich Przywara of the Thomist concept of the analogy of being (*analogia entis*), and the significance of that development for the theology of Rowan Williams.

## Gethsemane[6]

> Who said that trees grow easily
> compared with us? What if the bright
> bare load that pushes down on them
> insisted that they spread and bowed
> and pleated back on themselves and cracked
> and hunched? Light dropping like a palm
> levelling the ground, backwards and forwards?

Visitors to Gethsemane will immediately resonate with Williams' description of the ancient olive trees growing in that garden. 'Bowed', 'cracked and hunched', the trees seem weighed down as though under immense pressure. The poet attributes the source of the pressure to the intense Jerusalem light which, in its relentless brightness, becomes almost a tactile weight, akin to the palm of a human hand pressing heavily on the trees beneath, twisting them into distorted shapes.

> Across the valley are the other witnesses
> of two millennia, the broad stones
> packed by the hand of God, bristling
> with little messages to fill the cracks.
> As the light falls and flattens what grows
> on these hills, the fault lines dart and spread,
> there is room to say something, quick and tight.

In the second stanza, the metaphor of the palm-like weight of light is extended to become the 'hand of God' packing together the 'broad stones' of the Wailing Wall, all that remains of the temple once central to the life of the city. Such is the pressure of that divine palm that it 'flattens' all that lies beneath, creating 'fault lines' in the solid matter of the wall and surrounding landscape, making cracks into which may be pressed prayers, 'messages' to God, a 'quick and tight' human response to the divine insistence.

> Into the trees' clefts, then, do we push
> our folded words, thick as thumbs?
> somewhere inside the ancient bark, a voice
> has been before us, pushed the densest word
> of all, abba, and left it to be collected by
> whoever happens to be passing, bent down
> the same way by the hot unreadable palms.

The third stanza returns us to Gethsemane, its trees having acquired the same significance as the Wailing Wall. It is in their 'clefts' that human messages may now be deposited, since the One who prayed there 2,000 years ago left behind him, in the twisted bark of the trees, the tender word 'abba' to be 'collected' and used by all who, like him, are 'bent' sufficiently low by the weight of God's 'unreadable' presence to experience for themselves the true significance of the small but humanly inconceivable word, 'abba'.

The poem provides insight into the functioning and purpose of analogy and the ways in which it differs from metaphor, even as it uses metaphor to achieve its effect. Through metaphor, exposure to the heaviness of Middle Eastern sunlight is experienced as the pressure of an open hand pressing down on both humans and the trees of the garden in which they stand. The garden has multiple distinctive associations. Its very name evokes scriptural references – not only to Jesus' anguished prayer on the night before his death but also to the city of Jerusalem where the garden is located.

In that city the stones carry memories of the God whose temple was once erected there. Through these associations, the metaphor of light as a hand pressing down is extended to become the hand of God and the analogical meaning of the poem begins to become clear. It communicates the message that, in that place, God's presence is inescapable, exerting pressure on its human inhabitants to respond. The analogy takes the Aristotelian form of ὡς αλλο προς αλλο: as light bears down on human heads so God bears down on human consciousness.

The third stanza offers a complementary, complex analogy[7] which clarifies the nature of God's insistent presence in human lives. The reference there is to Christ's anguished prayer of submission to his Father. The analogy is accordingly as follows: as Jesus Christ bowed to the Father's will, so we humans must bow to the purposes of God. The emotional resonance of the analogy is, however, transformed by the inclusion of the word 'abba'. As a consequence, it must be read in the following way: as Jesus Christ, in accepting the Father's purpose, knew the closeness of the love relationship of Son to Father, so humans, by submitting to God, will also know that God is close to them as their loving Father. The weight pressing down upon that place is shown to be the pressure of God's passionate desire to draw humanity into a relationship of boundless love.

From the poem we discern that analogy goes beyond metaphor in establishing not only relations of similarity between diverse entities but also relations between different experiences, and relations between relations. In contrast also to metaphor, analogies have an explanatory purpose in showing how one experience or relationship may throw light on another, bringing out a more comprehensive meaning. This explains why analogy is a vehicle whereby finite beings may gain some conception of God. As Aquinas insisted, language used of finite reality may be applied to God only analogically, as a means of indicating a relationship of similarity-in-difference between a known finite phenomenon and God who is beyond human comprehension. Analogical language thus makes talk of God possible while at the same time acknowledging the significant difference that exists between finite reality and the infinite God.

In contemporary thought, interest in analogy is less concerned with the metaphysical relation between finite and infinite than with the analogical basis of concept formation. In both instances, what is involved is a conceptual leap from known to unknown. I argue that the capacity to make such leaps is what we call 'imagination'.

## Analogy in cognition

The cognitive scientists Gentner, Holyoak and Kokinov argue that 'analogy lies at the core of human cognition', underpinning 'language, art, music, invention and science'.[8] They describe analogy as 'a special kind of symbolic ability – the ability to pick out patterns, to identify recurrences in these patterns despite variation in the elements that compose them, to form concepts that abstract and reify these patterns, and to express those concepts in language'.[9] The ubiquity of analogy in human thinking was studied by the cognitive psychologists Hofstadter and Sander, who concur that the human capacity for analogy-making is responsible for the phenomenon of categorization and thus for the formation of concepts.[10] Their claim is that cognition involves a 'constant flow of categorizations' produced through the process of analogy-making, and that this capacity for analogy-making enables us to develop 'mental representations of situations' which are then linked by inference to new situations. Daily life thus involves a constant drawing on the categories produced through analogy to enable us to negotiate new and strange experience.[11]

The characteristic feature of such analogies is that they share a conceptual skeleton enabling comparisons to be made between previous and new experience.[12] This conclusion is supported by the work of Holyoak and Thagard, who argue that analogy-formation is determined by three main constraining factors: similarity, structure and purpose, such that similarities and structural parallels between the source and target domains are accessed according to the reasoner's purpose.[13] One such purpose is the communication of emotion, as employed in the processes of persuasion, empathy and reverse empathy. In all these cases, analogies with familiar emotional situations facilitate emotional identification with new situations.[14]

In her discussion of the significance of both metaphor and analogy for scientific thinking, Daniela Bailer-Jones concludes that 'the use of analogies is central for scientific modeling as well as for metaphorical language use.'[15] Noting that, in scientific reasoning, analogy and metaphor often occur together, Bailer-Jones points to the more limited application of metaphor, citing the conclusion reached by Max Black that 'every metaphor may be said to mediate an analogy or structure correspondence.'[16] She remains agnostic, however, in determining whether analogy underlies metaphor formation or whether 'the recognition of an analogy' is 'prompted' by the use of a metaphor.[17]

## Aristotelian and Thomist conceptions of analogy

Turning to the historical origins of analogy, we find that Aristotle is credited with the most extensive early exploration of the concept. Roger White's study of analogy highlights Aristotle's expansion of analogy beyond the field of mathematics into such areas as biology, justice, poetics and metaphysics. White states that 'In Aristotle's hands, analogy becomes an all-important tool of research ... show[ing] by example the extraordinary power of the concept and the diversity of uses to which it can be put.'[18]

Aristotle's insight lay in the realization that the concept of mathematical ratio is applicable to situations in which it is possible to identify *relations* common to two phenomena. These analogical comparisons take the form of αλλο προς αλλο, expressed mathematically as a:b::c:d, or $R(a,b)= R(c,d)$, to be read as: 'As "a" stands in relation to "b", so "c" stands in relation to "d".' So we can say that 'As wings are to birds, so fins are to fish.' This analogical formulation, termed 'analogy of proportionality', allows for comparisons to be made between things that are 'different in kind'.[19]

White argues that Aristotle's use of the word 'analogy' is restricted to the analogy of proportionality. A second pattern of relating is that of 'focal meaning'.[20] This pattern designates the primary referent of a word such as 'healthy', while secondary meanings (food, lifestyle, medicine) indicate the sorts of relations that exist between the primary referent and various aspects of that referent's situation. Characterized by 'a definite ordering of priority and posteriority',[21] this pattern was later called the 'analogy of attribution'. According to White, Aristotle used the analogy of attribution only in reference to the Divine Mover, finite existents being posterior to, and deriving meaning from, that primary cause. It was this exceptional usage that was taken up by medieval theories of analogy.

The application of analogy to Christian theology is generally attributed to Thomas Aquinas. Scattered throughout his major texts, his discussions of analogy are not developed into a systematic theory, resulting in serious disagreements among his interpreters about the classification of analogical relations.[22] For the purpose of this study, discussion of Thomist understandings of analogy will be confined to the contrasting interpretations provided by recent commentators Roger White and Steven Long.

White's thesis is that Aquinas rejected the analogy of proportionality in reference to God since it presupposes a symmetrical relation between the two terms of the analogy.[23] Arguing that the 'qualitative superiority of God over His creation' reveals the divine/human relation to be one of priority and posteriority, White states that Aquinas concluded that the divine/human relation is that which is proper to analogies of attribution.[24]

White then seeks to harmonize the two types of analogy by pointing to many of Jesus' parables which operate according to the model: 'If the inferior is such, all the more must the superior be such.' The example quoted by White is that of Luke 11.11–13,[25] the earthly situation being comparable to a heavenly one, on the model of 'how much more so'. He concludes that 'Despite the fact that analogical modeling is a symmetric relation, we can use such modeling in such a way that an inferior situation can be used as a model of a superior situation, and vice versa.'[26] The model of 'how much more' allows for human language to be used of God on the understanding that the primary sense of the word is its divine meaning, since the chronologically prior human usage is nevertheless dependent on the perfection attached to the divine meaning.[27]

Steven Long disputes White's contention that Aquinas discarded the analogy of proportionality in favour of that of attribution. He argues that the metaphysical relation between God and creation is conceptually coherent only in terms of the analogy of proper proportionality. The argument he proposes depends on a subdivision of the analogy of proportionality into two types: the simple analogy of proportion, in which the relations of the analogates are symmetrical, and the analogy of *proper proportionality*, where the relations are not symmetrical and cannot be reversed, but stand in proper proportion to each other, the proportions being those of the limitless perfection of God as compared with the limited perfectibility of creatures.

Only the analogy of proper proportionality may be accurately used to express the proper relation between God and the created order, a relation of dependence of creature upon God whose being is pure act without limit, whereas creatures are limited in potency and perfection.[28] Labelled the *analogia entis*,[29] it specifies that being cannot be predicated univocally of both God and creatures. God alone is pure Act/Being. Creaturely being stands in analogical relation to pure Being, the relation being that of proper proportionality.[30]

The *analogia entis* is critical for the development of this study. My claim is that it is the key to understanding Rowan Williams' theology and aesthetics. I also argue that Erich Przywara's treatment of the *analogia entis* provided Williams with a theological metaphysic supportive of his critical symbolic realism, his anthropology and his conception of imagination.[31]

## Przywara and the analogy of being

Subtitled *Metaphysics: Original Structure and Universal Rhythm*, Erich Przywara's *Analogia Entis*[32] is an exposition of the metaphysical structure of reality and of the rhythmic nature of human knowledge, which oscillates between the universal and the particular.[33] He contends that reality is essentially analogical, the finite realm existing in a relation of proper proportionality to that which is infinite, the relation being that of similarity-in-always-greater-difference. As the unifying metaphysical principle, the *analogia entis* holds in tension the absolute and the particular, thus embracing the oppositions that have dogged the history of philosophy, with its two main strands of Platonic idealism and Aristotelian realism. Key to the structure of reality, the *analogia entis* designates the proper relation between philosophy and theology, nature and grace.[34]

Employing Husserl's phenomenological method, Przywara begins with a series of philosophical questions on the nature of human existence and human knowledge. He observes that, in human experience, a person's essence is never identical with her actual existence. At any moment, the potentialities of finite being are never fully realized but are always in the process of becoming. Human *being* is accordingly experienced as *becoming*; it is never complete in itself; it requires something beyond itself to complete its essence. So Przywara concludes:

> In view of the undeniable character of 'becomingness' in the creaturely, which excludes the idea of an identity between essence and existence ... there remains then no other alternative than the completely open *tension* between essence and existence; essence as an inward process essentially *within* existence and yet never as complete essence, essentially *over* or *above* existence; essence *in-over* existence.[35]

Suspended in this way between nothingness and fullness of Being, and between becoming and being, the human experience of existence is that of tension, the tension inherent in analogy. It is the tension of existing 'within the interval between being and otherness, being and non-being, God and creation ... without any collapse into identity or contradiction'.[36] Unlike the tension of dialectic which ultimately results in identity or contradiction, the tension of analogy maintains human being as a 'suspended middle' between absorption into identity with the infinite and separation into absolute difference. The tension of the suspended middle also accounts for what Przywara calls the 'universal rhythm' of human thinking, which oscillates between the poles of the universal and the particular, the ideal and the real, neither being finally resolvable into the other.

Human *being* is thus held to be fundamentally analogous. In itself, it is experienced as a relation of likeness and unlikeness between essence and existence, existence never fully coinciding with essence. In respect of what is 'in and above existence', it is experienced as existing in a dependent relation to that which completes its essence, that relation being the analogous relation of likeness within greater unlikeness, since only in ultimate Being is there identity of essence and existence. The relation between finite human *being* and absolute *Being* is accordingly one of proper proportionality, the proportion being that of limited finite being to limitless ultimate Being.

Commenting on these two experiences of analogical relation, John Betz notes that the *analogia entis* 'refers not just to the God–world relation (the transcendent analogy of being), but also to the analogical nature of creaturely being ... the immanent analogy, or the immanent aspect, of the analogy of being'. He points to Przywara's assertion that 'the full form of the *analogia entis* is an intersection of two different analogies – an immanent ("horizontal") analogy and a transcendent ("vertical") analogy – and, as such, has a cross-like structure.'[37]

Przywara's phenomenological approach is thus seen to open the way not only to a metaphysics of being but also to a claim concerning the central significance of the *analogia entis* for Christian theology. Arguing that revelation points us to the God who is in-and-above creation, both immanent and transcendent, Przywara finds implicit support for the *analogia entis* in scripture, in the writings of Augustine and Aquinas, and in the Fourth Lateran Council's conclusion that 'One cannot note any similarity between creator and creature, however great, without being compelled to observe an even *greater* dissimilarity between them.'[38]

In its clarifying of the relation between immanent and transcendent, the *analogia entis* may be considered central to such fundamental Christian doctrines as creation, incarnation, redemption and sanctification. The doctrine of creation *ex nihilo* holds in tension both the essential difference between Creator and creation and the dependence of the latter on the former. The incarnate Christ is both divine and human, without confusion, the true analogue of divine presence. Redemption is a divine act within the immanent realm made possible by the analogical event of the incarnation. Sanctification is the process whereby existence and essence/becoming and being are gradually drawn together through the Holy Spirit. The nature/grace debate finds its resolution in the *analogia entis*, which gives support to the Thomist contention that grace does not supplant nature but 'perfects' it. Linked to that conclusion is the doctrine of secondary causation also proposed by Aquinas. All the above depend on the vertical analogical relation between the transcendent God and the world created by, and dependent on, the God who is in-and-beyond creation.

A theological understanding of the human person necessarily draws on both the vertical/transcendental analogy of God/world relation and the horizontal/immanent analogy of creaturely being. In his 2006 study of Przywara's *analogia entis*, Betz argues that the *analogia entis* entails not only an 'insuperable' difference between Creator and the beings created from nothingness but also a difference between created essence and existence. As a result, difference is the mark of creaturely identity and of the 'dynamism of becoming'.[39] On this analysis, it is the *difference* between creaturely being and divine Being that, in a constant movement of becoming, draws humans beyond their present state towards as yet unspecified future being.

Such a conclusion implies the existence within humanity of the energy of desire impelling them towards the God who is radically Other yet present within as the impulse towards change. The issue of desire as impulsion towards the divine is the theme of Part Two of this study and will be discussed more fully there. Here, however, we find further support for that claim in Przywara's 1923 article, 'God in us and God over us'.[40]

There Przywara compares the human experience of God to a dynamic rhythm oscillating between the poles of divine immanence and divine transcendence. Citing the cry addressed to God by Augustine, *tu autem eras interior intimo meo et superior summo meo* ('you were more interior to me than my own inmost being, and higher than what is highest in me'), he argues that:

> The fundamental disposition of the soul that believes in God is one of 'fearing love' and 'loving fear' ... the element of love corresponds to 'God in me'; the element of fear to 'God above me.' Both, however, are bound together so that the immanence of 'God in me' does not make God into man, and so that the transcendence of 'God above me' does not ultimately make man into God.[41]

Oscillating between immanence and transcendence, love and fear, human consciousness thus functions in analogical tension. Described elsewhere by Przywara as the tension 'between "'self-containedness" (immanence) and a "stretching-beyond-self" (transcendence)',[42] it is the tension between known and unknown, between security and risk, between finite and infinite. The image thus evoked by Przywara's anthropology is that of humanity suspended between earth and heaven, drawn downwards by the desire for the security of self-sufficiency, impelled upwards by a yearning for the infinite unknown beyond the self. Captured by the image is the dynamic restlessness of human consciousness, ever stretching-beyond-self to new experience, understanding, and knowledge, while simultaneously constrained by fear of that which is other, different and unknown. Held in analogical tension, desire and foreboding, love and fear are considered by Przywara to be constitutive of the human condition.

Particularly significant for the development of this study is the notion of consciousness as a process of 'stretching-beyond-self'. Such a notion coheres with the conclusions of Chapter 1 concerning the nature and functioning of imagination. There it was argued that imagination is the capacity of human cognition to transcend the known present in a kind of leap towards the as-yet-unknown. The fundamentally analogous character of the theological anthropology advanced by Przywara serves as the metaphysical underpinning for the development of a theology of imagination.

Rowan Williams' engagement with Przywara's thought is significant for an understanding not only of his overall theology but also, and most importantly, for an insight into his theology of imagination. To that end, I now turn to an exploration of the place of analogy in Williams' writings, where I will argue that the concept of analogy is key to Williams' metaphysic, his anthropology and his aesthetics.

## Rowan Williams and analogy

Williams' earlier writings contain few references to Przywara, the exception being a footnote in the 1982 essay, 'Balthasar, Rahner and the Apprehension of Being'.[43] Explicit attention to Przywara's thinking on analogy is to be found only in three later works, the 2013 essay 'Dialectic and Analogy',[44] the 2013 Gifford Lectures published as *The Edge of Words*[45] and the 2018 Christological study, *Christ the Heart of Creation*.[46] It may nevertheless be postulated that Williams' conclusions concerning the theological significance of analogy drew their initial inspiration from Balthasar's conception of the *analogia entis* as expounded by Przywara.[47]

If that is the case, the 1982 essay, 'Balthasar, Rahner and the Apprehension of Being' may be considered foundational for Williams' understanding of analogy as the metaphysical and epistemological principle which enables finite beings to apprehend the nature of their existence.[48] There Williams argues that, according to Balthasar (and Heidegger), human consciousness is an experience of participation as a 'unique, non-necessary concrete being', existing in relation to other non-necessary concrete beings, in 'a system of contingent and flexible interdependence, in which novelty and gratuity are possible'.[49] Such a world points to a context of 'infinite freedom', the personal freedom of love which, in granting limitless possibility to finite beings, holds nothing back. Balthasar's conclusion is that the *analogia entis* is accordingly the *analogia libertatis*, the freedom of the creature to realize its essential being in a similar gift of self in self-dispossessive love.[50] Implicit in that conclusion is the intersection of the horizontal and vertical analogies of being, finite human freedom and love being analogous to, and dependent on, the freedom of the God whose Being is infinite self-dispossessive love.

Consistent with this conclusion is Williams' own metaphysical vision, a vision of a world created and sustained by the freely willed gift of divine love. While the language of analogy may be largely absent from Williams' earlier writings, an analogical conception of being may be held to underpin his repeated insistence that the divine/human relation is generated by, and reflective of, the Trinitarian relations of freely outpoured love.[51] Only in the 2018 study of the intersection of immanent and transcendent being in *Christ the Heart of Creation* is there a fully developed account of the analogical structure of reality and of human nature, as expounded by Przywara.[52]

In that study, Williams follows Przywara in arguing that metaphysical speculation brings awareness only of what God is *not*. Never finally conclusive, the oscillating rhythm of human cognition leads only to an intuition of the 'transcendental unity' which gives coherence to the tension of form and matter.⁵³ Intuition cannot go beyond that point. Knowledge of who God is, knowledge that is relational and personal, is dependent on revelation, and specifically on the enactment of divine life in Jesus Christ.⁵⁴

It is only through Christ that humanity has insight into 'the non-dual, non-identical grammar of divine relation' and thus into 'divine relatedness to what is not divine'.⁵⁵ Key to these relations is analogy, 'the "in and beyond" relation of two terms', indicative of 'the irreducibly "layered" character of finite reality and the ultimate layering that grounds the finite in the infinite'.⁵⁶ Infinite reality thus exists in an 'in and beyond' relation to the finite, a relation that, according to the Chalcedonian formula, is enfleshed in the person of Jesus Christ.

In line with Przywara, Williams argues that Jesus Christ is the 'heart' of creation, the true 'middle' who not only gives coherence and meaning to finite reality⁵⁷ but also signifies the proper relation of finitude to divinity. His further assertion is that the most accurate specification of the divine/human relation is the figure of the crucified Christ.⁵⁸ Fully human and fully divine, Jesus on the cross reveals both the proper human response to God and the infinite difference of God from all human expectation. In his response of obedient love, the crucified one enacted the proper relation of human to divine, a relation of 'direct openness to infinite activity' no matter how humanly impenetrable that divine activity may be. As scandalous figure of failure and disgrace, he also shattered all human conceptions of God, thus making evident that God is always Other, infinitely different from human notions of divinity.

It is therefore the *crucified* Christ who, according to Przywara, 'reveals what the analogical relation of finite and infinite actually and abidingly must be'.⁵⁹ In the scandal of the cross, we grasp a whole metaphysic, the metaphysic of non-dual, non-identical being, the metaphysic which is, I argue, the crux of Williams' theology of imagination.⁶⁰ As Williams states:

> God repeats God's self non-identically in the Trinity; God repeats God in another kind of non-duality, in and as the finite creation which lives from the divine Word and Wisdom; creation repeats God in the analogical tension between abiding intelligible form and diverse historical specificity. Not one of these relationships allows a deduction of one term from the other: they are different levels of a single ontological fact, 'non-dual non-identity' – which is eternally and unchangeably at the root of all being in the form of the Word's and the Spirit's relation to the Father.⁶¹

Revealed by the crucified Christ is not only the difference of God but also the answer to the question of what God is like. The disgraced and broken figure on the cross is the embodiment of the divine as self-gift, as life poured out for the sake of that which is other than God. In the face of human violence, the vulnerable powerlessness of Jesus' death 'exhibits', says Williams, 'the divine will – the divine passion, we could analogically say, God's "wanting-to-be" – as wholly other than any finite assertion of one being against other beings'.[62] The relation of God to humanity is therefore not the otherness of opposition but the otherness of self-giving.[63]

Williams' distinctive voice is to be heard in this emphasis on the character of divinity as self-gift to that which is other. The self-gift of Christ's life and death is the finite expression of the divine life as Trinitarian, as 'the giving of life between Father, Son and Spirit, the giving *from* each of these "moments" in God *to* all in the divine circulation of life'.[64] The divine life is thus revealed as 'a plurality in unity, a plurality of reciprocal gift' with created reality intended as 'the analogue of that inner-Trinitarian movement'.[65]

The gift of self to the other is thus shown to be the purpose of finite existence, a purpose made possible by Christ's self-gift, which 'releases into the world ... new forms of relation and possibility'.[66] Incorporated into Christ, into Christ's relation of responsive self-giving to the Father, created beings may learn to live in 'life-giving responsiveness' to their Creator and to each other, which is 'the goal and fulfilment of all creaturely process'.[67] Only through the human enactment of lives of 'radical selflessness' may the infinite God be discerned as present and active within the finite world. Humanity thus realizes in Christ its goal of being the analogical middle, the intersection of finite and infinite, of differentiation and connectedness.

## Conclusion

In the light of the above discussion of analogy, Williams' 'Gethsemane' poem offers further insight into the significance of analogy for Williams' theology and for his conception of imagination. As discussed earlier, the poem is an instance of a complex succession of analogies. It now becomes clear that, for Williams, analogy is not merely a literary device but represents the in-and-beyond structure of reality, finite creation subsisting in a relation of dependence on its infinitely greater and infinitely different Creator. So it is that the insistent presence of God impinges not only on the holy city of Jerusalem but on the whole creation since the finite is inextricably related to its divine origin.

As a consequence, far from being self-contained and static, the created order is seen to be a dynamic process of becoming, open to the energy of divine desire, analogous, in its multiple interconnectedness, to the divine life of 'Trinitarian plurality in mutuality'.[68] 'What we encounter in any finite substance,' says Williams, 'is a kind of *excess*, an overflow of connectedness and so of possible meaning.'[69] Discerned by poets and artists, the excess within the finite entices humanity towards the abundance that is divine life. That abundance is correctly identified, however, only when it is made explicit in the person of Jesus Christ. Jesus, both God and human, is the middle, the infinite who is the true form of the finite, and the proper relation between created and Creator as manifested by the crucifixion. In that event, as the final stanza of the poem suggests, we are shown both the divine kenosis of ecstatic other-focused self-giving love and the trust maintained by the human Jesus in the One who is eternally the 'abba' of the divine Son.

In Part Two, Williams' image of the divine pressure of love ever impinging on finite creation will be explored in greater detail. There it will be argued that it is the energy of divine desire that drives the created process of becoming, and that the created analogue of divine desire is the energy of human imagination with its passion to explore the excessive abundance of created reality and thereby discover ever new relations of similarity-in-difference.

## Notes

1 Oxford Dictionary on *Lexico*.

2 Roger White, *Talking about God: The Concept of Analogy and the Problem of Religious Language* (Farnham: Ashgate, 2010), p. 6.

3 White, *Talking About God*, p. 83.

4 John R. Betz, 'Translator's Introduction' in Erich Przywara, *Analogia Entis: Metaphysics: Original Structure and Universal Rhythm*, trans. John R. Betz and David Bentley Hart (Grand Rapids, MI: William B. Eerdmans, 2014), pp. 33–5.

5 Betz, 'Translator's Introduction', pp. 37ff.

6 Rowan Williams, *The Poems of Rowan Williams* (Oxford: Perpetua Press, 2002), p. 59.

7 White argues that complex analogies of this kind may be compared to models consisting of a series of analogical relationships between two domains, elements of the better-known domain being correlated with corresponding elements in the lesser known/unfamiliar domain, thus giving rise to fresh insights and a richer experience. White, *Talking About God*, pp. 41, 52.

8 Dedre Gentner, Keith J. Holyoak and Boicho N. Kokinov, eds, *The Analogical Mind: Perspectives from Cognitive Science* (Cambridge, MA: MIT Press, 2001), pp. 1–2.

9 Gentner et al., *The Analogical Mind*, p. 2.

10 Douglas Hofstadter and Emmanuel Sander, *Surfaces and Essences: Analogy as the Fuel and Fire of Thinking* (New York: Basic Books, 2013).

11 Hofstadter and Sander, *Surfaces and Essences*, pp. 3, 20–21.

12 Hofstadter and Sander, *Surfaces and Essences*, p. 354.

13 Keith J. Holyoak and Paul Thagard, 'The Analogical Mind', *American Psychologist* 52.1 (1997), pp. 35–44.

14 Paul Thagard and Cameron Shelly, 'Emotional Analogies and Analogical Inference' in Gentner et al., *The Analogical Mind*, pp. 335–62.

15 Daniela M. Bailer-Jones, 'Models, Metaphors and Analogies', in *The Blackwell Guide to the Philosophy of Science*, ed. Peter Machamer and Michael Silberstein (Malden, MA: Blackwell, 2002), p. 108.

16 Bailer-Jones, 'Models, Metaphors and Analogies', p. 114.

17 Bailer-Jones, 'Models, Metaphors and Analogies', p. 114.

18 White, *Talking about God*, p. 27.

19 White, *Talking About God*, p. 173.

20 The term was coined by G. E. L. Owen and was not employed by Aristotle.

21 White, *Talking about God*, p. 75.

22 The fifteenth-century Italian cardinal Thomas Cajetan was for centuries regarded as the principal interpreter of Aquinas' theory of analogy. His conclusions are disputed by more recent scholars seeking to offer a fresh analysis of the Thomist position on analogy. Ralph McInerny, for example, begins his study with a chapter entitled, 'Where Cajetan Went Wrong' in *Aquinas and Analogy* (Washington: Catholic University of America Press, 1996). Long argues that a proper understanding of the Thomist theory of analogy is dependent on Aquinas's analysis of the *analogia entis*. Steven A. Long, *Analogia Entis: On the Analogy of Being, Metaphysics, and the Act of Faith* (Notre Dame, IN: University of Notre Dame Press, 2011).

23 White, *Talking about God*, p. 176.

24 White, *Talking About God*, p. 178.

25 'Is there anyone among you who, if your child asks for a fish, will give a snake instead of a fish? Or if the child asks for an egg, will give a scorpion?'

26 White, *Talking About God*, p. 180.

27 White, *Talking About God*, p. 182.

28 Long, *Analogia Entis*, pp. 31–41.

29 Long, *Analogia Entis*, p. 2.

30 In reference to the relation of proper proportionality, David Bentley Hart writes that 'The proportion – the analogy that created things declare – is that of an ever-greater distance from God, even in God's expression of himself in creation; the proportions of created things, their orders of magnitude, quantity and beauty, tell of an infinite proportion – an infinite interval – of ever yet greater magnitude, "quantity" and beauty.' David Bentley Hart, *The Beauty of the Infinite: The Aesthetics of Christian Truth* (Grand Rapids, MI: William B. Eerdmans, 2003), p. 300.

31 Williams' first reference to Przywara was in a footnote to the chapter 'Balthasar, Rahner and the Apprehension of Being' included in John Riches (ed.), *The Analogy of Beauty* (Edinburgh: T&T Clark, 1982) and republished in Mike Higton, ed., *Wrestling with Angels: Conversations in Modern Theology* (Grand Rapids, MI: William B. Eerdmans, 2007), pp. 85–105. Here he acknowledges his debt to Christopher Seville, whose study of analogy in Balthasar introduced him to the work of Przywara.

32 Erich Przywara, *Analogia Entis*, originally published in German in 1932.

33 Przywara's translator and commentator, John Betz, asserts that the *analogia entis* is concerned with 'the very nature of reality, the relation between the finite and the infinite, and the ontological similarity-in-ultimate-dissimilarity between God and the world [and that it] bears at the end of the day on everything'. John R. Betz, 'The *Analogia Entis* as a Standard of Catholic Engagement: Erich Przywara's Critique of Phenomenology and Dialectical Theology', *Modern Theology* 35.1 (2019), p. 88.

34 Przywara's account of the analogical structure of reality has been influential, not only for certain of his contemporaries including Balthasar, but also for such later scholars as John Milbank and David Bentley Hart. His theory remains contentious among traditionalists, as evidenced by Christopher Malloy's review of the 2014 English translation of *Analogia Entis*, which lists eight 'critical points' requiring further justification. Christopher J. Malloy, *Notre Dame Philosophical Reviews*, 22.08.2014.

35 Cited by Niels C. Nielsen, 'Przywara's Philosophy of the "Analogia Entis"', *The Review of Metaphysics* 5.4 (1952), p. 607.

36 Jonathan M. Platter, 'Holiness in Excess: Between Holiness and Metaphysics in the Wake of Rowan Williams', *The Heythrop Journal* 62.5 (2020), p. 2.

37 Betz, 'The *Analogia Entis*', p. 92.

38 Betz, 'The *Analogia Entis*', pp. 86–7, 89.

39 John R. Betz, 'Beyond the Sublime: The Aesthetics of the Analogy of Being (Part Two)', *Modern Theology* 22.1 (2006), p. 17.

40 Published as Erich Przywara, 'Gott in uns und Gott über uns' in *Ringen der Gegenwart*, vol. 2 (Augsburg: Benno Filser Verlag, 1929), pp. 543–78.

41 Cited by Betz, 'The *Analogia Entis*', p. 91.

42 See Nielsen, 'Przywara's Philosophy of the "Analogia Entis"', p. 608. The reference is to Przywara's 1927 monograph, *Religionsphilosophie Katholischer Theologie*, trans. A. C. Bouquet, which was published as *Polarity* (Oxford: Oxford University Press, 1935), pp. 3, 4. The term 'stretching-beyond-itself' is accordingly that of the translator but expresses the dynamism of the German employed by Przywara.

43 Williams, 'Balthasar, Rahner and the Apprehension of Being', p. 101.

44 Rowan Williams, 'Dialectic and Analogy', in *The Impact of Idealism: The Legacy of Post-Kantian German Thought*, Volume IV, ed. Nicholas Boyle et al. (Cambridge: Cambridge University Press, 2013), ch. 11.

45 Rowan Williams, *The Edge of Words: God and the Habits of Language* (London: Bloomsbury, 2014), p. 20.

46 Rowan Williams, *Christ the Heart of Creation* (London: Bloomsbury Continuum, 2018), pp. 228–41. Here we find Williams' most extensive exposition of Przywara's concept of the *analogia entis* as both metaphysical method and grounding for Christology. 'Dialectic and Analogy' is primarily concerned with analogy as a metaphysical and theological method, a means of moving beyond dialectic to hold in tension the oppositions of God and world, infinite and finite, in an analogy of unity-in-difference. *The Edge of Words* (pp. 20–1) draws on Przywara as support for Williams' conception of 'representation' which presupposes a universe in which form is expressed in multiple ways and knowledge involves a participatory relation between subject and object.

47 See Williams' discussion of Balthasar's use of the *analogia entis* in 'Balthasar, Rahner and the Apprehension of Being', pp. 92ff.

48 In view of Williams' familiarity with the Orthodox theological tradition from his doctoral studies, he may also have been aware of the work of Gregory Palamas, discussed in his 2021 study of Orthodoxy, *Looking East in Winter: Contemporary Thought and the Eastern Christian Tradition* (London: Bloomsbury Continuum, 2001). There he notes (p. 38) that 'Palamas implies that there is in the divine life an analogical foundation for the awareness of the incompleteness of the self in finite experience.'

49 Williams, 'Balthasar, Rahner and the Apprehension of Being', p. 93.

50 Williams, 'Balthasar, Rahner and the Apprehension of Being', p. 93.

51 See Part Two. It is interesting to note that Williams' theological methodology of seeking ongoing conversation between opposing positions without resorting to closure is consistent with Przywara's 'oscillating rhythm' of human knowledge and finds expression in the final sentence of 'Balthasar, Rahner and the Apprehension of Being', where he states (p. 101) that 'Balthasar's Christ remains a question to all human answers, and to all attempts at metaphysical or theological closure.'

52 In Williams' 2021 study of Eastern Orthodox thought, *Looking East in Winter*, there is reference (pp. 38–45) to the Orthodox conception of the analogous relation between the Trinity and the structure of finite reality. While the concept is similar, the Orthodox treatment is theological rather than philosophical.

53 Williams, *Christ the Heart of Creation*, p. 233.

54 Williams, *Christ the Heart of Creation*, p. 225.

55 Williams, *Christ the Heart of Creation*, p. 245.

56 Williams, *Christ the Heart of Creation*, p. 240.

57 Williams, *Christ the Heart of Creation*, p. 225.

58 Williams points out that the significance for Przywara of the crucified Christ was brought to prominence by Kenneth Oakes, 'The Cross and the *Analogia Entis* in Erich Przywara', in *The Analogy of Being: Invention of the Antichrist or the Wisdom of God*, ed. Thomas Joseph White (Grand Rapids, MA: William B. Eerdmans, 2011), pp. 147–71.

59 Williams, *Christ the Heart of Creation*, p. 225.

60 See Williams, *Christ the Heart of Creation*, p. 252, where Williams concludes that 'The "in-and-beyond" of [Przywara's] analysis … implies that what we encounter in any finite substance is a kind of *excess*, an overflow of connectedness and so of possible meaning which cannot be detached from a sense of life and of participation in abundance.'

61 Williams, *Christ the Heart of Creation*, pp. 236–7.

62 Williams, *Christ the Heart of Creation*, p. 238.

63 Williams, *Christ the Heart of Creation*, p. 241.

64 Williams, *Christ the Heart of Creation*, p. 226.

65 Williams, *Christ the Heart of Creation*, p. 226.

66 Williams, *Christ the Heart of Creation*, p. 242.

67 Williams, *Christ the Heart of Creation*, p. 225.

68 Williams, *Christ the Heart of Creation*, p. 232.

69 Williams, *Christ the Heart of Creation*, p. 252.

PART TWO

# Desire in Rowan Williams' Theology

## Introduction

Part One established the foundation for this study of Rowan Williams' theology of imagination. In Part Two we turn to a consideration of Williams' conception of divine desire. Here I argue that, in Williams' theology, the notion of divine desire is the interpretative key to a proper understanding of the analogous relation between God and creation. I further contend that the synthesizing and transformative power of human imagination is to be considered as the finite analogy of the ecstatic, kenotic energy of divine desire permeating creation and impelling it towards its ultimate fulfilment.

Chapter 4 examines the significance of the concept of divine *eros* in Williams' theology, drawing on his Christological study, *Christ the Heart of Creation*, and his analyses of divine desire in the work of Augustine, Aquinas, St John of God and Balthasar. Chapter 5 examines the analogous energy of human desire, first in its distorted modes of rivalry and violence and second in its true expression as Christlike, other-oriented, self-dispossessive love. I argue that imagination provides the otherness-oriented focus of human desire, directing desire either towards death-dealing fantasy or, when renewed by grace, towards the positive transformation of the whole created order. Chapter 6 identifies the role to be played by the Christian Church as the context in which, renewed and enabled by grace, followers of Christ learn to direct the transformative energy of imagination towards the eschatological vision of the Kingdom.

# 4

# Divine Desire

## Introduction

This chapter examines Rowan Williams' conviction that divine desire is the energy activating creation and enticing our human response. The mode of celebratory theology offers the most vivid expression of his personal experience of the nature and intensity of that divine energy. Through poetry and meditative reflection, he shares with us his awareness of God's passionate desire for our human response, as evidenced in his poetic meditations on the twelfth-century icon *Our Lady of Vladimir*.[1] In this chapter they set the scene for his scholarly conversation with theologians on the theme of divine desire.

## *Our Lady of Vladimir*: Icon of divine desire

The icon *Our Lady of Vladimir* shows the Christ child clambering up his mother's breast, thrusting his face against hers, and clinging to her with both hands. In reflecting on this icon in *Ponder These Things*, Williams muses that here we see God in Christ 'positively *shameless* in his eagerness ... to embrace and be embraced' by his human mother and, in her, by the whole of humanity.[2] Portrayed in visual form is the 'hungry', passionate intensity of God's love for humanity, for that which was created as 'not God' so that it may be loved 'as if it were God'.[3] Such love, says Williams, is 'terrible' in its intensity, since it is not God's distance that we fear, but rather his overwhelming closeness and passionate 'hunger' for our response.[4]

The intensity of God's desire for humanity is expressed even more powerfully in the poem of the same name.

> Climbs the child, confident,
> up over breast, arm, shoulder;
> while she, alarmed by his bold thrust
> into her face, and the encircling hand,

> looks out imploring fearfully
> and, O, she cries, from her immeasurable eyes,
> O how he clings, see how
> he smothers every pore, like the soft
> shining mistletoe to my black bark,
> she says, I cannot breathe, my eyes
> are aching so.

The strength of God's desire is communicated to the listener by the force of the first word 'Climbs'. Here the inverted word order, with the verb preceding the subject, focuses attention on the Christ child's sheer determination to cling as closely as possible to his human mother. For the mother, however, the child's 'bold thrust' and 'insistent pushing warmth' become a smothering source of torment, choking all breath, driving away any possibility of sleep, peace and forgetfulness.

> The child has overlaid us in our beds,
> we cannot close our eyes,
> his weight sits firmly,
> fits over heart and lungs,
> and choked we turn away
> into the window of immeasurable dark
> to shake off the insistent pushing warmth;
> O how he cleaves, no peace
> tonight my lady in your bower,
> you, like us, restless with bruised eyes
> and waking to
>
> a shining cry on the black bark of sleep.

The child, like all babies, demands attention. But this child, claims Williams, will never desist. What impels him is not his need but our human need to know and respond to the love which has no limits, and which persists despite all obstacles. From our human perspective, such love is too demanding. With Mary, we feel smothered by the pressure of his desire. Our impulse is to turn away from him, wishing to escape his 'insistent pushing warmth'. Ultimately, however, we too, like Mary, find that we cannot escape the 'shining cry' of his indefatigable love.

Both poem and meditation assert the 'violent' insistence of divine love. Both declare that finite humanity cannot but react with dread to that intensity.[5] Such love, says Williams, confronts us with the truth about ourselves and with our terror at the mystery of otherness, human and divine. The self-dispossessing urgency of God's love for the created other forces us to recognize our human fear of difference, and the resultant compulsion to possess and 'absorb' the other into the self.[6] It is perhaps only 'the shock of seeing God ... as hungry child' that opens for us the possibility of loving the infinite Other who is God, and thus of learning to love the human 'other as if it were God'.[7]

These artistic representations of divine desire confront us with the mystery of the Child, the Word made flesh, who is both infinite God and mortal human being. They confront us with the total otherness of God, an otherness incomprehensible to finite humanity and accordingly a source of fear. Yet they also present us with a vision of a God who grasps us tightly and refuses to abandon us. Held together by the imaginative sensibility of iconographer and poet are the contradictory longing and fear which, in Williams' view, haunt the human sense of the divine.[8] The question is forced upon us: Who is this child who is so different from all human expectations of God? What do his insistent demands on our attention and commitment tell us about God and what do they tell us about ourselves? Those are questions Rowan Williams seeks to answer in his Christological study, *Christ the Heart of Creation*.[9]

## Jesus Christ: Icon and revelation of God

In this work, Williams explores the Christian Church's struggle to find adequate language to express the conviction that Jesus Christ is both fully human and fully divine. While the fifth-century Council of Chalcedon succeeded in formulating a definition asserting that Jesus Christ is one person (hypostasis) in two natures, divine and human, which remain 'unconfused, unchanged, indivisible and inseparable', the issues of the nature of the unity and the mode of relation between the two natures continue to tease theologians.

Williams argues that the synthesis developed by Aquinas is the most satisfactory clarification of the question of the unity of Christ. According to Aquinas, the principle of unity is the *esse/suppositum*/Person of the divine Word.[10] The union is that of personal active presence (*esse*). Jesus as acting subject lives out in human existence the receptive, responsive self-giving of the Son/Word. The whole of his human existence is 'the eternal living out of the divine life in the mode of "filiation"',[11] the conclusion being that 'the active human presence of Jesus in the world is indistinguishable from the active presence of the eternal Word in the world.'[12] Since he is the finite embodiment of the eternal Word through whom creation came into being and is given coherence, his life and death have the power to be transformative for humankind.[13] Those who through faith align themselves with Jesus are thus enabled to 'share the direction of the Word's own agency, and the Word's [filial] relation to the Father', living as the Body of Christ, 'a *communal* embodiment of the Word'.[14]

The main concern of Williams' study is, however, the second area of continuing contention, namely the mode of relation between the infinite God and finite creation. Taking Nicholas of Cusa's *non aliud* principle as his starting point,[15] he sets out to clarify what he calls the 'non-dual, non-identity' relation between the two extremes of divine infinity and created finitude.[16] He argues that the metaphysical model of 'non-duality, non-identity' holds in tension the theological assertions that the finite creation has its source in the infinite God but is incommensurably other than God. Existing in a 'non-dual' asymmetrical relation to God, the created order has its own integrity, 'made to be and act according to its own logic and structure'.[17] The relation is thus 'non-identical', the consequence being that the infinite God does not intervene directly in finite creation.

In exploring this non-dual, non-identical model, Williams turns to the insights of both the Anglican theologian Austin Farrer and the Jesuit Erich Przywara. As discussed in Chapter 3, it is Przywara's conception of the *analogia entis* which provides Williams with a metaphysic capable of accounting for the relation between finite and infinite. In the current chapter the emphasis is on the insight provided by Przywara into humanity's access to knowledge of God.

Williams' line of argument is as follows. Following Farrer, he stresses the importance of clarifying the 'grammar' of finite and infinite causality, which do not operate within the same frame of reference. Finite creation, says Farrer, has its own integrity. There is no need for supernatural operation to fill in the gaps. 'Personal *will*' is the phenomenon that enables the relation between finite and infinite to be a matter of 'personal relatedness' rather than that of 'universal causal activation'.[18] As a result, finite beings are enabled to bring their will into alignment with the infinite divine will, thereby realizing hitherto unforeseen possibilities within finite creation. In this way, God may be said to operate through the openness of finite beings to the divine will. Revelation is such an instance.

Williams expands Farrer's argument through reference to Przywara's discussion of the 'meta' in 'metaphysical', 'meta' referring to 'what is *beneath, behind, above or within*' whatever is spoken of. Generalities presuppose particulars and vice versa, but both levels of description cannot be thought at the same time. There is a relation between the two levels but there is no language for that relation. It exists as method, as a '*rhythm*, a reciprocal movement back and forth between the two'.[19] It is a movement of difference-in-continuity since phenomena exist not in isolation but in relation to their context. This means that:

> [our] 'ordinary' perception of the world we inhabit is always analogical in the sense of showing us a world in which participatory relations always hold between particulars and forms, but in which neither can be said to be the origin of the other or the level to which the other ultimately reduces.[20]

Since there is no finite form that exists independently as ultimate, none of these forms can serve as ground for finite existence. It may therefore be surmised that the finite universe as a system, as 'intelligible unity', must also exist in a relation of 'difference-in-continuity', a relation with that which is different, such that 'all finite relations [are grounded] in that from which they are absolutely different, the infinite.'[21] The relation of finite to infinite is thus that of 'non-dual non-identity'.[22] The finite is non-dual in its dependence on the infinite but it is absolutely different and so non-identical.[23] The relation is analogical in that its difference-in-continuity is that of the 'in-and-beyond'. The finite exists 'in' that which is absolutely 'beyond' and different from it.[24]

This has implications for the process of human thinking which, says Przywara, is a continual 'intellectual oscillation' between object and form.[25] Far from being a detached observer viewing an array of discrete objects, the thinking subject is always already a participant within the situation, moving from particular to general and vice versa, without the possibility of attaining an ultimate controlling perspective. The oscillating rhythm of thought constitutes what Przywara calls 'analogy as method', the method of constant movement between likeness and difference.

While it is impossible to get beyond the method, the oscillating rhythm itself evokes an intuition of 'depth', which gives 'coherence' to the whole. It may thus open a 'space in which recognition of God, but not a concept of God, can occur'.[26] Such metaphysical thinking is necessarily negative. It terminates in awareness only of what God is not. All it can do is 'gestur[e] towards the generative mystery'.[27]

It is the person of Jesus Christ who enables us to go beyond the purely negative. As Word made flesh, truly God and truly human, Christ embodies the 'transforming *coincidence* of finite and infinite',[28] this finite embodiment being the only way in which finite beings may truly apprehend the infinite God. God who is infinite, and thus ever beyond finite conceptualization, may nevertheless be known by finite beings in a personal encounter with the One who is self-dispossessing love, analogously enacted in the finite reality of the human life.[29]

Drawing together the contributions of Farrer and Przywara, Williams argues that the man Jesus is the finite embodiment of the infinite God[30] and, as such, he realizes within the conditions of finitude 'the relatedness of the Word to the Father which is the eternal ground of all finite existence'.[31] It is henceforth possible for human beings to experience for themselves the filial relation existing between the eternal Son and the Father. Knowledge of God is accordingly not primarily conceptual but relational and analogical. It is in relation to Jesus that finite human beings can know something of the infinite God within the conditions of finite creation.

What can be known is 'beyond paradox', says Przywara. Dramatically highlighted by the scandal of the cross is the utter difference of God from any human conception of divinity. Williams asserts that:

> The extreme tension between the paradoxical assertion of the divine in Christ and the actuality of the cross is the ultimate clarification of what analogy implies: the ultimate level of the 'meta' in metaphysics. That which is above and beyond any similarity or continuity, that which is definitely beyond any category of description, the infinite itself, speaks itself or embodies itself *only* in that which makes no claim to similarity or continuity – the finite, but more especially the mortal, and still more especially the abandoned and despised mortal.[32]

What the cross makes known is therefore the truth about God's relation to humanity. In accepting human limitation, powerlessness and a scandalous death, Jesus Christ who is God incarnate, fully divine and fully human, reveals that God is utter self-dispossession, 'loving self-gift for the sake of the healing and remaking of the finite'.[33] The 'foundational reality' of creation and of the Christian Church is thus discovered to be an 'endless ... mutual outpouring of life and bliss'.[34] Opened up for finite minds is the vision of God as Trinitarian relationships of infinite self-dispossessive love, overflowing in an excess of bliss to bring creation and humanity into being. This excess of divine desire is the subject of what follows.

## Divine desire as kenotic *ekstasis*

The poem 'Rublev',[35] inspired by the icon of the angels' visit to Abraham, offers a further glimpse into Williams' vision of divine kenosis.

One day, God walked in, pale from the grey steppe,
slit-eyed against the wind, and stopped,
said. Colour me, breathe your blood into my mouth.

I said Here is the blood of all our people,
these are their bruises, blue and purple,
gold, brown, and pale green wash of death.

These (god) are the chromatic pains of flesh.
I said, I trust I make you blush,
O I shall stain you with the scars of birth

For ever. I shall root you in the wood,
under the sun shall bake you bread
of beechmast, never let you forth

to the white desert, to the starving sand.
But we shall sit and speak around
one table, share one food, one earth.

Williams imagines God walking in from the open plain, 'pale' and unblemished, squinting against the bitter wind of human existence. In entering Abraham's tent, God takes the initiative in making the totally unexpected request to be stained with the colours of humanity. As the representative of humanity, 'I' (Abraham/Rublev) respond by offering the hues that mark human history, the shades characteristic of suffering: the red of blood, the 'blue and purple/gold, brown' of bruising and the 'pale green' of death. Reproachful, I want to make God 'blush' in full awareness of the scars that result from being born a mortal human being. I therefore insist on his sharing human experience, by ensuring that he is 'rooted' in the wood that is his fate among humanity. Henceforth I keep him bound to finite existence, not allowing him to escape again into the 'starving, white emptiness' of the infinite, since it is only here, on earth, that we can know God. It is only here that we can 'sit and speak around/ one table, share one food, one earth.'

The 15 lines of Williams' reflection on God's initiative in instigating relationship with humanity hold divine *ekstasis* and *kenosis* inseparably together. Here God is depicted as humbly going out from self in order to encounter the different human other and to share the pain, scarring and death of finite human existence.

As is true of 'Our Lady of Vladimir', this poem points to God's ecstatic persistence in seeking out finite beings so that they might share divine bliss. Here too the divine initiative encounters a paradoxical human reception. In this case, the response is to compel God to experience our human 'scars of birth' and the 'wash of death'. Divine love for humanity is met with either avoidant fear or lethal rejection.

The paradox is explored in one of Williams' earliest publications, *The Wound of Knowledge*.[36] The title is taken from a poem by R. S. Thomas, 'Roger Bacon'.[37] It refers to knowledge which is both a divine gift to humanity and the means of death. Access to knowledge results not only in death for humanity but also in 'the hole/in God's side' inflicted at the crucifixion. Here again we are presented with the dual theme of divine initiative and divine cost. The kenotic *ekstasis* that is the energy of divine love overflowing into creation is distorted by created beings into acts of death-dealing, leading to the wounds of the crucified Christ.

In this early work, the frightening 'violent' intensity of divine desire is particularly emphasized in Williams' discussion of the spirituality of Augustine:

> The initiative is always God's, God's love breaking in with 'sweet violence'... and irresistible force.[38]

> Where, in Pelagianism, was the sense of this 'violence' of God, the utterly gratuitous and unpredicted flow of mercy to his creatures, the sense of being grasped, overwhelmed and intoxicated?[39]

> The violent love of God breaks through deafness and blindness.[40]

> Augustine's genius is in the wholeness, the sweeping comprehensiveness, of his picture of the believer shattered and compelled by God's violent beauty; the genius of classical monasticism is ... In the believer's attempt ... To be accessible to the violent, reshaping love of God.[41]

These relatively early references to the impelling force of God's love for humanity are an indication of how powerfully Williams' vision was shaped by his study of Augustine in the first years of his theological teaching,[42] the effect being that his whole opus is tinged with an Augustinian hue.[43] His 1986 sermon celebrating the 1600th anniversary of Augustine's conversion reiterates that God 'seeks us, urgently, relentlessly, passionately, out of the changeless movement of a love that seeks the joy and fulfilment of everything in its createdness and limitation'.[44] While the word 'violence' is less evident in his later writings, the power of divine desire remains an important theme, fundamental to his perception of the North African saint's doctrines of creation and redemption.[45]

## Augustine: The triadic structure of *Caritas*

Augustine's analysis of the Trinitarian relations in *De Trinitate* is the source of one of Williams' most extended reflections on the theme of divine desire. In the essay '*Sapientia*: Wisdom and the Trinitarian Relations'[46] he follows Augustine's argument that the triadic nature of love as it is known in human experience allows for conclusions to be drawn concerning the Trinitarian dynamic of divine love.

In that essay Williams sets out to demonstrate that, in Books 8–15 of *De Trinitate*,[47] Augustine points to the triadic structure that characterizes authentic human love. We love the Good we see in another, which we recognize as Good and therefore desirable. Such love involves first the act of loving, second the person who is the object of that loving, and third the Good loved by that person. It is a triad of lover, beloved and what is loved by, and hence lovable in, the beloved.

In following Augustine's argument, Williams concludes that the analysis of human love offers insight into divine love because the process of self-awareness leads to a recognition that we already have within us some knowledge of the eternal Good which we desire. Beyond ourselves is that which 'underl[ies] our existence' and which we recognize as 'the eternal Good as turned towards us and sharing itself with us'.[48] Such sharing presupposes that we are the object of God's love and that we are 'sustained and embraced by this self-communicating action of God'.[49] Awareness of God's 'sustaining love' (*caritas*) is 'wisdom' (*sapientia*), the knowledge that God desires to share his life with us, that God desires for us ultimate Good. Wisdom (*sapientia*) and love (*caritas*) are thus inseparable. To know God is to know that God is love. The triadic structure of human love is thus shown to mirror the eternal dynamic of divine love, which is an eternal self-giving in love to another and to that which is loved by that other.

Expressed in Trinitarian terms, the source of life and love is the Father, who is love by 'generating an other', and by being actively *for* that other, the Son. The Son exists as *from* the Father, as recipient of, and loving response to, the Father's love. The Spirit exists as the relation of love between Father and Son, 'the act of everlasting love which is given form but not exhausted by the mutual gift of Father and Son'.[50] It is the inexhaustible nature of divine love for the other which gives rise to the possibility and fact of finite creation. It is what brought the world into being and gives it coherence and meaning.[51] Embodied in the crucified Christ, that same love is the source of human redemption and 'nuptial union' with Christ, thus enabling human beings to realize the fullness of their created humanity in sharing 'the pattern of divine gift and bliss'.[52]

From the protracted argument in Books 8–15 of *De Trinitate*, Williams has extracted Augustine's conclusions about the triadic structure of love, human and divine. In doing so, he has accorded these conclusions greater prominence than is evident in the original text. Williams' commentary is therefore to be viewed as evidencing his own distinctive perspective on the nature of divine love rather than as a faithful exegesis of Augustine's text.

Absent also from Augustine's Latin vocabulary are the equivalents of the Greek terms, *ekstasis* and *kenosis*, which feature prominently in Williams' discussions of the relations of love within the Trinity. Those terms became important in the Eastern Church largely through the works of Pseudo-Dionysius and Maximus the Confessor. Paraphrasing Dionysius, Williams writes:

> The divine *eros* ... is fundamental to all we say of God ... God comes out from his selfhood in a kind of 'ecstasy' (*ekstasis*, literally a 'standing outside') when he creates; and his ecstasy is designed to call forth the ecstasy of human beings, responding to him in selfless love, belonging to him and not to themselves. Thus in the created order there is a perpetual circle of divine and human love, *eros* and ecstasy.[53]

In summarizing Maximus's thought, Williams says that 'God's *kenosis* of love, his *ekstasis* from his own nature in becoming human must be answered by human love and human *ekstasis* into the divine life.'[54] While the equivalent terminology may be missing from Augustine's discussion of divine *caritas*, the concepts are certainly present. *Caritas* implies a dynamic of self-gift (*kenosis*) expressed as a moving out from the self towards the other (*ekstasis*) for the good of the other (*kenosis*). As will become increasingly evident, the interrelated concepts of *kenosis* and *ekstasis* are at the heart of Williams' understanding of the analogical relation between God and humanity.

## Aquinas: Knowing and loving

As with Augustine, the notion of divine movement towards, and for the good of, the other is central to Williams' analysis of Trinitarian relations in the theology of Thomas Aquinas. In *The Wound of Knowledge*, he asserts that 'the notion of love, *caritas*, is the great unifying theme of the *Summa Theologiae*', his claim being that Aquinas is 'a theorist of ecstasy', despite his infrequent use of the word *caritas*.[55] Justification for that claim is to be found in the lecture 'What Does Love Know? St Thomas on the Trinity', delivered in 2001.[56]

In that lecture, Williams focuses on the Thomist notions of participation and differentiation in reference to the Trinitarian relations of love and knowledge.[57] His argument is as follows. Scriptural accounts of God's acts lead us to the conclusion that God is revealed as both 'intellection' (*intellectus*) and love (*caritas*), the term *intellectus* having the sense of responsive understanding rather than mere cerebration.[58] Understanding, by its very nature, is participatory, since it involves an inner movement of consciousness that goes out towards an object so as to 'bring it into' the thinking subject, such that the object is now held within the subject as '*verbum*, [an] inner word, that is the fruit of the encounter between mind and object'.[59]

Such participatory knowledge involves a disposition towards the object known. It is never neutral since the act of knowing includes an assessment of the object's value in relation to our desires. It therefore resembles the act of loving which also involves an 'inclination', a 'programme for action' in respect of the object. In the case of love, however, the object is not fully encompassed by the mind but continues, both within and external to the subject, as a stimulus to change.

The conclusion is that while the act of knowing is participatory by bringing the object into the subject, the act of loving not only brings the object into the subject but also retains awareness of the otherness of the object of love.[60] As a consequence, knowing is a process of participation while loving is a process of differentiation.

In human existence, both knowing and loving can become possession by assimilating the other into the self and thus rejecting its otherness. By contrast, divine knowing and loving maintain their integrity as participation and differentiation. The result is that divine knowledge is always perfect love and, as such, is a process of differentiation, giving rise to difference. Divine love is generative not only of the reflection of the Father, the Son/Word, but also of that which 'overflows'[61] and 'exceeds that repetition', the Spirit.[62] The Spirit, concludes Williams, is 'God's life as it is shaped and directed towards the good of the other by the recognition of divine life as self-bestowal'.[63] The Spirit is the gift of self-dispossessive, other-oriented love.

In Williams' analysis, the interrelation of participation and difference is the key to the Thomist doctrine of the Trinity. The life of the other brought into the subject (participation) is balanced by the abiding difference of that other. There is accordingly no possession of the other since the coincidence of divine knowledge and love means that each remains other to the other in a way that generates an excess of otherness, the excess of the Spirit's love freely overflowing as gift into creation. Williams can thus sum up Aquinas's Trinitarian theology in the following words:

> In God ... that is, in the reality that is formative of the entire universe, there is perfect reflection or participation, and there is endless invitation, the stimulus of difference; *as if* God is utterly familiar to God and utterly 'strange' to God. Love knows divine life as bestowal and self-emptying; it knows a bestowal and self-emptying so complete, in the relation of Father and Son, that it knows that there can be no 'terminus' to the act of self-giving. Its perfect repetition in the Son is the ground of its overflow and excess in the Spirit. The Spirit as love is what comes from seeing that the Father's understanding of the Son or of himself in the Son is not an enclosed mutual mirroring ... but the understanding of a life that moves inexhaustibly in gift, even dispossession.[64]

In this passage we have Williams' perspective on Thomist theology. As with Augustine, we again find many of Williams' favourite terms in relation to God: 'participation', 'bestowal', 'overflow', 'excess', 'inexhaustible', 'gift', all suggestive of *ekstasis*, together with the kenotic terms 'self-emptying' and 'dispossession'. His conclusion is that 'the irreducible structure of God's *esse*' is 'a movement to which desire is analogous – self-projection, intention, what Thomas calls impulsion.'[65] Creation is the result of the inexhaustible impulsion of divine desire towards that which is other than God. From this, we may draw the tentative conclusion that human imagination, with its orientation towards the different other, may be conceived as the finite analogue of the divine impulsion towards otherness.

## St John of the Cross: The excess of desire

The title of Rowan Williams' 2002 essay 'The Deflections of Desire: Negative Theology in Trinitarian Disclosure',[66] provides the clue to Williams' argument that the essence of the divine life is both hidden and revealed in the *relations* of the Trinity. While God's 'nature evades all description',[67] it is nevertheless disclosed in the encounter with God as Trinitarian relationship of love. The 'rhythm'[68] of that relationship is what strains human comprehension. It is a rhythm that never culminates in a loved object as terminus but is endless and thus beyond conceptual conclusion. It may nevertheless be known in the darkness of prayerful encounter with God as a movement of endless deflection of love towards what is loved by the beloved.

These insights are derived from St John of the Cross, and specifically from the poetic meditations, known as the *Romanzas*. In this work Williams notes the use of the term *quería*, which has the meaning of 'desire' and which thus carries with it the human connotations of desire, namely the energy associated with '"erotic" movement towards a goal'.[69]

Whereas human desire implies a lack to be filled by the other, divine desire has no closure, no object which terminates desire. On the contrary, as discerned in Williams' accounts of Augustine and Aquinas, it is characterized by excess. The love of the Father for the Son does not terminate in the Son but is also love for what the Son loves. Similarly, the Son's love for the Father is love for what the Father loves. The excess of the mutual love of Father and Son is the Spirit. The excess of the Spirit means that the love of Father and Son is not completed in a 'mutual reinforcement of identity'. Instead, God's life is represented as a rhythm of circling movement, an eternal going-out from self towards the other and towards that which is loved by the other.[70]

In this way, divine desire is shown to be an eternal movement or rhythm of deflection, love for the other being deflected from the other to include the object of the other's love. Williams can therefore conclude that 'in the divine life "desire" has to be reimagined as love for the love of the other, the passion for an other to be fulfilled.'[71]

This pattern of circling deflection, observes Williams, is startlingly similar to the Rublev icon's visual representation of the Trinity.[72] Unlike the 'Rublev' poem, Williams' emphasis here is not on God's initiative in making contact with humanity but rather on the position of the three figures seated around a table. At the front of the table is an open space which is the position of the viewer in relation to the three figures. The viewer's gaze is held in an endless circling motion: the central figure is looking towards the person on his right who in turn is looking towards the third person. That figure, however, is not looking at either of the others but towards the viewer, whose gaze is directed back to the central figure, traditionally identified as Jesus. The viewer is thus drawn in and included in the unending circle of deflected, dispossessive love which is the Trinitarian life of God. The viewer, says Williams, becomes 'the "site" where the eternal movement of dispossession is being enacted'.[73] Creation and, specifically, humanity have their being through the excess of divine love, ever overflowing to include that which is loved by the beloved.

Paradoxically, the excess of deflected love is to be most clearly discerned in the dereliction of Jesus on the cross, where all sense of the Father's love is completely missing from Jesus' consciousness. The Father is absent as the goal of desire. All that remains for Jesus is the divine purpose for creation, for that which is the excess of the Father's love and to which his own love is deflected. As Williams argues, 'The Son's love must enact the Father's, not simply reflect it back to him; so, on Calvary it acts in an experienced darkness with respect to the knowledge or feeling of a divine other.'[74] The dark absence of Calvary is the most startling evidence of the nature of divine love: a movement ever deflected beyond any form of final gratification, love directed outward towards the object of the beloved's love.

Revealed at Calvary is divine love as utter self-bestowal. Here excess, *ekstasis* and *kenosis* may be seen to coincide. The Son's kenotic giving of himself for love of the Father's love is an ecstatic movement towards that which is loved by the Father as excess of love for the Son. Divine love is shown to be complete self-gift.

## Balthasar and divine self-alienation

Similar themes are reprised in 'Balthasar and Difference', Williams' discussion of Balthasar's Trinitarian theology.[75] Here God is analogously revealed in what is different from God, in the temporal imperfect unfinishedness of creation and, supremely, in the vulnerable finite mortality of the crucified Jesus. Jesus, crucified, shows God to be self-alienation for love of that which is other, in order that the other may freely remain other, having its own identity and integrity. Highlighted by the crucifixion is not only the 'gulf of immeasurable otherness' of Father from Son but also the fact that 'the divine life ... [s]ustains itself as unqualified unity across the greatest completeness of alienation that can be imagined.'[76]

Divine life is thus revealed as an eternal movement of self-alienation, realized as the opening up of distance in order that the other may remain differentiated as other, rather than being a repetition of sameness. As Williams states, 'the self-alienating of divine life in the Father's self-gift to the Son itself "alienates" itself, posits itself as *more* than a symmetry of self-sacrifice, becomes [the Spirit], that which the Son gives, realizes, liberates, from the depth of his distance from the Father.'[77] It is this maintaining distance in love, the act of kenotic self-alienation in the ecstatic gift of self-bestowal, which allows for the continuing differentiation of the other as other, and thus for the possibility of further self-alienating self-bestowal on the part of the beloved other.

Despite differences in emphasis and language, the above accounts of Trinitarian relations are markedly similar. All hold that love/*eros*/*caritas* is the essence of the life of the Godhead; all describe the nature of divine love as excess, using such terms as 'inexhaustible', 'overflowing', 'without terminus/closure'. Common also is the notion that divine love involves a movement out from sameness towards the other (*ekstasis*), that movement being one of self-bestowal/self-dispossession/self-alienation (*kenosis*). Held together in these Trinitarian theologies are the notions of participation/unity and differentiation, of subsistent but differentiated relations.

It is difficult to disagree with Andrew Moody's questioning of 'whether [Williams'] readings truly reflect the way Augustine, Aquinas, and John of the Cross *actually* see the Trinity'.[78] As Mike Higton has pointed out, Williams' discussions of the ideas of other theologians may be described as 'interpretative performances' rather than faithful exegesis.[79] This judgement is supported by the similarities I have discerned among the readings, giving strength to the conclusion that these essays cannot be considered as dispassionate analyses of the Trinitarian theology of the theologians in question. What we are presented with is Williams' own distinctive vision of the divine life as an inexhaustible excess of ecstatic, kenotic love, overflowing into creation.

## Conclusion

In this chapter I have argued that the impelling force of Williams' theological vision is the notion of divine desire. Drawing on Williams' analysis of the analogical relation between infinite divinity and finite humanity in the work of Austin Farrer and Erich Przywara, I have sought to show that the nature of divine desire is made evident in the person of the crucified Jesus, revealed as the analogue of that desire. From an examination of Williams' accounts of the Trinitarian theologies of Augustine, Aquinas, St John of the Cross and Balthasar, the conclusion is drawn that divine desire may be described as the excess of ecstatic, kenotic love overflowing into creation.[80] A further tentative conclusion is that the impulsion towards otherness characteristic of human imagination is a finite analogue of the ecstatic, other-oriented energy of divine desire.

The focus of Chapter 5 will be the human experience of desire, the distortions to which it is subject within finite existence, and the relation between desire and imagination.

### Notes

  1 These meditations take the form of a poem, 'Our Lady of Vladimir' (Rowan Williams, *The Poems of Rowan Williams* (Oxford: Perpetua Press, 2002), p. 14), and an address to pilgrims, *Ponder These Things: Praying with Icons of the Virgin* (Mulgrave, Vic: John Garratt, 2002), pp. 21–39.
  2 Williams, *Ponder These Things*, p. 25.
  3 Williams, *Ponder These Things*, p. 38.

4 In his reflections on icons, Williams stresses the 'terrible weight of divine love' (*Ponder These Things*, p. 31), which is 'hungry' for our response (*Ponder These Things*, pp. 25, 28), an 'alarming', 'violent ... explosive force' (Williams, *The Dwelling of the Light: Praying with Icons of Christ* (Mulgrave, Vic: John Garrett, 2003), pp. 13, 11), operating on 'the dangerous border between love and terror' (*Ponder These Things*, p. 30). In the 1995 collection of sermons *A Ray of Darkness* (Lanham, MD: Cowley, 1995), Williams declares Christmas to be 'a beauty that is the beginning of terror' (p. 3) and the 'seeing of God' as akin to a 'refining fire' (p. 101).

5 For the experience of fear of the divine, see Rudolf Otto, *The Idea of the Holy*, trans. John W. Harvey (London: Oxford University Press, 1924), pp. 12ff. See also my Chapter 3, p. 71, for the mingling of love and fear in Przywara's conception of the divine/human relation.

6 Williams, *Ponder These Things*, p. 36.

7 Williams, *Ponder These Things*, p. 38.

8 Williams, *A Ray of Darkness*, p. 3.

9 Rowan Williams, *Christ the Heart of Creation* (London: Bloomsbury Continuum, 2018).

10 Williams, *Christ the Heart of Creation*, pp. 26ff. *Esse*, as used by Aquinas, 'designates the particular acting subject.'

11 Williams, *Christ the Heart of Creation*, p. 29.

12 Williams, *Christ the Heart of Creation*, p. 31.

13 Williams, *Christ the Heart of Creation*, p. 38.

14 Williams, *Christ the Heart of Creation*, pp. 38, 39.

15 See Brett Gray's discussion of Williams' conception of the *non aliud* principle in relation to God. Williams, in Mike Higton, ed., *Wrestling with Angels: Conversations in Modern Theology* (Grand Rapids, MI: William B. Eerdmans, 2007), p. 80, argues that God is not '*an* other, an item in a list along with the contents of the universe'. Equally, *non aliud* indicates that God is the source of all that exists. Brett Gray, *Jesus in the Theology of Rowan Williams* (London: Bloomsbury, 2016), pp. 9–11.

16 Gray, *Jesus in the Theology of Rowan Williams*, p. xiv. In his analysis, Williams acknowledges his debt to the writings of Hans Urs von Balthasar, Thomas F. Torrance, Kathryn Tanner, John Webster and Herbert McCabe.

17 Williams, *Christ the Heart of Creation*, p. xiv.

18 Williams, *Christ the Heart of Creation*, p. 2.

19 Williams, *Christ the Heart of Creation*, p. 230.

20 Williams, *Christ the Heart of Creation*, p. 230.

21 Williams, *Christ the Heart of Creation*, p. 230.

22 Williams, *Christ the Heart of Creation*, p. xiv.

23 See also Rowan Williams, 'Augustine on Creation' in *On Augustine* (London: Bloomsbury, 2016), p. 75, where, following Augustine, Williams affirms 'creation's integrity ... as a limited and fluid whole that is not God, yet is saturated with God'.

24 See Williams, *Christ the Heart of Creation*, p. 240.

25 Williams, *Christ the Heart of Creation*, p. 232.

26 Williams, *Christ the Heart of Creation*, p. 233. As noted by Williams in his essay on 'Trinity and Revelation' (*On Christian Theology: Challenges in Contemporary Theology* (Malden, MA: Blackwell, 2000), p. 133), Ricoeur also concludes that 'The truth with which the poetic text is concerned is not verification, but manifestation.' As a result, the text may be said to 'embod[y] the reality with which it is concerned simply by witness or "testimony"'.

27 Williams, *Christ the Heart of Creation*, p. 233.
28 Williams, *Christ the Heart of Creation*, p. 236.
29 Williams, *Christ the Heart of Creation*, p. 234.
30 Williams, *Christ the Heart of Creation*, pp. 222–5.
31 Williams, *Christ the Heart of Creation*, p. 242.
32 Williams, *Christ the Heart of Creation*, p. 240.
33 Williams, *Christ the Heart of Creation*, pp. 250–1.
34 Williams, *Christ the Heart of Creation*, p. 251.
35 Williams, *The Poems of Rowan Williams*, p. 35.
36 Rowan Williams, *The Wound of Knowledge: Christian Spirituality from the New Testament to St John of the Cross*, 2nd rev. edn (London: Darton Longman & Todd, 1990). The first edition was published in 1979.
37 R. S. Thomas, *Collected Poems* (London: Phoenix, 2000), p. 354.
38 Williams, *The Wound of Knowledge*, p. 85.
39 Williams, *The Wound of Knowledge*, p. 86.
40 Williams, *The Wound of Knowledge*, p. 91.
41 Williams, *The Wound of Knowledge*, p. 117. The 'fierceness' of Williams' vision of divine love is also noted by Higton who says, of this vision, 'to know God is to be caught in this fierce [torrential] current, and to have all the comforting accretions which have cushioned us against its flow stripped away'. Mike Higton, *Difficult Gospel: The Theology of Rowan Williams* (London: SCM Press, 2004), p. 59.
42 In *The Wound of Knowledge*, p. ix, Williams states that the book was based on four years of lectures on Christian spirituality. See also the 'Introduction' to *On Augustine*, p. vii, where he refers to the many years spent teaching and reflecting on Augustine's thought. Rupert Shortt (*Rowan's Rule: The Biography of the Archbishop*, rev. edn (London: Hodder & Stoughton, 2014), p. 35) holds that Augustine may be considered Williams' 'single greatest influence', an opinion supported by Benjamin Myers (*Christ the Stranger: The Theology of Rowan Williams* (London: T&T Clark, 2012), pp. 33ff.).
43 It must be noted that Williams is often concerned less with a detailed exegesis of Augustine's thought than with demonstrating its relevance for contemporary Western debates. See *On Augustine*, p. ix.
44 Williams, *On Augustine*, pp. 209, 211.
45 Williams, *On Augustine*, pp. 76–7. In Williams' *Looking East in Winter: Contemporary Thought and the Eastern Christian Tradition* (London: Bloomsbury Continuum, 2001), a primary emphasis is on the centrality of divine desire (*eros*) in the Trinitarian theology of such Orthodox theologians as Gregory Palamas and Maximus the Confessor. Again, Williams' early interest in Orthodox theology may have significantly contributed to the insistence he places on desire as key to Trinitarian and finite relations.
46 Williams, *On Augustine*, pp. 171–90.
47 Augustine of Hippo, *On the Trinity*, ed. Gareth B. Matthews, trans. Stephen McKenna (Cambridge: Cambridge University Press, 2012).
48 Williams, *On Augustine*, p. 178.
49 Williams, *On Augustine*, p. 174.
50 Williams, *On Augustine*, p. 183.
51 Williams, *On Augustine*, p. 190.
52 Williams, *On Augustine*, p. 77.
53 Williams, *The Wound of Knowledge*, p. 121.

54 Williams, *The Wound of Knowledge*, p. 123. See also Williams, *Christ the Heart of Creation*, pp. 106–7, 120–1 and Williams' discussion of Maximus's conception of divine *eros* in *Looking East in Winter*, p. 51, with its reference to 'the infinite act of God, which generates finite *eros* as an echo of its own love for itself in the mutual inexhaustibility of trinitarian life'.

55 Williams, *The Wound of Knowledge*, p. 124. In this early work, Williams provides no evidence on which to base this sweeping claim. It is, however, supported by a paper published in 2006 by Peter Kwasniewski, who argues that 'while the term "ecstasy" does not occur with much frequency in Aquinas's writings, the concept signified by it turns out to play quite a crucial role in his articulation of a doctrine of love.' Peter A. Kwasniewski, 'The Ecstasy of Love in Aquinas's Commentary on the Sentences', *Angelicum* 83.1 (2006), p. 93.

56 Williams, 'What Does Love Know? St Thomas on the Trinity', *New Blackfriars* 82.964 (2001).

57 Williams, 'What Does Love Know?', p. 262. Aquinas's conception of the interdependence of knowledge and love is the subject of a study by Michael Sherwin, entitled *By Knowledge and Love: Charity and Knowledge in the Moral Theology of St Thomas Aquinas* (Washington: Catholic University of America Press, 2005).

58 Williams, *The Wound of Knowledge*, p. 125.
59 Williams, 'What Does Love Know?', p. 262.
60 Williams, 'What Does Love Know?', p. 265.
61 Williams, 'What Does Love Know?', p. 271.
62 Williams, 'What Does Love Know?', p. 265.
63 Williams, 'What Does Love Know?', p. 265.
64 Williams, 'What Does Love Know?', p. 271.
65 Williams, 'What Does Love Know?', p. 272.
66 Rowan Williams, 'The Deflections of Desire: Negative Theology in Trinitarian Disclosure' in *Silence and the Word: Negative Theology and Incarnation*, ed. Oliver Davies and Denys Turner (Cambridge: Cambridge University Press, 2002).
67 Williams, 'The Deflections of Desire', p. 116.
68 Williams, 'The Deflections of Desire', p. 117. It should be noted that the notion of 'rhythm', as used here, is similar to the 'rhythm' of Przywara's analogical method.
69 Williams, 'The Deflections of Desire', pp. 118, 126.
70 Williams, 'The Deflections of Desire', pp. 118–19.
71 Williams, 'The Deflections of Desire', p. 132.
72 Williams, 'The Deflections of Desire', pp. 128–9.
73 The inclusion of humanity in the circle of deflected divine love will be discussed further in Chapter 5.
74 Williams, 'The Deflections of Desire', p. 122.
75 Williams, 'Balthasar and Difference' in Higton, ed., *Wrestling with Angels*, pp. 77–85.
76 Williams, 'Balthasar and Difference', p. 81.
77 Williams, 'Balthasar and Difference', p. 81.
78 Andrew Moody, 'The Hidden Center: Trinity and Incarnation in the Negative (and Positive) Theology of Rowan Williams', in *On Rowan Williams: Critical Essays*, ed. Matheson Russell (Eugene, OR: Cascade Books, 2009), p. 35. The same reservation is expressed by Myers, *Christ the Stranger*, pp. 124–5, and Higton, 'Editor's Introduction', *Wrestling with Angels*, pp. xxii–xxiii.
79 Higton, 'Editor's Introduction', p. xxii.
80 Williams, *On Christian Theology*, p. 74.

# 5

# Human Desire

## Introduction

> This is the only way to dis-illusion my prayer and my life, by bearing the oppressive shapelessness of a dark without agency, blind desire, blind trust, the sparkle from the coal ... that sharp dart of longing love, the ache of wanting, the decision to be faithful ... That is the mercy which will never ... let us be content with less than itself and less than the truth. I must be found in God ... and so that void draws and calls us, the magnet of all our hearts and the lodestar of all truth.
> (Rowan Williams, 'Address to the 1983 Conference of Anglo-Catholics')[1]

We have now reached the heart of Williams' theology of imagination. It is our human desire for God, the 'sparkle from the coal', 'that sharp dart of longing love' that draws us onwards towards 'the magnet of all our hearts'. Repeatedly Williams returns to the theme of the 'endless character of desire',[2] considered by him to be central to Augustine's thinking and to Orthodox spirituality. In his recent study of the collection of Orthodox texts known as the *Philokalia*, he points to its emphasis on 'the impulsion' at the centre of human nature, an '"erotic" drawing towards the [divine] source without which it is incomplete and imprisoned in unreality'.[3]

Human desire is thus attributable to the inexhaustibility of divine desire overflowing as finite creation. According to Williams, the limitless love of the triune God for the beings created in the divine image is the 'void that draws and calls us', igniting 'the sparkle' from the coal of our finite existence. Yet as a critical observer of the human condition and of his own inner struggles, he is also aware, with Augustine, of the paradoxical nature of human desire and of the distortions to which it is subject.

In this chapter, I set out to explore Williams' account of our human response to divine desire as it is experienced within finite existence. I argue that just as human desire is the finite analogue of the other-oriented energy of divine love, so the human capacity for imagination, with its impulsion towards otherness, difference and seemingly infinite possibility, is to be conceptualized as the finite analogue of the inexhaustible ecstatic energy of divine desire. My further claim is that, for Williams, our response to God's desire determines the direction of our imagination. Directed towards that which is other-than-God, imagination is liable to degenerate into what he calls 'fantasy', a term imbued by him with decidedly negative connotations. Desire and imagination must accordingly be reoriented towards their true end, Jesus Christ, this reorientation being effected only through the operation of divine grace.

Williams' meditation on the Icon of the Transfiguration leads us into a consideration of the paradoxical tension associated with human desire, which, drawn towards that which is other, simultaneously longs for and fears the other's closeness.[4] For insight into that tension I turn to the conclusions of René Girard and Jacques Lacan, with whose writings Williams engaged in analysing the distortions of desire evident in human relations.[5] Lacan's discussion of fantasy leads to an exploration of the significance of fantasy for Williams, my conclusion being that fantasy is the distorted form of imagination, a misdirection of desire towards finite ends.

In the second half of the chapter, I follow Williams' argument that human desire finds its true *end* only in Jesus Christ.[6] Through engagement with the thought of Augustine, Maximus the Confessor, Aquinas and St John of the Cross, he concludes that human desire must be renewed in Christ, thereby becoming self-dispossessive (kenotic) and other-oriented (ecstatic). In view of the inextricable relation between desire and imagination, it follows that the renewal and transformation of desire also involves a refocusing of imagination, such that its energy is directed towards the fulfilment of the divine purposes for creation.

## The Icon of the Transfiguration

Reflection on icons, says Williams, is 'the basis for a transformed vision of the world in the transfigured and transfiguring reality of Jesus'.[7] Asserting the impossibility of representing the divine through a material medium, he declares that icons are intended not to depict God but rather to position us correctly in relation to the divine.[8] Unlike Western art in which the viewer stands outside the frame to examine what is depicted, iconic representation reverses the perspective so that it converges on the viewer. The icon thus 'bears down on' and interrogates the one who is viewing it.[9] 'The skill of looking at icons', says Williams, 'is the strange skill of letting yourself be seen, be read.'[10] In this way the finite human is positioned correctly in relation to the infinite God and the icon acts as a kind of window into otherwise unrepresentable reality.[11]

The traditional Icon of the Transfiguration shows Jesus, in startlingly white robes, emerging from the dark depths of infinity, with the figures of Moses and Elijah on either side, while the disciples lie 'sprawled in disorder' at the bottom of a rocky slope.[12] In allowing himself to be 'read' by this icon, Williams focuses initially on the gleaming whiteness of the central figure, showing 'Jesus' human life ... shot through with God's ... eternal life ... bringing with him all the fullness of the creator'.[13] Encompassed by this transfigured presence are time and history, creation and its fulfilment. In that presence, the figures of Elijah and Moses are revealed as contemporary with the disciples, and with us, the viewers.

Williams' reflection then shifts to the human bystanders, the three disciples, depicted as though 'physically thrown down'. They cover their faces to shade their eyes from the brightness and turn away from the terrifying energy of what they are seeing. For them, says Williams, the 'explosive', 'violent force' of that transfigured presence is experienced as unbearable to finite beings.[14] In their glimpse of the transfigured Jesus, the eternal life of God the Son is 'translate[d] into human terms'.[15] It is a glimpse that shatters all their previous conceptions of God. And yet as these disciples will soon discover, a further shattering is about to occur with the humiliation, brokenness and death of that transfigured figure. Presented through the medium of the icon is the radical otherness of God who is most clearly seen in the broken body of the crucified Jesus.

In the conditions of finite creation, says Williams, God is known either as light so blinding that it becomes an alarming 'ray of darkness',[16] or as a despised figure on a cross. Only from the position of the beholder of an icon, a position of openness to the confronting truthfulness of the divine gaze, are we able to begin to know God. For finite human beings such knowledge may be so terrifyingly alien that we direct our desire elsewhere, to that which is familiar and subject to our control.

The various ways in which the relation between desire and otherness becomes distorted within finite existence are the subject of what follows.

## Human desire within the parameters of finite existence

As discussed in Chapter 3, Przywara identifies the analogous relation between the infinite God and finite creation as that of continuity-in-difference. The continuity is revealed as the relational dependence of finite creation on God; the difference lies in the limitations inherent in creation: temporality and materiality. In respect of this continuity-in-difference, Augustine's account of creation is particularly significant for Williams' understanding of the relation between divine and human desire.

Williams follows Augustine in conceiving of the world as an interconnected whole, a 'network of sensitive interaction',[17] which is constantly in the process of seeking equilibrium. As conceptualized by Augustine, that process is 'the "desire" of things for divine stability'.[18] The meaning we human beings seek to give to the fluctuations of human existence is evidence of our human desire for stability.[19] When, directed towards God, the source of coherent meaning in instability, finite desire finds its true end.

By contrast, evil, for Augustine and for Williams, is the misdirection of desire towards objects of fantasy. Summarizing Augustine's position, Williams asserts that 'the nature of evil [is] the perversion of my own capacity to see or know, and to become open in love and knowledge to the reality of God.'[20] Instead of being directed towards God, human desire seeks a fantasized fulfilment in finite, temporal experience. The result is a distortion of the relation between desire and otherness in the finite conditions of temporality, and materiality. These distortions are explored by Williams in dialogue with the thought of Girard and Lacan.

## René Girard and mimetic desire

In a 1989 lecture,[21] Williams draws on the mimetic theory of the anthropologist René Girard to account for the ubiquity of violence in human behaviour.[22] According to Girard, the origin of violence lies in the fact that, from infancy, human beings learn by imitation.[23] In imitating the sounds and gestures of those around us, we learn to reach for, and thus desire, what significant others desire. The other is a model who subsequently becomes a rival and a potential threat. Girard postulates that, within society, such rivalrous threats are initially kept in check by the development of rituals and taboos that control the scope of imitation. When a disaster or an outbreak of violence occurs, the ensuing crisis demands a more drastic solution. A scapegoat, identified as 'other', is held to be the source of the disaster, his/her sacrificial elimination being considered necessary for the restoration of peace and stability within the society.[24]

Once a link is established between social stability and the scapegoat mechanism of the sacrificial ritual, the notion of the sacred is henceforth associated with violence.[25] Society's security is thus dependent on ritual sacrifice. Paradoxically, therefore, the sacrificial victim who is the solution to society's ills is thereby seen as its saviour and is accorded the status of mythical hero.[26] With the establishment of the myth, the arbitrary nature of the sacrifice is forgotten, and no learning occurs. The cycle of violence and sacrifice continues, becoming a 'generative principle which works unconsciously in culture and society'.[27]

Girard's argument is that this 'mechanism of victimage' is identified for what it is only when the victim is shown to be completely innocent, as was the case with Jesus. In refusing to respond to violence with violence, the dying Jesus exposed the arbitrariness of the victimage mechanism, and so subverted the whole sacrificial system with its link to the sacred.[28] While history confirms that the scapegoating of victims continues to operate, Girard's account reminds us that such a system may no longer be accorded divine sanction.

The significance of Girard for Williams lies not only in his identification of the way in which the victimage mechanism operates in human relationships but also, and primarily, in his recognition that the God revealed in Jesus is *'wholly* outside the processes of sacred violence'.[29] The death and resurrection of Jesus is the revelation of the absolute ontological difference of God; it shows us that that divine desire is totally free of mimetic imitation and therefore free of violence.[30] It demonstrates that God's relation to humanity has no element of rivalry but is solely a gift of grace, the gift of unmerited divine love.

## Jacques Lacan: The *telos* of desire and the role of fantasy

The relationship between desire and otherness is also the core of the reinterpretation of Freudian psychoanalytic theory by the French psychoanalyst Jacques Lacan. Lacan reconceptualizes desire as insatiable lack, a lack fuelled by the ultimately unattainable Other.[31] Desire, he argues, is desire for the ever-elusive, unsignifiable desire of the Other, the Other being 'an unfathomable abyss' of impenetrable unknowability,[32] derived from the infant's initial relationship with the mother.[33] Originating in the infant's experience of the need to satisfy hunger, desire becomes a demanding cry which is met not only by the mother's breast but also by the mother's closeness.

Demand thus becomes more than a demand for food; it is also a demand for love.[34] That love can never be adequately met since the core of the mother's desiring is not a 'static, stable thing' to be given on demand, but is itself a restlessness, incapable of reaching fulfilment.[35] In this way the mother becomes the desired, but inaccessible, Other, ever beyond the satisfaction of desire since the (m)Other's desire is itself unattainable.

Sociocultural mediation of desire occurs as the infant develops and learns to identify him/herself with the body-image seen in a mirror or as reflected by significant others. Of significance in such development are what Lacan terms the 'orders' of 'the imaginary' and the 'symbolic' as opposed to the 'Real'.[36] The imaginary designates the 'basic and enduring dimension of experience that is oriented by images, perceived or fantasized'.[37] The symbolic is the sociocultural mediation of the imaginary as names and meanings are given to specific objects of desire that have no significance in themselves but derive their importance from the culturally acceptable significance attributed to them by others.

No longer the expression of basic need, desire is now a matter of fantasy, the fantasies learned from what the growing child imagines to be the desires of others.[38] Being insatiable and unconscious, driven by libidinous energy, desire is transferred from object to object but finds no terminus, since that which is ultimately desired is the desire of the unattainable Other. Desire, for Lacan, is therefore 'an insistent circuitry' of never satisfied lack,[39] with fantasy as the means that not only sustains the subject's desire but also confirms the subject him/herself as essentially desirous.[40]

As conceptualized by Lacan, fantasy is an unconscious solution to unattainable desires by providing a shifting focus for desire. At the core of a subject's psyche is, however, the 'fundamental fantasy', the internal schema of 'who I am for others', which constitutes the framework for the subject's perception of reality, and which governs attitudes and behaviour. Functioning as the mechanism which protects the psyche from the intolerable fact of insatiable lack, it remains inaccessible unless exposed in psychoanalysis as the 'unbearable truth that I have to learn to live with'.[41] That unbearable truth is what Lacan terms the order of the Real, conceived 'as lack or absence, as the impossible, as the unspeakable force of trauma, or as the ineffable exigence of the body'.[42] Fantasy thus serves to create a reality which protects against awareness of the intolerable negativity at the heart of Reality.

Williams' interest in Lacan lies primarily in the French psychoanalyst's decisive dismantling of the popular Western notion of the naked, authentic self, hidden beneath imposed layers of social construction. Williams agrees with Lacan that the self is the construct of social interaction, and that self-knowledge lies in the awareness 'that there is nothing prior to reciprocity'.[43] He also follows Lacan in differentiating between the ego and the subject. According to Lacan, the ego is an object, 'the fundamental fantasy', constituted by the imagined desires and projections of others, whereas the subject is the unconscious energy of negativity which propels desire. Williams concurs that the ego seeks to assert its possession of the objects of desire, while, for him, 'the subject is constituted as what does not possess, desiring and desiring to be desired.'[44]

Williams argues that the demands of the ego for gratification of desire exist in tension with the unfulfillable desire of the subject, and this tension accounts for the movement of both language and history.[45] Truthful consciousness consists in the recognition of this tension, and of the need for constant questioning of self in relation to the other. Such questioning may be assisted by the analytic process where the analyst refuses to be the object of ego gratification, thus 'lay[ing] bare the fraudulence of the ego' and its projections and making possible the recognition of another person as desiring subject rather than ego object.[46]

Williams and Lacan part company in their conception of the source and *telos* of desire and in their understanding of fantasy. In the essay '"Know Thyself": What Kind of an Injunction?', Williams identifies the source of Lacanian desire as primordial need and its *telos* as the unattainable Other; it thus becomes a desire for death, for the negativity of the Real.[47] By contrast, he follows Augustine and St Bernard of Clairvaux in locating the inexhaustible source of human desire in the divine love evidenced in creation,[48] and he sees its goal as Augustinian *iustitia*, 'a universally shareable good', to be worked out in the conditions of created finitude.[49]

In a corrupted world, with 'misidentification' of the Good and 'fictions of rivalry', desire is readily misdirected.[50] The essay '"Know Thyself"' claims that what is needed to free humanity from its inevitable enmeshment in rivalrous desire is an 'ego-less interlocutor'. Such a figure, who does not hold 'even a residual position in the world where desires are negotiated',[51] is in no way a rival, and can therefore provide a 'horizon against which other perspectives may be tested'.[52] As truly egoless, Jesus Christ is, for humanity, the non-rivalrous interlocutor who enables the testing of desire.

Williams' assertion that this interlocutor should have no place in the world of desire would seem to demand an absolute separation between divinity and humanity. Such an assertion contradicts his repeated contention that 'unchanging truth [can] be touched' only 'in the non-finality of historical relationships and historical "satisfaction"'.[53] From the latter statement we would conclude that the ego-less interlocutor must be available within the conditions of finite reality. Whereas '"Know Thyself"' asserts the liberating force of 'the inaccessib[le] ... divine perspective',[54] Williams' most consistent position is to affirm that humanity's experience of a perspective completely free of rivalry and ego-compulsive desire is to be found in the accessibility of the life and death of Jesus of Nazareth.

## Desire, fantasy and imagination

The relation between desire and fantasy is made explicit in the Freudian psychoanalytic tradition as reworked by Lacan. In that tradition, fantasy serves as protection against awareness of prohibited erotic desire for the (m)other (Freud) and against the intolerable inaccessibility of Real Otherness (Lacan). For Rowan Williams, it is the God revealed in Jesus who is the Real Other, the authentic *telos* of desire and who is known through the exercise of properly focused imagination.[55] Fantasy is a misdirection of the human imaginative capacity to transcend the limits of finite actuality. Only through the identification and rejection of fantasy does desire find its true *telos* in God.

While Williams recognizes that, in human development, fantasy plays a necessary role in giving children the opportunity to test various identities and to learn responsible decision-making, he insists on alerting his audiences to the danger of unchecked fantasy in adult relations. In line with Freud and Lacan, he knows that fantasy has a protective function, serving as it does as a defence against the fearsome depths of the human psyche and the uncontrollable aspects of finite existence. He is alert, however, to the damaging consequences of such evasion, both for the individual and for society, arguing that the danger of fantasy lies in its denial of the time-bound and interdependent nature of finite existence. The result of such a denial is an abdication of responsibility for the outcome of one's actions.

In an early work, *The Truce of God*,[56] Williams examines the 'collective neuroses'[57] evident in popular obsessions with the catastrophic and paranormal in advertising, cinema and literature. Depicting humans pitted against uncontrollable, alien forces, these fictional scenarios give expression to the sense of powerlessness experienced in a world threatened by nuclear annihilation, terrorism and environmental disaster. In these fictions, the threats are depersonalized, with violence seen as an acceptable solution. Williams contends that disaster fantasies represent an evasion of personal responsibility for the sources of real-life conflict and are indicative of 'a deep sickness of the spirit', an unwillingness to develop the inner resources required for acknowledging guilt and pain.[58]

His most extended treatment of the spiritually destructive effects of fantasy is to be found in his 2008 study of the work of Dostoevsky. Pointing to the 'diabolical' outworking of the fantasies of absolute autonomy and freedom, represented by such characters as Stavrogin and Shigalyov, Williams concludes that 'The triumph of the diabolical is when we cannot bear to see what we cannot deny is the truth in ourselves and in the world.'[59] Evasion into fantasy constitutes a denial of the 'fluidity' of human existence in time; it is an abnegation of the labour and responsibility of making choices in each new situation. It is also a refusal to recognize the obdurate fact of otherness, the impenetrable otherness of another person and the uncompromising otherness of the world in which we live.

In Williams' view, Dostoevsky's extreme fictions demonstrate the necessity of subjecting 'our commitments [to] repeated imaginative testing' for the purpose of assessing whether our 'decisions [and] moral trajectories are life-bound or death-bound'.[60] Unlike fantasy, which is an evasion of truthfulness, imagination is the means whereby we may explore the possible consequences of our desires in an effort to determine whether they are life-giving or death-dealing.

According to Myers, the 'dread of self-deceptive fantasy is ... the secret engine of Williams' work',[61] spurring him to develop his 'doctrine of divine desire'.[62] Such a conclusion alerts us again to the tension at the heart of Williams' anthropology, which views human beings as both drawn towards, and burdened by, the overwhelming Otherness of the Love for which we are created. Open to question, however, is the direction of the movement between abhorrence of fantasy and insight into divine desire. It is arguable that it is awareness of the intensity of divine desire that keeps Williams mindful of the human counter-desire to escape into self-enclosed fantasy.

The examination of Williams' discussion of desire and otherness in the thought of Girard and Lacan has shown that, within finite reality, the inextricable interrelationship between desire and otherness readily leads to the distortions of fantasy. Such fantasies serve to justify either possession of the other, thus reducing otherness to the same, or suppression of the other through violence or mythical sacralization. Williams' conclusion is that human desire may be freed from these distortions only through encounter with the One whose desire is completely dispossessed of rivalrous ego-demands and whose Otherness is not a threat, but a source of inexhaustible love.

## Christ-focused desire

In Williams' vision of human existence, a life-changing encounter with Jesus Christ brings about a transformation of desire. It is then that the human vocation of *imaging* God finally begins to be realized, as desire is gradually directed away from the egotistical self towards God, the source and end of finite existence. Drawn irresistibly towards its source in God, human desire becomes a 'sudden stirring ... speedily springing unto God as a sparkle from the coal'.[63] In the process, desire becomes ecstatically nuptial and kenotically filial, an increasingly true human reflection of the divine image.

## The source and end of human desire

As we have seen, Girard and Lacan concur concerning 'the fundamentally desirous nature of [human] beings', a conclusion also reached by Augustine.[64] In his *Confessions*, Augustine identified desire as the spur that led him from sexual exploration to intellectual inquiry and finally to the realization that God alone was both the source and end of his desire.[65] As he wrote in addressing God, 'You have made us for yourself, and our heart is restless until it rests in you.'[66] The restlessness Augustine experienced is integral to desire; it is a restlessness that has its source in the endlessness of divine desire, generating, within created beings, an infinite longing which cannot be sated by anything less than God.[67]

This theme is explored by Williams in his first book, *The Wound of Knowledge*, which follows the history of Christian spirituality from the New Testament to St John of the Cross. Here we are reminded that saint after saint was impelled along the dark and difficult pathway of Christian discipleship by an ever-deepening desire for God. So, says Williams, Gregory of Nyssa saw 'the Christian life [as] a journey into God ... always marked by *desire* ... a longing and trust directed away from itself towards an object ... which it will never comprehend'.[68] According to Bernard of Clairvaux, our experience is of 'a searching never satisfied ... that eternal inexplicable longing that knows no dissatisfaction and want'.[69] Aquinas, in Williams' reading, is concerned with 'the natural life in its entirety gathered up and taken beyond itself in the act of desire for God and exposure to God'.[70] Meister Eckhart is likewise held to assert that 'Christian life is ... [a] conversion of behaviour grounded in the transforming of desire, the naked receptivity of the self to God's graceful act.'[71] St John of the Cross describes the dark and painful process whereby desire is gradually purified until, within human beings, intellect is transformed into faith, memory into hope, and will into love.[72]

These saints recognized that human desire must learn to seek its proper end, an end that is clarified by Augustine's distinction between *res* and *signum*.[73] Willliams' analysis of that distinction is to be found in the 1989 essay, 'Language, Reality and Desire in Augustine's *De Doctrina*'.[74] As with his discussion of Augustine's conception of divine desire, Williams' concern is to bring out the contemporary relevance of the North African saint's insights.[75] In this essay, he follows Augustine's argument that God, 'determined by nothing else', is the only *res* to be enjoyed for his own sake;[76] all finite objects are signs that point to their divine source and have their purpose and meaning in God.[77] They exist not primarily to be enjoyed of themselves but are to be used to direct human desire towards the supreme *res*, God.

Finite signs are, however, ambiguous and open to misinterpretation. As such they become misleading objects of desire. The one sign that does not mislead is Jesus Christ, both infinite Word/Son and finite human being. His life and death are for humanity the finite sign that points unerringly to God, the proper end of desire.[78] As Jesus used the transient object-signs of human existence to point to God as their true meaning, so we human beings find our true vocation by learning from Christ the proper use of the signs of everyday existence, namely, growth in love for God. We thus discover that desire directed towards God, 'the sparkle from the coal', brings fulfilment that has no terminus, but which becomes ever more intense.

## Desire and the image of God

As the sign that points truthfully to God, the man, Jesus, is the true image of God,[79] the perfect imprint of God's being. Central to Williams' conception of the image is Augustine's notion that the image exists *ad ipsum a quo imprimatur*;[80] that is to say, it exists 'towards him from whom its impression is received'.[81] To image God, for Augustine and for Williams, is to be a mirror turned towards God and, in this way, to become, like Jesus, a reflection, an imprint, an image of God.[82]

A mirror provides an accurate reflection of a person only when the mirror is fully pointed towards that person. Williams is accordingly concerned to correct the misconception that the Augustinian image is the reflection of the Trinity simply by virtue of the threefold structure of the human mind: namely, intellect, memory and will.[83] As a reflection of God, the image may be realized only when intellect, memory and will are focused on God,[84] and that cannot be achieved merely by human effort. Grace alone has the power to 're-form [the mind] in *sapientia*'[85] in an awareness of the love and goodness of God.

Such awareness brings the realization that we exist because God desires 'to impart his life',[86] thereby sharing with created beings the divine capacity for wisdom, goodness and love (*sapientia, iustitia* and *caritas*).[87] In a vivid image, Williams stresses that 'human life [receives] its unity and intelligibility from outside ... [w]hen God pulls taut the slack thread of desire, binding it to himself.'[88] God alone effects the renewal of the human mind, using our experiences of failure and helplessness[89] to make us aware of the futility of our fantasies of self-formation.[90] In this process, desire is directed away from self-fulfilment towards its true goal in God.

Using Pauline baptismal imagery, Williams suggests that the renewal of our minds is a matter of 'being unmade to be remade'.[91] It 'involve[s] going down into the chaotic waters of Christ's death, so that the Spirit can move to make a "new creation"'.[92] The related imagery of new birth and adoption emphasizes that the remaking of human identity is by reception of the gift of divine grace with consequent incorporation into the identity of Christ Jesus. Henceforth our identity consists in sharing, through adoption, Christ's relation to the Father, the filial relation of son or daughter of God.[93]

The identity thus bestowed involves the gradual replacement of human knowledge by divine wisdom (*sapientia*) and brings with it a new vision of God and a new understanding of the human vocation. In that process, previous conceptions of divine power and glory are dismantled. In place of the majestic, omnipotent god of popular belief, we see the broken figure of Jesus hanging on a cross.[94] Imaged for us in the One who suffered the vulnerability of incarnation and crucifixion is the truth about God and about the nature of divine desire. Jesus' death on the cross reveals God to be kenotic, self-dispossessive love poured out for the sake of humanity.[95] His fragile, broken body is the proof that God is not an overwhelming force to be feared but is with us and 'for us', participating in our human weakness. Also evidenced by that death is the true mode of finite human existence. The crucified Jesus, who is the image/reflection of divine love, is the sign that all human life is to be lived in as *kenosis* and *ekstasis*, as 'self-sacrifice, other-directed love'.[96]

## Desire as *kenosis* and *ekstasis*

The kenotic ecstatic character of Christ-focused desire is further elaborated in *Christ the Heart of Creation,* where Williams follows Maximus the Confessor in identifying the incarnation as the finite actualization of the Word's relation of Son to the Father.[97] Jesus of Nazareth, the Word incarnate, is evidence of a human life that is completely filial in its dependence on, and response to, the Father. The filial relation of the human Jesus to the divine Father brings human nature into its proper alignment with God, thereby enabling created beings to share with Jesus the '"ecstatic" relation [of] radically self-emptied and other-directed love'.[98] In summarizing Maximus's argument, Williams writes:

> When [divine] filiation is embodied unsurpassably and uninterruptedly, as in the humanity of Jesus, the image of God in which humanity was first created is fully activated, and human beings in communion with the Word incarnate are made able to live in kenotic love and mutual gift, reflecting the life that belongs to the Trinitarian persons in eter-

nity. And just as the Trinitarian God lives eternally in a relation to the created order that is free from conflict and competition, so the finite self united with the infinite reality of the Word is able to live in reconciled communion with other human persons and to overcome the various life-denying divisions that characterize the fallen finite world.[99]

The 'kenotic love and mutual gift' that characterize the Trinitarian life point to the inseparable link between *kenosis* and *ekstasis*. Life in Christ, according to Maximus and Williams, is not a matter of sacrificial self-denial for its own sake.[100] It draws its vitality and otherness-orientation from the mutual love of the Persons of the Trinity, eternally overflowing in ecstatic self-gift towards the Other. Trinitarian love makes possible what is otherwise impossible for finite beings, namely 'a movement of "desire, *erōs*" [that is] a moving beyond what the intellect can master and a growth in love'.[101] Renewed in Christ, and incorporated into his life, Christians find that desires are redirected from self to others, so that we are enabled to live 'our own *kenosis* and *ekstasis*, our self-emptying and self-transcending in love'.[102]

Williams' association of desire with movement from self to other and from known to unknown echoes his argument that, for Aquinas, love and knowledge involve a movement from self towards the different other, such that the other is brought into the self while remaining other.[103] Knowing and loving thus become not only participatory, a mutual bestowal of self to the other, but also exploratory, an invitation to change by going beyond self in a process of self-emptying. The movement of desire towards an exploration of as-yet-unknown possibilities highlights the integral relation between desire and imagination. Renewed in Christ, desire activates the energy of imagination towards ever-increasing otherness.

## Filial and nuptial desire

The notion of 'movement towards an other' also underlies another pair of images employed in reference to divine and human desire, the images of erotic and filial love. Repeatedly found in studies of spirituality,[104] the image of erotic love holds particular significance for St John of the Cross.[105] As we saw in Chapter 4, the Spanish saint considers the essence of divine life to be mutual love, 'the movement of one into the other in desire'.[106] Divine desire accordingly has an erotic quality; it resembles an eternal nuptial embrace. Far from being a 'closed mutuality', it opens outward as excess, as desire for the desire of the other.[107] In its outward-directedness, nuptial desire, says Williams, is a 'mimesis without rivalry'.[108]

Incorporated into Christ, believers share, by adoption, the eternal relation of the Son to the Father, a relation of both filial and nuptial desire. Within finite existence the erotic and the filial exist in constant tension; it is the tension between erotic desire for the closeness of the Father's love and filial desire for the realization of the Father's purpose for creation.[109] This tension prevents the closure of human desire. Whereas we may wish to find gratification in an enclosed, nuptial, relation to the divine, such gratification is ultimately beyond reach, since God cannot be turned into an object that will terminate desire.[110]

The human experience of God may instead involve the darkness of absence and even abandonment, as was evidenced by Jesus' cry of dereliction on the cross. In that anguished cry we hear our own confused groaning at being confronted with the eternal other-orientation of divine love which allows of no closure.[111] Such love, says St John of the Cross, is felt as a 'wound'. It is a wound inflicted by the 'burning' desire of the Father, who, through the Son, arouses desire within us that is constantly intensified by the Spirit and cannot be satisfied by any finite object. In that process, our human desires are progressively 'purged' of finite attachment to become increasingly identified with the filial desire of the Son.[112] Seeking no return of love for itself, filial desire wishes only for what the Father desires.[113]

The example of Jesus also serves to clarify the meaning of nuptial desire in human relations. In finite existence, erotic desire is frequently experienced as a lack to be filled, the other person being merely an object of gratification.[114] Jesus, by contrast, embodies love towards others that frees them to grow and flourish.[115] His love desires only the other's good.[116] It elucidates the meaning of vows of marriage or celibacy with their pledges to place the good of the other ahead of personal gratification.[117] Such love is 'gratuitous and non-functional'. It is love that, like divine *eros*, overflows as excess for the benefit of the other.[118]

## Desire and imagination

In this chapter I have pointed to the connection Williams draws between desire and imagination. The way they are related is illuminated in *The Edge of Words* by a crucial reference to the link between the ecstatic energy of divine *eros* and the otherness-oriented energy of human imagination:

> In the theological perspective, the notion that what we perceive is a facet of eternal activity, unconditioned 'energy', the divine Logos, will

further intensify this impulse to imaginative expansion, the quest for more and more relatedness.[119]

In this statement, Williams identifies the quest for ever-greater relatedness with the energy of the divine Logos, thus pointing to the *erotic* nature of divine energy. Activated by that energy, human imagination is directed outwards, in an ever-expanding movement of desire for otherness. Its purpose is to bring about an increase of relatedness within the created order. Imagination is thus shown to be the finite expression of the otherness-oriented energy of divine desire that impels creation towards its fulfilment in the ever renewed and renewing relations of divine love.

Whereas no disjunction exists between the energy of divine desire and its goal of loving relatedness, that is not so in the case of human desire and imagination. In the conditions of finitude, distrust and fear of the other effect a separation between desire and its purpose of greater relatedness. The energy of imagination thus degenerates into fantasy, focusing desire on such distorted relations as possession or destruction or evasion of the other.

The role Williams accords to imagination in the realization of God's purposes for creation accounts for his abhorrence of the destructive effects of fantasy. He argues that the 'manipulative' myths and fantasies of 'the contemporary cultural and technological world' result in a kind of 'paralysis'.[120] Fantasy impedes relatedness and is ultimately death-bound. Imagination, when renewed by grace, orients our desires towards ever-increasing relatedness with that which is other. It points us to the goal which is the divinely appointed end of human desire, life in kenotic, ecstatic relationship with God, so that 'what is not God may be suffused with God's joy.'[121]

## Conclusion

This chapter has focused on the nature and expression of desire in human beings and the relation between desire and imagination. I have shown that, for Rowan Williams, human desire has its source and end in God's desire for created beings to participate, by adoption, in the divine life through the Son. Diverted from its true end in the finite conditions of temporality and materiality, human desire readily becomes distorted into the death-dealing fantasies of possessive violence and sacral fear. Through his life, death and resurrection, Jesus of Nazareth, Word made flesh, has effected the transformation of human desire, thus enabling created beings to image God in relationships of filial, nuptial love, relationships which, being both self-sacrificial and other-oriented, mirror the ecstatic, kenotic love that is the life of the Trinity.

Imagination is seen to be inseparably linked to desire. It may be conceived as the goal-directed energy of desire, providing ends towards which desire tends. Whereas distorted desire seeks its end in death-dealing fantasy, the renewal of the human person by grace effects a reorientation of both desire and imagination, such that desire is now directed towards the envisioned end of the restoration of all things in Christ, the vision of a universe that reflects the kenotic, ecstatic relatedness of the divine life.

In the next chapter I shall examine the process whereby, within the Christian Church, human beings are enabled, through the Holy Spirit, to reorient desire towards the vision of self-dispossessive, other-oriented interrelatedness. In view of the temporal nature of human existence, the process of transformation is necessarily gradual as believers learn and practise the habits that strengthen the reorientation of desire and imagination.

## Notes

1 Quoted by Shortt, *Rowan's Rule: The Biography of the Archbishop*, revised edition (London: Hodder & Stoughton, 2014), pp. 105–6.

2 Rowan Williams, *On Augustine* (London: Bloomsbury, 2016), p. 7.

3 Rowan Williams, *Looking East in Winter: Contemporary Thought and the Eastern Christian Tradition* (London: Bloomsbury, 2021), p. 41.

4 As noted in Chapter 3, the tension of desire and fear is likewise considered by Przywara to be constitutive of the human condition.

5 Williams' commentary on these scholars is found in the following essays: 'Girard on Violence, Society and the Sacred' in Mike Higton, ed., *Wrestling with Angels: Conversations in Modern Theology* (Grand Rapids, MI: William B. Eerdmans, 2007), pp. 171–85, and '"Know Thyself": What Kind of an Injunction?', in Michael McGhee, ed., *Philosophy, Religion and the Spiritual Life* (Cambridge: Cambridge University Press, 1992), pp. 211–27. There are also references to Lacan in *Looking East in Winter*, pp. 50–1 and 56.

6 The term 'end' is used here in the sense employed by the Westminster Shorter Catechism question: 'What is the chief end of man?' Here end has the sense of 'purpose' and is not to be confused with 'terminus' since Williams insists that desire for God is endless.

7 Rowan Williams, *The Dwelling of the Light: Praying with Icons of Christ* (Mulgrave, Vic: John Garrett, 2003), p. xx.

8 Rowan Williams, *Lost Icons* (Harrisburg, PA: Morehouse, 2000), p. 184.

9 Williams, *Lost Icons*, p. 185.

10 Williams, *Lost Icons*, p. 185.

11 Williams, *Lost Icons*, p. 184.

12 Williams, *The Dwelling of the Light*, p. 3.

13 Williams, *The Dwelling of the Light*, pp. 6–7.

14 Williams, *The Dwelling of the Light*, p. 11.
15 Williams, *The Dwelling of the Light*, p. 12.
16 *A Ray of Darkness* is the title of the American edition of the collection of Williams' sermons, originally published as *Open to Judgement*. It is also the subject of one of the sermons in the collection, the phrase being attributed to Pseudo-Dionysius.
17 Williams, *On Augustine*, p. 66. According to Williams, the notion that the human mind intuitively recognizes the universe as a 'whole' and cannot conceive of a particular is also to be found in Hegel, Wittgenstein and Przywara. See Rowan Williams, *The Edge of Words: God and the Habits of Language* (London: Bloomsbury, 2014), p. 20, and Rowan Williams, *Christ the Heart of Creation* (London: Bloomsbury Continuum, 2018), p. 229.
18 Williams, *On Augustine*, p. 67.
19 Williams, *On Augustine*, pp. 66–7.
20 Williams, *On Augustine*, p. 83.
21 Williams, 'Girard on Violence, Society and the Sacred', pp. 171–85.
22 See, for example, 'Mimesis and Violence' in *The Girard Reader*, ed. James G. Williams (New York: Crossroads, 1996), pp. 9–19.
23 Girard asserts that 'mimesis is rooted deep in our biology', and that 'the human brain is a kind of mimetic machine.' James G. Williams, 'The Anthropology of the Cross: A Conversation with René Girard' in *The Girard Reader*, p. 268.
24 James G. Williams, 'The Anthropology of the Cross', p. 15.
25 Williams, *Wrestling with Angels*, p. 173.
26 James G. Williams, *The Girard Reader*, p. 265.
27 James G, Williams, *The Girard Reader*, p. 266.
28 Girard, 'The Nonsacrificial Death of Christ' in *The Girard Reader*, p. 182.
29 Williams, *Wrestling with Angels*, p. 181.
30 Williams, *Wrestling with Angels*, p. 181.
31 Richard Boothby, *Death and Desire: Psychoanalytic Theory in Lacan's Return to Freud* (London and New York: Routledge, 1991), pp. 164–5.
32 Slavoj Žižek, *How to Read Lacan* (New York: W.W. Norton, 2006), pp. 42–3.
33 Lacan distinguishes between the 'little other' and the 'big Other'. The 'little other' is the ego-image formed from the reflected views of others. It is accordingly a false image, rendering the ego 'a repository for the projected desires and fantasies of larger others'. The 'big Other' is both the symbolic order of law and language, and the radically unassimilable otherness of the desired other.
34 Néstor A. Braunstein, 'Desire and Jouissance in the Teachings of Lacan', in *The Cambridge Companion to Lacan*, ed. Jean-Michel Rabaté (Cambridge: Cambridge University Press, 2003), p. 110.
35 Braunstein, 'Desire and Jouissance in the Teachings of Lacan', p. 111.
36 I am following Žižek in capitalising the 'Real', considered as the dimension held by Lacan to be inaccessible to consciousness, as contrasted with the fantasized nature of everyday reality.
37 Boothby, *Death and Desire*, p. 18.
38 Boothby, *Death and Desire*, p. 18.
39 Paulo Padilla Petry and Fernando Hernández Hernández, 'Jacques Lacan's Conception of Desire in a Course for Fine Arts Students', *Visual Arts Research* 36.2 (2010), p. 67.

40 Jacques Lacan, *Écrits: A Selection*, trans. Alan Sheridan (London: Tavistock, 1977), p. 272.
41 Žižek, *How to Read Lacan*, p. 3.
42 Boothby, *Death and Desire*, p. 19–20.
43 Williams, '"Know Thyself": What Kind of an Injunction?', p. 212. See also Rowan Williams, *On Christian Theology: Challenges in Contemporary Theology* (Malden, MA: Blackwell, 2000), p. 267.
44 Williams, '"Know Thyself": What Kind of an Injunction?', p. 213. See also Williams, *On Augustine*, p. 5: 'I know myself as an act of questioning, a lack and a search ... a sort of eros without the anxiety to possess.'
45 Williams, '"Know Thyself": What Kind of an Injunction?', p. 213.
46 Williams, '"Know Thyself": What Kind of an Injunction?', p. 214. Williams adds on p. 224 that 'Lacanian analysis goes a long way to removing the pathos of the victim from the destiny of the self', a judgment qualified by his further statement that 'liberation as overthrowing the bondage of the other's (oppressive) desire remains determined by that desire so long as it remains primarily negative and does not move on to address the question of how we might *now* imagine shared satisfactions.'
47 Williams, '"Know Thyself": What Kind of an Injunction?', p. 224.
48 Williams, '"Know Thyself": What Kind of an Injunction?', p. 219. Divine love is identified as 'the sparkle from the coal ... the magnet of all our hearts' in Williams' 1983 address to a Loughborough conference of Anglo-Catholics. Shortt, *Rowan's Rule*, pp. 105–6.
49 Williams, '"Know Thyself": What Kind of an Injunction?', p. 222.
50 Williams, '"Know Thyself": What Kind of an Injunction?', p. 223. See also Rowan Williams, *The Tragic Imagination* (Oxford: Oxford University Press, 2016), p. 112.
51 Williams, '"Know Thyself": What Kind of an Injunction?', p. 224.
52 Williams, '"Know Thyself": What Kind of an Injunction?', p. 223.
53 Williams, *On Augustine*, p. 50. Jan-Olav Henriksen seeks to resolve this dilemma by noting Williams' distinction in *Lost Icons* between Jesus as the embodiment and as the representation of God. Henriksen argues that it is as God's representative rather than God's embodiment that Jesus may be considered as totally Other to the human subject. In the passage cited by Henriksen, Williams is not, however, referring to Jesus but to the *therapist*, his argument being that the *therapist* must represent but not embody the completely Other. Jan-Olav Henriksen, *Desire, Gift, and Recognition: Christology and Postmodern Philosophy* (Grand Rapids, MA: William B. Eerdmans, 2009), pp. 135–6.
54 Williams, '"Know Thyself": What Kind of an Injunction?', p. 223. The italics are mine.
55 Williams, *On Augustine*, p. 5.
56 Rowan Williams, *The Truce of God* (London: Fount Paperbacks, 1983).
57 Williams, *The Truce of God*, p. 9.
58 Williams, *The Truce of God*, p. 23.
59 Rowan Williams, *Dostoevsky: Language, Faith and Fiction* (London: Bloomsbury, 2008), p. 71.
60 Williams, *Dostoevsky*, p. 242.
61 Benjamin Myers, *Christ the Stranger: The Theology of Rowan Williams* (London: T&T Clark, 2012), p. 107.

62 Myers, *Christ the Stranger*, p. 112.
63 *The Cloud of Unknowing In the Which a Soul Is Oned with God*, 2nd edn, with Introduction by Evelyn Underhill (London: Merchant Books, 2021), p. 22.
64 Williams, *On Augustine*, p. 43. See also Jonathan Jameson, 'Erotic Absence and Sacramental Hope: Rowan Williams on Augustinian Desire', *Anglican Theological Review* 102.4 (2020).
65 Augustine of Hippo, *Confessions*, trans. Henry Chadwick (Oxford: Oxford University Press, 1998). See also Williams, *On Augustine*, p. 50.
66 Augustine, *Confessions*, p. 3.
67 Williams, *On Augustine*, pp. 7, 45.
68 Rowan Williams, *The Wound of Knowledge: Christian Spirituality from the New Testament to St John of the Cross*, 2nd rev. edn (London: Darton Longman & Todd, 1990), pp. 57–8.
69 Cited by Williams in *The Wound of Knowledge*, p. 114.
70 Williams, *The Wound of Knowledge*, p. 131.
71 Williams, *The Wound of Knowledge*, p. 138.
72 Williams, *The Wound of Knowledge*, p. 174.
73 The *res/signum uti/frui* distinctions are found in Augustine's treatise *On Christian Doctrine*, trans. J. F. Shaw (Mineola, NY: Dover, 2009), 1:2–4, 2:1–3.
74 Rowan Williams, 'Language, Reality and Desire in Augustine's *De Doctrina*', *Literature and Theology* 3.2 (1989), pp. 138–50. It was republished in *On Augustine* as 'Language, Reality and Desire: The Nature of Christian Formation'. My references are to the book version.
75 Williams, *On Augustine*, pp. viii–x.
76 Williams, *On Augustine*, p. 44.
77 Augustine, *On Christian Doctrine*, Bk 1, ch. 4.
78 Williams, 'Language, Reality and Desire: The Nature of Christian Formation', p. 45.
79 Colossians 1.15.
80 Williams, *On Augustine*, p. 173.
81 Luigi Gioia, *The Theological Epistemology of Augustine's De Trinitate* (Oxford: Oxford University Press, 2008), p. 295.
82 See also Williams, *Christ the Heart of Creation*, p. 234, where Christ is described as '"icon" or "mirror" of the Father'.
83 As pointed out by Williams (*On Augustine*, p. 135), the Augustinian *mens* (mind) encompasses the three mental activities of thinking, remembering and willing.
84 Williams, *The Wound of Knowledge*, p. 85.
85 Williams, *On Augustine*, p. 174.
86 Williams, *On Augustine*, p. 175.
87 Williams, *On Augustine*, p. 175.
88 Williams, *The Wound of Knowledge*, p. 92.
89 Williams, *The Wound of Knowledge*, p. 6.
90 Williams, *On Christian Theology*, p. 273.
91 Williams, *The Wound of Knowledge*, p. 8.
92 Williams, *The Wound of Knowledge*, p. 8.
93 In *Christ the Heart of Creation*, Williams turns to the thought of Maximus the Confessor (pp. 101–2), Aquinas (p. 13), Calvin (p. 142), Barth (p. 182) to justify the significance he gives to the concept of 'adoptive filiation' (p. 250) in

respect of the divine purpose for humanity. Rowan Williams, 'The Deflections of Desire: Negative Theology in Trinitarian Disclosure', in *Silence and the Word: Negative Theology and Incarnation*, ed. Oliver Davies and Denys Turner (Cambridge: Cambridge University Press, 2002) explores this concept in the work of St John of the Cross.

94 Williams, *Christ the Heart of Creation*, p. 242.
95 Williams, *Christ the Heart of Creation*, p. 106.
96 Williams, *Christ the Heart of Creation*, p. 56.
97 See Williams, *Christ the Heart of Creation*, pp. 99–109.
98 Williams, *Christ the Heart of Creation*, p. 107.
99 Williams, *Christ the Heart of Creation*, p. 108.
100 This charge is sometimes levelled against Williams. Higton asserts that Williams' 'focus falls too consistently on the "No" of the cross rather than on its encompassing "Yes"'. Mike Higton, *Difficult Gospel: The Theology of Rowan Williams* (London: SCM Press, 2004), pp. 35–6.
101 Williams, *Christ the Heart of Creation*, p. 107.
102 Williams, *Christ the Heart of Creation*, p. 106.
103 Rowan Williams, 'What Does Love Know? St Thomas on the Trinity', *New Blackfriars* 82.964 (2001), p. 271.
104 See, for example, Williams, *The Wound of Knowledge*, p. 14; *On Augustine*, p. 76. See also Mark A. McIntosh, *Mystical Theology: The Integrity of Spirituality and Theology* (Malden, MA: Blackwell, 1998), pp. 56–7, 205–8, inter alia.
105 Williams draws on the *Romanzas* and *The Living Flame of Love*, as well as *The Ascent of Mount Carmel*.
106 Williams, 'The Deflections of Desire', p. 118.
107 Williams, 'The Deflections of Desire', p. 118.
108 Williams, 'The Deflections of Desire', p. 127.
109 Williams, 'The Deflections of Desire', p. 119.
110 Williams, 'The Deflections of Desire', p. 120.
111 Williams, 'The Deflections of Desire', p. 121.
112 Williams, 'The Deflections of Desire', pp. 125–6.
113 Williams, 'The Deflections of Desire', p. 122.
114 Williams, 'The Deflections of Desire', p. 131.
115 Williams, 'The Deflections of Desire', p. 132.
116 Williams, 'The Deflections of Desire', p. 132.
117 Williams, 'The Deflections of Desire', p. 132.
118 Williams, 'The Deflections of Desire', p. 133. Williams' notion of love as 'pure gratuity ... the unqualified wanting of another's good' is also expounded in 'What Does Love Know? St Thomas on the Trinity', p. 260.
119 Williams, *The Edge of Words*, p. 122.
120 Rowan Williams, 'Changing the Myths We Live By' in *Faith in the Public Square* (London: Bloomsbury, 2012), pp. 175, 184.
121 Williams, 'Changing the Myths We Live By', p. 178.

# 6

# The Church and the Transformation of Desire

## Introduction

Chapter 5 set out to explore Rowan Williams' insights into the operation of human desire within finite existence. In that chapter, I argued that desire finds its true end only when directed towards Christ and towards his vision of the self-dispossessive, other-oriented relatedness which is the divine purpose for creation. Desire and imagination were seen to be interconnected, imagination providing the Christ-focused, ecstatic, kenotic vision towards which the energy of desire is to be directed.

In this chapter, I examine the role played by the Christian Church in the refocusing of desire towards Christ and, in that process, towards that which energizes Christ's desire, the vision of universal 'erotic' relatedness which scripture calls the 'Kingdom of God'. Williams argues that, empowered by the Holy Spirit, the Christian Church becomes a *workshop* for the refocusing of desire and imagination. It is primarily within the Church that, renewed by grace and in-breathed by the Spirit, Christians learn and practise the habits that gradually transform and redirect human desires and imagination. Oriented towards God and others, desire is thus transformed into sacrificial self-bestowal, and imagination is refocused towards the vision of a transfigured creation suffused with divine love and joy.[1]

It should be noted that the discussion of the Church in this context does not aim to provide an exhaustive critical analysis of Williams' ecclesiology. My purpose is to highlight the transformative role accorded to the Church in his vision for the realization of God's creative purpose. In the context of that theological vision, Williams' use of the term 'Church' refers not so much to its various institutional expressions as to the 'assembly' of those for whom there is 'a fresh configuring of the whole of experienced reality – a new set of human relations, a new horizon for what human beings are capable of, a new understanding of the material world and its capacities'.[2] Elsewhere he describes it as 'the community assembled by divine initiative and divine love'[3] for the purpose of 'reconstructing the entire human race'.[4] This vision of the Church's transformative role encompasses the many different forms taken by Christian communities across time and space.

To set the theme for the chapter, I begin with Williams' poem 'Sarov, August 2003: the Outer Hermitage',[5] which offers insight into the struggle and discipline involved in the transformation of desire. I then move on to examine the image that may be considered as key to Williams' ecclesiology: the Pauline image of the Church as the Body of Christ. Pointing to the source of the Church's life, the Body of Christ image is indicative of the Church's ontological status as the community re-created through the Holy Spirit to share Christ's filial relation with the Father. The final section focuses on the disciplines of worship, prayer and sacrament, which are considered by Williams to be the Spirit-empowered means whereby believers are gradually transformed into Christlikeness and their desires and imagination redirected towards the vision of the Kingdom.

### Sarov, August 2003: the Outer Hermitage

The riverbed, between the road
and the railway line is dry
in summer;

Soft sand, like air or water
welcomes and at once forgets
your step.

Eyes closed, you could be walking
shallow dunes, walking the edge
of ocean;

Open your eyes, go on across
the bridge, under the peeling birch
and pine.

The swaying leaves and needles
spin light from shafts, crests,
faces, hands,

As if, under the sea, you looked up
into the lightning, into the firing
circuits above,

## THE CHURCH AND THE TRANSFORMATION OF DESIRE

Where the crisp waves are catching
the sun's wild leap from plane
to plane.

The forest fingers the summer sky,
a child's stubby arm from the pram
waving.

In search of nose and lips and breast,
feeling; not knowing; recognising;
feeling.

Being seen. The leaping and the firing,
learning your way round a face against
the sky.

The poem is an account of a visit to the rock on which the Russian saint Serafim knelt for three years to learn the arduous task of directing his desire towards God. The poet sets out on a kind of pilgrimage to encounter the saint, walking in his footsteps along the riverbed and through the forest, an experience akin to being plunged into ocean depths. Submerged in this baptismal-like ocean and dazzled by sunlight wildly leaping from 'wave to wave', he becomes again a helpless infant, groping for the breast that brings sustenance, and for the face that provides security and love. In his reversion to an infant's helpless dependency, the poet thus replicates to some extend the saint's lengthy labour in seeking the love which alone can satisfy human desire.

At night, Serafim knelt on the same rock
three years long, walked from the sand
into the sea,

And drowned, night after night,
when the sun did not dance,
or the trees

Caress, and like a bear he rubbed
and nuzzled into the dark, blind
and appalled.

And hungry, until the rock began
to smell of honey. Quickly he made
for the surface,

Breathed, was blinded again by the first
dry lined leaf falling from the birch,
the first

Dry lined face falling from the forgotten
worlds of sand and hurt, of death
and shining drought.

In the barrel of your lungs,
father, the hammer swung for the first
leaping blow

Of Paschal Matins, fingers closing
like a child's on the found flesh.
my joy. My joy.

In his blind search for God in the oceanic darkness of emptiness and unknowing, Serafim nuzzled hungrily, like a bear, for the only food that would satisfy, the 'honey' of God's presence.[6] Finally sated with the gift that has restored him to the pain and suffering of the world, Serafim can now view that world through resurrected Easter eyes. Henceforth, with the joy of the infant who has rediscovered the security of his mother's breast, Serafim finds God in everyone he meets. All have become 'joy' to him.

The poem articulates the intertwined themes which, with desire, are at the heart of Williams' theological anthropology, the themes of imaginative vision and discipline. Something of Serafim's initial vision is caught by the poet as he makes his way through the forest towards the rock of the outer hermitage. Here the sun glinting through the canopy of 'swaying leaves' becomes the lightning flash of divine light glimpsed from the oceanic, baptismal depths of earthly existence. Instantly, desire is generated, inchoate desire, the desire of the infant for the mother's breast.

That same desire, born of our human need for the Other, was what impelled and sustained Serafim in his three-year-long dark search for God, when all he could hold on to was the vision and the desire. For Serafim, that was the time for discipline, the discipline of learning the essential human habits of patience, attentiveness and love.[7] In Serafim's case, the faithful practice of these habits led finally to the realization of his desire. At last, his grip could close 'on the found flesh' of God discovered in his fellow human beings, those beings who are henceforth his 'joy'.

In this poem the corporate life of the Christian Church is evoked by the images of baptismal immersion and eucharistic feeding. Implicit here is the important claim made by Williams concerning human desire:

generated by God, as the sparkle from the coal, and having its end in God, desire finds its meaning and vocation in the other-oriented life of the Spirit-breathed community of the Church. Baptism is entry into that community. The Eucharist is the life-renewing food that sustains desire and focuses it outward towards others. The community exists because, through the Spirit, it is brought into being by the life, death and resurrection of Jesus Christ. The image of the Church as the Body of Christ clarifies the Church's vocation of realizing, in its life and mission, God's eschatological purpose for creation. The tension experienced by the poet as he walks towards Serafim's place of encounter with God is the biblical tension between the 'already' of actual experience and the 'not yet' of imaginative vision.[8]

## The Church as the Body of Christ

Williams turns to Aquinas for a theological elucidation of the scriptural image of the Body of Christ.[9] As we saw in Chapter 4, Williams' reading of Aquinas leads him to conclude that the person of the eternal Word is 'the activating principle in the life of Jesus'.[10] As a consequence, Jesus' historical actions and relations have cosmic significance in that they are completely consistent with the eternal activity of the Word who sustains and brings order and coherence to creation.[11] The actions of the human Jesus are thus 'the vehicle of the Word's universal action'[12] and, as such, they have the power to bring meaning and fulfilment to humanity. Those 'aligned' with Jesus in love and trust are thereby brought into the relationship of the Word/Son with the eternal Father.

Whereas Christ is Son by eternal divine generation, finite human beings may become sons and daughters of the Father by *adoption*.[13] Williams can therefore conclude that, for 'those whose relation with Jesus is one of loving trust and "alignment" of will or desire, the effect is what the New Testament calls incorporation into the identity of Jesus – becoming a member of 'the "Body" of Christ'.[14] Henceforth, as members of his Body, they share Christ's relation to God and to the world.[15] It is a relation of (adoptive) filiation to the Father, now addressed and experienced as 'Abba'.[16] It is a relation too of sharing the breath, life, and other-directedness of Jesus, that is a sharing of the Holy Spirit.[17] In-breathed by the Spirit,[18] believers also share Jesus' relation to other believers and to creation, their desire and their vision being now directed 'towards the good and the healing of the world'.[19]

Made up of all who are incorporated into Christ Jesus, the Church may therefore be considered as a '*communal* embodiment of the Word'.[20]

In its life and actions, it is not a mere human institution but, insofar as it remains faithful to Christ, it is the 'visible community' through which the Word is 'recognisab[le] in history'.[21] In this sense, the Augustinian expression *totus Christus* may be used to 'denote the complex unity that is not only the Word and Jesus, but Jesus and the members of his Body, understood as making up together a single *persona*, a single acting and speaking subject'.[22]

The consequence is that it is when the Church is truly aligned with Christ that its actions and words may be considered as those of Christ, as expressive of 'the inexhaustible action that pervades and structures it'.[23] The Church therefore shares Christ's mission of bringing into being 'a new people',[24] a new humanity,[25] a covenant people,[26] who, in their life together, enact within finite existence the other-oriented 'self-imparting, self-sharing',[27] kenotic, ecstatic love that is the life of the Trinity.[28]

## The Holy Spirit: The breath of the Body of Christ

The Church's mission cannot be realized by human effort. As Williams is careful to emphasize, the relation between Christ and the believer is pure gift and comes about solely through the agency of the Holy Spirit.[29] As the divine agency of overflowing, other-oriented love, the Spirit, says Williams, re-creates and translates 'the relation of Father and Son in the medium of human existence'.[30] It is therefore the Spirit who, as the 'breath of Jesus' life',[31] enables the relation of incorporation into Christ and adoption as son or daughter of the Father, giving new life and a new identity to those baptized into Christ.[32]

Baptism, according to Williams, is literally life-changing. In its symbolism, it enacts the transition from the death of sin to new life in Christ, but, as Williams is adamant to argue, what actually occurs is a 'divine reality'.[33] A new identity is bestowed through the Spirit, the identity originally given at creation.[34] This identity may or may not be consciously 'appropriated',[35] but when such appropriation occurs, it restores not only the relationship with God, but also the relation between self and others, and between self and creation.

Incorporated into the Body of Christ, the baptized believer is now brought into the community of all those who share Christ's life and who thus come to share his passionate desire for the healing of the world. In this community, it is the Spirit who brings about the transformation of human desire such that it is gradually freed 'from competitive patterns or rivalry' and learns to seek instead only the good of the other.[36] Williams therefore concludes that the Spirit's role is that of bringing about 'response to and *conformation* to the Son', so that finite beings may live Son-like lives in the world.[37]

As the Spirit of Christ, the Spirit is active in refocusing desire outwards towards solidarity, not only with the community of the Church but also with the whole of humanity. In a 2002 address at Trinity College in Melbourne, Williams reminded his hearers that to be part of the body of Christ is to live in a '*wounded* body', a body with 'defences lowered' and open to 'the need, the chaos, the darkness of the world'.[38] It is to live, as Christ lived, in solidarity with those whose lives are broken, defiled, or chaotic, so that they may come to experience the embrace of the God who loves humanity in all its brokenness.[39]

Also enabled by the Spirit is the act of prayer. As Williams stresses in the Trinity lecture, the prayer of the baptized is caught up in the prayer of Jesus for the world, a prayer not only of advocacy and thanksgiving, but one which also takes us into 'the darkness of faith'.[40] Here again the emphasis is on the painful struggle involved in growing into the likeness of Christ. It is a journey into the darkness of Gethsemane and Calvary where the Father was experienced as absent. To pray at such times is to pray solely in faith, without consolation. It is prayer which necessitates the turning away from 'the comforting emotional and intellectual patterns that ... [w]e use to keep ourselves safe'.[41] Such prayer takes us into the absolute self-emptying of Christ on the cross and, through the Spirit, brings us more deeply into the divine life of kenotic, ecstatic love. So, Williams writes: 'To discover in our "emptying" and crucifying the "emptying" of Jesus on his cross is to find God there, and so to know that God is not destroyed or divided by the intolerable contradictions of human suffering.'[42] The Spirit's work is therefore the difficult task of forming finite beings whose subjectivity is such that they are capable of existing in 'the tension between security and powerlessness', and of maintaining hope in the darkness of human existence 'without illusion but also without despair'.[43] The development of such subjectivity is a lifelong process, the gradual transformation of human consciousness as the Spirit shapes us increasingly into the likeness of Christ.

The significance Williams attaches to the Holy Spirit as the renewing and sustaining life of the Church cannot be emphasized too strongly. His repeated references to the Spirit in terms of 'movement', 'pressure' and 'energy' convey the power of the Spirit, as does his favourite image of the 'relentless stream' of divine love 'driving' the life of the Church.[44] So we read that:

> We are caught up in the 'slipstream' of th[e] great energy driving towards the Father from Christ.[45]

> Running through the life of [the Church] like a steady, relentless stream is the reality of mutual love and delight that is God's life ... It keeps flowing through because it is driven on by the Spirit.[46]

> In the history of the Jews, God's sanctifying power, God's Spirit, has been for centuries pressing this people towards a complete openness, receptivity, and vulnerability that will 'clear a space' for renewing grace to flow freely.[47]

> Spirit is the pressure upon us towards Christ's relation with the Father, towards the self secure enough ... to decide for the cross of powerlessness.[48]

These images highlight Williams' awareness of the kenotic, ecstatic love that, for him, is the essence of Trinitarian relations, the love that persistently seeks a response from beings created to mirror that love. The images are also indicative of Williams' own response to the Spirit's pressure to form human lives into the shape of Jesus' life. Arguing that Jesus' life took the form of a decision for 'the cross of powerlessness',[49] Williams concludes that human lives are intended to follow the same pattern of vulnerable openness to divine grace even in the darkest of circumstances. For him, the 'grammar' of finite human existence is 'the interplay ... between the given and the future ... between Good Friday and Easter'.[50]

Living in that interplay is to live, as Jesus did, both with the threatening insecurity of present reality and with hope-filled trust in God's promised future. Williams himself is very aware of that tension having experienced his own 'Good Friday' during his period as Archbishop of Canterbury. During that time, the inconsistencies in the outworking of his beliefs were acknowledged even by his supporters,[51] and his vision of the Church was repeatedly subjected to the criticism that it lacks grounding in the complex reality of everyday life and is incapable of practical implementation.[52] In the face of such criticism, Williams has nevertheless maintained his trust in the Church's role as a community that both challenges society by its 'rootedness in something beyond the merely political'[53] and offers the hope-filled promise of a 'renewal of creation'.[54] As he has stated, the work of the Holy Spirit is to 'span the unimaginably great ... gulf between suffering and hope'.[55] Since the future belongs to God, it is necessarily a 'future of healing and promise',[56] which can be neither predicted or planned, but is nevertheless to be trusted.[57]

The notion of Spirit-generated hope in a future of healing and promise highlights once again the relation between desire and imagination. I argue that, for Rowan Williams, human desire, when oriented towards Christ, is expressed as the imaginative vision of hope. In his writings, the Holy Spirit is imaged as the divine energy of love pressing humanity forward towards the realization of the divine desire for creation. In that process, human desire is enabled by the Spirit to embrace not only the difference of subjective otherness, both created and divine, but also the difference of temporal otherness, the difference between present reality and future possibility. Hope amid suffering is made possible by the Spirit because the life-breath of the crucified and resurrected Christ sustains the life of Christ's Body on earth.

Incorporated into that Body, believers share the vision and desire of Christ himself, the vision of the Kingdom. It is the vision of the 'new heaven and the new earth', the vision of 'where the world in God's purpose is meant to be heading'.[58] Described in *Tokens of Trust*, the vision is of 'a "peaceable kingdom", a realm in which God directs, shapes and draws the variety of human and non-human reality towards a state where humanity and the whole material world speak clearly of his glory'.[59]

Such a vision requires the imaginative capacity for analogy, the capacity to hold together the continuity of divine loving purpose amid the difference of human distrust, destruction and the suffering that results. As will be discussed in Part Three, Christian imagination is considered by Williams to be the Spirit-enabled capacity to see with that analogous double vision. It is the capacity not only to see the present surface reality, but also to glimpse, within the processes of the world, the divine presence active in the unfolding of the eternal purpose for creation.

## The Eucharist: The central practice of the Body of Christ

Williams' ecclesiology places the Eucharist 'at the centre of ... Christian practice'.[60] His belief is that the vocation of humanity is to become 'Homo Eucharisticus'.[61] To live eucharistically is, he claims, a 'distinctive style of being human'.[62] It is a way of living that views the world with thanksgiving as the gift of God and which recognizes that the death and resurrection of Jesus Christ have radically transformed the possibilities for human existence.[63] With Jesus' identification of himself with the material objects of bread and wine, given for human nourishment, matter is revealed as it truly is, as 'the sign of divine renunciation'.[64]

Williams' argument is that, in the act of creation and in the events of the Last Supper, the divine presence is evidenced by 'the renunciation of control'.[65] Created matter is the gift of that which is *not God*. It exists in its own integrity, subject to its own natural laws. Jesus, in 'passing over' into passive matter, both at his incarnation and in this final meal, enacts for human beings the ecstatic kenotic nature of God. In place of the human image of divine power and control, God is shown by Jesus to be sacrificial love, the love which gives unstintingly of itself.

Demonstrated also by Jesus' action at that Supper is the meaning of the term *homo eucharisticus*. To live eucharistically is to live as Jesus lived, by the renunciation of 'the controlling ego'.[66] Eucharistic living is kenotic in its abnegation of self-focused control. It is ecstatic in its directedness of desire towards the good of the other. It is, says Williams, 'our own "passover" into the need of the other, wherever and whoever the other may be'.[67]

Such a form of life is made possible by the 'real presence' of Christ in the Eucharist. Treading the delicate path between transubstantiation and memorial, Williams claims that 'By eating [the bread and wine], the believer receives what the literal flesh and blood have within them, the radiant action and power of God the Son, the life that makes him who he is.'[68] To support that claim, Williams draws on Calvin, arguing with him that:

> Eucharistic presence ... is the freedom of God to make both the finite elements of Jesus' humanity and the finite elements of the bread and wine which Jesus adopts as signs of his identity *effective vehicles of transforming relation with God* and thus *effective vehicles* of the *transformation of relations* within the finite order.[69]

Participation in the Eucharist may thus be life-changing. The material elements of bread and wine, consumed by the believer, become the 'vehicles' of divine grace, 'effecting' what they represent, namely, incorporation into Christ and thereby into his relation with the Father and into his relation as gift to the world.[70] Williams can therefore claim that, in the Eucharist, God's grace is active in gradually dismantling the firmly defended ego so as to bring about a new way of seeing and acting.[71] Transformation of the relation with God brings awareness of 'the passion and intensity and relentlessness' of the divine desire for our responsive love.[72] Transformation of the relation with the finite order brings a sense of our interdependence with all people and with creation.[73] In this process of gradual grace-enabled transformation, we learn to live eucharistically, as gift to the world and to one another.[74]

Noteworthy also is the transformation of perception. The Eucharist is perceived not only as the renewal of Christ's life in the believer but also as an anticipation of God's intended future.[75] In its enacted symbolism, the Eucharist thus has eschatological significance. Inclusive of all people, irrespective of class, gender, ability and ethnicity, it is a realization of the world as it is intended to be, 'non-competitive, non-territorial',[76] a world where 'the universe in all its complexity ... and inner relationships' reflects the radiant self-giving love of God.[77] Enacted in the Eucharist is the proleptic vision of the future which, as Williams reiterates, will be brought about by God alone.[78]

The eschatological character of the Eucharist highlights again the connection between hope-filled desire, vision and imagination. As noted earlier, eschatological hope gives rise to a kind of analogical double vision. Those renewed in Christ have the capacity to view time from a dual perspective, seeing the present in the light of God's purpose and the future as open to ever-unforeseen divine possibilities. The transformative power of God active in the sacramental life of the Church is accordingly one of the means whereby there is a reorientation not only of human desire but also of the end of desire, the vision of the divine Kingdom. Such a vision, being transcendent, may only be imagined.

Effected in the Eucharist is therefore the gradual transformation of the imagination as participants learn to imagine the Kingdom or, in a phrase borrowed from the Welsh poet Waldo Williams, to 'inhabit a great hall' between the narrow walls of finite existence.[79] Both phrases suggest the importance of learning to view the present world analogically in the light of its eschatological purpose.

## The schooling of desire and imagination[80]

Renewed in Christ in baptism, nourished by the Eucharist, members of Christ's Body must also learn the personal disciplines involved in growth into Christlikeness. The transformation of pre-existing attitudes, habits, thoughts and imaginings happens only gradually, through the painful process of self-examination, acknowledgement of failures in love of neighbour and of self, and the redirection of desire. It is a matter of learning to practise the habits which, under the pressure of the Spirit, gradually shape every aspect of daily existence in conformity with Christ. Williams turns to Christian monasticism to identify the disciplines that assist in the re-creation of the divine image in the members of Christ's Body.[81]

The monastic life is of abiding fascination for Williams.[82] It has been variously described by him as 'God's workshop',[83] a 'new model of *humanity*',[84] and an 'epiclesis in action'.[85] Its significance for Williams lies in his conviction that the monastic way of life, with its balance of solitude and community, prayer and service, acts as a model for the Church, and as an 'eschatological "sign" in the secular world'.[86] From monastic communities, believers may learn the practices and habits that, through the Spirit, shape desire into holiness of life, imagination into eschatological hope.

Williams repeatedly employs the images of workshop and toolbox in referring to the communities ordered in conformity with the Benedictine Rule.[87] Use of these images is intended to convey the prosaic, down-to-earth nature of the habits inculcated by that Rule. These are, says Williams, the habits of stability, peacemaking and accountability, habits considered fundamental to the development of mature, life-enhancing communal relations.[88]

Encompassing both spatial and temporal steadfastness, stability teaches the patient endurance necessary to counteract the urge to escape the difficulties of living with others. Stability of situation forces one to confront 'the otherness of others'. It imposes the discipline of learning to live openly with difference, without resentment, manipulation and rejection. It brings awareness of one's own faults of impatience and intolerance. Peacemaking is even more demanding since truthful peacemaking is not a matter of 'facile reconciliation' or the denial of the existence of conflict, but requires 'active and honest engagement' about differences of opinion and clashes of interest.[89] Accountability is a matter of taking responsibility not only for one's own actions but also for the flourishing of the other members of the community.[90] Proper accountability requires attentiveness to the distinctive gifts and needs of all others within the community.[91]

Practice of these habits, says Williams, must be accompanied by the discipline of self-scrutiny in the listening presence of a trusted other.[92] By this means, we learn to be honest with ourselves, able to 'diagnose' resentment, envy, self-deceit and fear, and to understand 'how deeply [the chains of fantasy] are rooted in a weak and flawed will'.[93]

More demanding still is the monastic practice of solitude, which serves as a balance to communal engagement. Solitude confronts us with our own emptiness; it forces us 'to recognise the strength and resilience of our selfishness and the need to let God dissolve the fantasies with which we protect ourselves'.[94] Solitude also provides the inner space for contemplation, the process of 'clearing the way ... into the depths of who we are, to reconnect with the buried image of God in us ... and to lead it to full liberation'.[95] Contemplation, claims Williams, is central to discipleship since it brings about 'the "reconditioning" of consciousness and the reorientation of understanding through the shattering of illusory self- and God-images'.[96] In Williams' view, contemplation, with its exposure of the illusory nature of ego-centred fantasies, will also lead to a reconditioning of the imagination.

The process whereby the whole person is reoriented towards the fulfilment of the divine purpose is accordingly painful. It is a process of 'dismantling' the old self to make way for the new creation in Christ Jesus. In support of this claim Williams draws on Abbot Edward Butler's monograph on *Western Mysticism*, stating that:

> Christian life is directed towards the radical purification of the soul, or decentring of the self ... The purgation of the classical 'nights' is not just some eccentric inner experience, but the condition *generally* for the union of the Christian with God's loving will ... Not everyone experiences the 'night' as ... the terrible dismantling of the sense of self and the self's worth at the level of full conscious self-awareness; but the process of 'dismantling' must be the same in all those who are being genuinely conformed to God's will. The nature and purpose of God's purgatorial fiery stripping of the self in Christian growth is one and the same, whatever the circumstances in which it is apprehended, wherever in consciousness it comes to the surface.[97]

Here again we see evidence of the painful intensity of divine desire. For Williams, to draw closer to God is to find oneself 'stripped' of all self-protective covering by the fierceness of the divine purgatorial fire. The experience is that of total exposure to the ardent fervour of divine love; it is the nakedness and helplessness of the cross.

Williams' insistence on the pain associated with growth into Christ-likeness has caused some to label his message as 'difficult' and unduly negative.[98] It is certainly true that, in Williams' view, Christian discipleship is a Spirit-driven kenotic process of dismantling previous habits and ways of thinking and imagining so as to effect a radical re-ordering of the believer's inner life.

While there is pain, Williams' vision also has place for joy. *Kenosis* is balanced by *ekstasis*, a movement of joyful love towards human others, the divine Other and the other-oriented relations of God's Kingdom. As is shown in the Sarov poem, it was Serafim's three-year-long 'inner dismantling' that made room within to savour the 'honey' of divine love and the joy of seeing Christ in all people. This joy in the otherness of others and the Otherness of God is what Williams sees as the fruit of contemplation.[99] It is the final purpose of human existence. As he states, in a 2012 address to the Roman Catholic Synod of Bishops:

> To be fully human is to be recreated in the image of Christ's humanity; and that humanity is the perfect human 'translation' of the relationship of the eternal Son to the eternal Father, a relationship of loving

and adoring self-giving, a pouring out of life towards the Other. Thus the humanity we are growing into in the Spirit, the humanity we seek to share with the world as the fruit of Christ's redeeming work is a *contemplative* humanity ... The face we need to show to the world is the face of a humanity in endless growth towards love, a humanity so delighted and engaged by the glory of what we look towards that we are prepared to embark on a journey without end to find our way more deeply into it, into the heart of the trinitarian life.[100]

## Conclusion

In this chapter, I have argued that Rowan Williams believes the Christian Church to be the community within which human desire may be gradually transformed by the Holy Spirit into other-directed self-bestowing love. Within the Church, those who are incorporated into Christ's filial relation with the Father through the Spirit undergo a lifelong process of inner dismantling whereby ego-centred imagination and desires gradually give way to delight in the otherness of the other.[101] The Church, as the Body of Christ, is seen by Williams as a major vehicle for nurturing and sustaining these other-oriented relations. Its calling is to be a visible symbol of the relations of divine love, the relations that characterize the divine life and which are God's purpose for the whole creation.[102]

Evident in such a vision is an exalted conception of the Church. It is an ecclesial vision that diverges markedly from the reality of imperfect, and even destructive, church communities. As noted earlier, Williams is certainly alert to the institutional Church's imperfections, and is not proposing a programme for the reform of the Church as an institution.[103] Offered instead is an imaginative vision of what the Church is called to become: communities of those who, renewed in Christ, are being gradually transformed by the Spirit to exemplify the otherness-oriented relations of God's Kingdom.[104] While this vision will not be perfectly realized before the eschaton, it may nevertheless find expression in the lives of Christians and communities committed to nurturing the disciplines of other-directed relationships.

In such lives and communities, the Church becomes, in Mike Higton's words, the 'the bearer of a question ... [about] a reality that cannot be exhausted by any system'.[105] The argument of this chapter is that, for Rowan Williams, it is imagination, transformed by grace and disciplined by the practices of the Christian Church, which enables finite beings to glimpse the reality which is God's life, uncontainable by any system and inaccessible to purely human vision.

## Notes

1 Rowan Williams, *Faith in the Public Square* (London: Bloomsbury, 2012), p. 178.

2 Williams, *Faith in the Public Square*, p. 92.

3 Rowan Williams, 'Foreword', in Nicholas Afanasiev, *The Church of the Holy Spirit*, trans. Vitaly Permiakov, ed. with Introduction, Michael Pleban (Notre Dame, IN: University of Notre Dame Press, 2007), p. vii.

4 Rowan Williams, 'The Authority of the Church', *Modern Believing* 46.1 (2005), p. 17. Elsewhere he cites Richard Hooker's claim that 'the Church is the totality of those who call upon the name of the Lord.' Rowan Williams, 'Theological Doubt and Institutional Certainty: An Anglican Paradox', *Studies in Church History* 52 (2016), p. 261.

5 Rowan Williams, *Headwaters* (Oxford: Perpetua Press, 2008), pp. 15–17.

6 According to legend, Serafim fed a bear who visited him.

7 Williams singles out these habits as essential for human living. See, for example, 'Bodies, Minds and Thoughts' in Rowan Williams, *Being Human: Bodies, Minds, Persons* (London: SPCK, 2018), pp. 49–68; and *The Way of St Benedict* (London: Bloomsbury, 2020), where the Benedictine Rule is held to inculcate these habits.

8 Rowan Williams, *Tokens of Trust: An Introduction to Christian Belief* (Louisville, KY: Westminster, John Knox Press, 2007), p. 97.

9 See Rowan Williams, *Christ the Heart of Creation* (London: Bloomsbury Continuum, 2018), pp. 36–40.

10 Williams, *Christ the Heart of Creation*, p. 36.

11 Williams, *Christ the Heart of Creation*, p. 38.

12 Williams, *Christ the Heart of Creation*, p. 40.

13 See Williams, *Christ the Heart of Creation*, p. 80, where Williams declares that 'the Word is *unconditional divine agency in its filial exercise.*'

14 Williams, *Christ the Heart of Creation*, p. 39.

15 The phrase 'To Stand where Christ Stands' is the title of Williams' chapter in *An Introduction to Christian Spirituality*, ed. Ralph Waller and Benedicta Ward (London: SPCK, 1999). It is an important concept for Williams, occurring also in his enthronement sermon (Rowan Williams, 'Enthronement Sermon', Canterbury Cathedral, 27 February 2003, http://rowanwilliams.archbishopofcanterbury.org/articles.php/1624/enthronement-sermon.html, accessed 5.07.2024) and his address to the World Council of Churches Plenary ('Christian Identity and Religious Plurality', *The Ecumenical Review* 58.1-2 (2006), pp. 69–75).

16 Williams, *Christ the Heart of Creation*, p. 2. Williams places great emphasis on the intimate relation of believers to their 'Abba' Father, holding that Christian prayer arises out of that relation. See, for instance, *Christ the Heart of Creation*, p. 4.

17 See 'Rowan Williams, Belief and Theology: Some Core Questions', in Rupert Shortt, *God's Advocates: Christian Thinkers in Conversation* (Grand Rapids, MI: William B. Eerdmans, 2005), p. 3.

18 Williams specifies ('To Stand Where Christ Stands', p. 2) that 'living … according to spirit … is a designation of the entire set of our human relations, to God and each other and our environment.'

19 Williams, 'To Stand where Christ Stands', p. 2. See also p. 11, where, incor-

porated into Christ, believers are 'identified with the movement of the Word from the Father into the heart of the world'. The same idea is repeated in the WCC address, 'Christian Identity and Religious Plurality'.

20 Williams, *Christ the Heart of Creation*, p. 39.
21 Williams, *Christ the Heart of Creation*, p. 76.
22 Williams, *Christ the Heart of Creation*, p. 74.
23 Williams, *Christ the Heart of Creation*, p. 77.
24 Rowan Williams, *On Christian Theology: Challenges in Contemporary Theology* (Malden, MA: Blackwell, 2000), p. 231.
25 Rowan Williams, *Tokens of Trust*, p. 101; *On Christian Theology*, p. 232. See also Williams' Enthronement Sermon where he declares that 'we only become completely human when we allow God to remake us.'
26 Williams, *On Christian Theology*, pp. 231, 233; *Tokens of Trust*, p. 114.
27 Rowan Williams, 'Afterword', in *The Blackwell Companion to Christian Ethics*, ed. Stanley Hauerwas and Samuel Wells (Oxford: Blackwell, 2004), p. 495.
28 Williams, *On Christian Theology*, p. 234. The emphasis here is on 'alignment with Christ'. Williams is all too aware of the Church's countless failures to be the 'visible community' in which Christ is recognizable. See, for instance, Rowan Williams, 'Making Moral Decisions', in *The Cambridge Companion to Christian Ethics*, ed. Robin Gill (Cambridge: Cambridge University Press, 2001), p. 12. See also *On Christian Theology*, p. 289.
29 Williams, *Christ the Heart of Creation*, p. 81.
30 Williams, *On Christian Theology*, p. 120.
31 Williams, *Tokens of Trust*, p. 100.
32 Rowan Williams, 'Sacramental Living', *Trinity Papers* 32 (Parkville, Vic: University of Melbourne, 2002), p. 5. See also 'Enthronement Sermon'.
33 Williams, *On Christian Theology*, p. 204.
34 Williams, 'Sacramental Living', p. 5.
35 Williams, *On Christian Theology*, p. 204.
36 Williams, *On Christian Theology*, p. 213.
37 Williams, *On Christian Theology*, p. 120.
38 Williams, 'Sacramental Living', pp. 6–8. See also *On Christian Theology*, p. 274.
39 Williams, 'Sacramental Living', p. 8.
40 Williams, 'Sacramental Living', p. 8.
41 Williams, 'Sacramental Living', p. 8.
42 Rowan Williams, *The Wound of Knowledge: Christian Spirituality from the New Testament to St John of the Cross*, 2nd rev. edn (London: Darton Longman & Todd, 1990), p. 182. This theme is also addressed in 'Word and Spirit' in *On Christian Theology*, pp. 124–5.
43 Williams, *On Christian Theology*, p. 124.
44 See Williams, *Tokens of Trust*, pp. 158, 135.
45 Rowan Williams, *Meeting God in Paul* (London: SPCK, 2015), p. 67.
46 Williams, *Meeting God in Paul*, p. 71.
47 Rowan Williams, *A Ray of Darkness: Sermons and Reflections* (Lanham, MD: Cowley, 1995), pp. 18–19.
48 Williams, *On Christian Theology*, p. 124.
49 Williams, *On Christian Theology*, p. 124.
50 Williams, *On Christian Theology*, p. 124.

51 See, for example, Andrew Goddard, *Rowan Williams: His Legacy* (Oxford: Lion Hudson, 2013), chs 6 and 7; Rupert Shortt, *Rowan's Rule: The Biography of the Archbishop* (London: Hodder & Stoughton, 2008), pp. 264ff.; Andrew McGowan, 'Conversations with Rowan Williams', *Eureka Street*, 22 March 2012, https://www.eurekastreet.com.au/article/conversations-with-rowan-williams, accessed 03.06.2020.

52 Theo Hobson has argued that his sacramentalism is innately violent, a form of 'ideological ... policing'. Theo Hobson, 'The Policing of Signs: Sacramentalism and Authority in Rowan Williams' Theology', *Scottish Journal of Theology* 61.4 (2008), p. 381. Giles Fraser has accused him of 'torturing' the Church of England by his adherence to 'a dead German philosopher (Hegel)', in 'Faith to Faith: Dialectical Anglicanism has many problems, foremost among them the damage to its champion – Rowan Williams', *The Guardian*, 17 June 2006. By contrast, Ben Myers asserts that Williams' intention was to 'articulate a distinctively political vision of the church, and to rethink the nature of contemporary society through the lens of Christian catholicity', with its concern for 'the good of the whole community'. Benjamin Myers, 'Rowan Williams and the politics of the empty tomb', *ABC Religion and Ethics Report*, 6 April 2012, https://www.abc.net.au/religion/rowan-williams-and-the-politics-of-the-empty-tomb/10100656, accessed 20.07.2021.

53 'Faith Communities in a Civil Society', in *Faith in the Public Square*, p. 306.

54 Williams, *Tokens of Trust*, p. 140.

55 Williams, *On Christian Theology*, p. 124.

56 Williams, *Tokens of Trust*, p. 96.

57 Williams, *Tokens of Trust*. Also *On Christian Theology*, p. 58.

58 Williams, *Tokens of Trust*, p. 133.

59 Williams, *Tokens of Trust*, p. 133.

60 Williams, 'Sacramental Living', p. 16. For a discussion of the significance of the eucharist in Williams' ecclesiology, see Alexander J. Irving, 'The Eucharist and the Church in the Thought of Henri de Lubac and Rowan Williams: Sacramental Ecclesiology and the Place of the Church in the World', *Anglican Theological Review* 100.2 (2018), pp. 267–89.

61 Williams, 'Sacramental Living', p. 16. The term is borrowed from Gregory Dix.

62 Williams, 'Sacramental Living', p. 16.

63 Williams, 'Sacramental Living', p. 18.

64 Williams, 'Sacraments of the New Society' in *On Christian Theology*, p. 217. Here Williams rejects the 'sacramental principle' which claims to discern divine presence in created matter.

65 Williams, 'Sacraments of the New Society', p. 218.

66 Williams, 'Sacraments of the New Society', p. 219.

67 Williams, 'Sacraments of the New Society', p. 219.

68 Williams, *Tokens of Trust*, p. 116.

69 Williams, *Christ the Heart of Creation*, p. 164. The italics are mine.

70 It is assumed that the caveat expressed by Williams in relation to baptism also applies to the eucharist; that is, that the grace offered must be received. See Williams, *On Christian Theology*, p. 211.

71 Williams, *Christ the Heart of Creation*, p. 214.

72 Williams, 'Sacramental Living', p. 15.

73 Williams, *On Christian Theology*, p. 219.

74 Williams' attachment to the Eucharist as central to the life of the Church has been called into question by Theo Hobson, who concludes that Williams' utopian vision of the Eucharist leaves him stuck 'in the ruins of Christendom', unwilling to pursue a more radical vision of the Church. Theo Hobson, *Anarchy, Church and Utopia: Rowan Williams on Church* (London: Darton, Longman & Todd, 2005), p. 101. In a later article, while not completely rejecting that earlier conclusion, Hobson concedes that, in the matter of 'the ritual essence of Christianity', Williams has 'got it right'. Here Hobson argues that Williams' transformative intention has been to present Christianity as a cultural tradition, its meaning lying in the 'true myth' of cross and resurrection enacted in the Eucharist. See Hobson, 'Rowan Williams got it right about Ritual', *The Guardian*, 31 October 2012.

75 Williams, *Christ the Heart of Creation*, p. 214.
76 Williams, *Christ the Heart of Creation*, p. 214.
77 Williams, 'Sacramental Living', p. 20.
78 Williams, 'Sacramental Living', p. 20.
79 Williams, *The Way of St Benedict*, p. 22.

80 Williams writes that 'We are such beings that living in bliss with God can never be other than something we *learn*.' Conversation with Rupert Shortt, *God's Advocates*, p. 11. Williams' emphasis on developing 'habits of imagination ... cultivated in the context of ... liturgical practices' is also stressed by Medi Volpe in '"Taking time" and "making sense": Rowan Williams on the Habits of Theological Imagination', *International Journal of Systematic Theology* 15.3 (2013), p. 354.

81 Shortt, *God's Advocates*, p. 127.

82 Williams' early study of the 'acrobats and jugglers' of desert and monastery was followed by a book on Teresa of Avila, reflections on the Desert Fathers and Thomas Merton, and more recently by a book on the Rule of St Benedict. See Rowan Williams, *The Wound of Knowledge* (1979/1990); *Teresa of Avila* (Harrisburg, PA: Morehouse, 1991); *Silence and Honey Cakes: The Wisdom of the Desert* (Oxford: Lion, 2003); *A Silent Action: Engagements with Thomas Merton* (London: SPCK, 2013); *The Way of St Benedict*.

83 Rowan Williams, *Holy Living: The Christian Tradition for Today* (London: Bloomsbury, 2017), pp. 53ff.

84 Williams, *The Way of St Benedict*, p. 52.
85 Williams, *The Way of St Benedict*, p. 60.
86 Williams, *The Way of St Benedict*, p. 104.
87 Williams, *The Way of St Benedict*, pp. 4, 22, 27, 83; Williams, *Holy Living*, pp. 53ff.
88 Williams, *The Way of St Benedict*, chs 1 and 2.
89 Williams, *The Way of St Benedict*, p. 33.
90 Williams, *The Way of St Benedict*, p. 33.
91 Williams, *The Way of St Benedict*, p. 33.
92 Williams, *The Way of St Benedict*, p. 14.
93 Williams, *The Way of St Benedict*, p. 14. See also *Holy Living*, pp. 182–3.
94 Williams, *The Way of St Benedict*, p. 55.
95 Williams, *Holy Living*, p. 126.
96 Williams, *The Way of St Benedict*, p. 130.
97 Williams, *The Way of St Benedict*, p. 126. See also *Holy Living*, pp. 97–8.
98 Mike Higton, *Difficult Gospel: The Theology of Rowan Williams* (London: SCM Press, 2004). Giles Goddard makes the telling observation that Williams saw

the role of Archbishop of Canterbury as defined by suffering and that during his tenure in that office the (Anglican) Church internalized the suffering he was projecting. Cited by Andrew Goddard in *Rowan Williams: His Legacy*, p. 291.

99 See, for example, Williams, *The Way of St Benedict*, pp. 70, 71; *Holy Living*, pp. 103, 120, 130, 161.

100 Williams, *Holy Living*, pp. 95–6.

101 Williams emphasizes the Church's call to offer a model of communal relations which, being other-oriented, run counter to the consumerist individualism of Western culture. See, for example, the account of the actions of Sofia Michaelovna in Rowan Williams, 'The Authority of the Church', *Modern Believing* 46.1 (2005), p. 27.

102 Rowan Williams, 'Authority Deferred: A Christian Comment', *Studies in Christian Ethics* 29.2 (2016), p. 215.

103 The relation between Church and society is certainly not neglected by Williams, as pointed out by Myers (note 52). Williams' focus is on general principles rather than sociological analysis.

104 Williams, 'Authority Deferred', p. 215.

105 Higton, *Difficult Gospel*, p. 69.

PART THREE

# Imagination in the Work of Rowan Williams

## Introduction

*The world's reality is always asymptotically approaching its fullness by means of the response of the imagination.*[1]
Rowan Williams

In Part Two, my exploration of the significance of imagination in Rowan Williams' writings focused on the relation between imagination and desire, divine and human. From his extensive reflections on the significance of desire in patristic and contemporary Christian theology, I drew the conclusion that, in its dynamic orientation towards otherness and transcendence, human imagination is held to be the finite analogue of the otherness-oriented energy of divine desire, its purpose being the focusing of human desire towards the eschatological vision of the divine Kingdom.

Part Three deals directly with the conception of imagination discernible in Williams' discussions of language, aesthetics, literature and art. A scrutiny of these writings provides evidence of the inseparable relation he establishes between the human capacity for remaking and transforming created matter and the inexhaustible excess of ecstatic, kenotic love activating, sustaining and transforming creation. I pay special attention to Williams' poetry as an expression of his intimation of created matter pulsating with the dynamic energy of divine desire.

In Chapter 7, I examine Williams' theological reflection on communication, with a specific focus on the phenomenon of human language and on humanity's capacity for symbolization. Chapter 8 is a discussion of his theory of aesthetics. Chapter 9 explores the outworking of his aesthetical theory in his poetry and literary criticism. Chapter 10 sets out to demonstrate that Williams' analogical conception of finite reality as excess of Trinitarian desire in-and-beyond divine being is the foundation for a coherent theology of imagination and is the impelling force of his theological vision.

## Note

1 Rowan Williams, *Grace and Necessity: Reflections on Art and Love* (London: Morehouse, 2005), p. 154.

# 7

# Language in a Communicative Universe

## Introduction

This chapter explores the claim made by Williams that human language re-presents a cosmos that is not only intelligible but also communicative. Implied by such a claim is the theological metaphysic identified in Chapter 3, the vision of finite reality as the analogical expression of infinite Love. In this chapter, I argue that this vision is the source of the passionate energy that impels Williams' reflections on language, delivered as the 2013 Gifford Lectures and published as *The Edge of Words*.[1] Listeners to the lectures would have sensed something of the energy imbuing Williams' words and may even have caught a glimpse of his view of the cosmos as a dynamic network of vibrant activity pulsating with divine love.[2]

The chapter begins with the poem 'Invocation: a sculpture for winter'. In this poem we share something of Williams' experience of the communicative power of divine *eros* permeating finite matter. That reflection leads into an examination of the metaphysical vision revealed in *The Edge of Words*, with its link to Augustine's theory of language. The chapter will continue with Williams' observations concerning the distinctive features and oddities of human language, with a view to discerning the implications of such language for a Christian theology of imagination. The conclusion to be drawn is that there exists an interrelationship between language, imagination and the energy of divine *eros*.

## 'Invocation: a sculpture for winter' (Monasterio di Bose, Northern Italy, January 2003)

The poem 'Invocation: a sculpture for winter' points to Williams' conception of the divine erotic energy permeating creation. Opening the *Headwaters* collection of Williams' poems, 'Invocation' presents the reader with a visual, almost tactile, experience of the theme loosely uni-

fying that collection: the sensed presence within the material world of the
One who is its source.

>  Landscape in pale concrete: the abstract downs,
>  hillocks and gullies, only adjusting slowly
>  into twin faces staring, cranium to cranium,
>  at the dove-grey, eagerly bending sky.
>
>  The first cold sting falls hours before dawn
>  out of the heavy miles of cloud, stirred
>  to an answer by the face seen only
>  from so far, only at night, and when
>
>  The cold has folded up the colours, shut down
>  wind and growing, and the rustle, crack and damp
>  of the short day. Sounds come sideways
>  like landscape at earth level, but then
>
>  They're put out for the night; we don't
>  have anything to go on but the sensed
>  profile alongside, whose eyes we can't see.
>  Into the fast-approaching heavy heaven
>
>  We look, guessing what open mouth brings down
>  the random, uninhibited and unrepeatable
>  designs that pile up in these gulfs,
>  guessing why what we can't see draws the lick and kiss
>
>  To our strange neighbour's skull.

The inspiration for this poem is the stunning location of the Monastery of Bose in Northern Italy, situated as it is in the hollow below the dark rocks of a glacial moraine, with the Italian Alps forming a jagged snow-covered backdrop. As the poet gazes upward, the late afternoon winter landscape becomes the sculptural form of 'twin faces staring, cranium to cranium/ at the dove-grey, eagerly bending sky.' As night falls, sound and sight are obliterated by 'the heavy miles' of dark cloud descending over the mountains' twin faces. Gazing upward, the poet can only 'sense' rather than 'see' the presence of those peaks, but what he does experience almost viscerally is the powerful pull of the mountains' 'open mouth', drawing forth from the impenetrable cloud the 'lick and kiss' of erotic love. Conveyed through that final image is the irresistible attraction between finite creation and its Creator: earth's yearning for heaven's response, heaven's drawing near in a kiss of love. The poet's experience, as witness to this interaction of cloud and mountain, is his heightened sense of the ever-present current of erotic love flowing between heaven and earth and giving divine significance to the material world.[3]

The invocation of the title may be mutual – who is calling to whom? Is this the earth calling to God or the reverse? The poem is infused with a sense of presence, an awareness of the material world as the uninterrupted object of God's loving gaze, an awareness that is at the heart of Williams' vision of created existence.[4] For this poet-theologian, poetry is primarily a vehicle for recognizing the divine as not only the source of all that exists but also as the eternal energy of *eros* animating creation. In the poet's imaginative response to the beckonings of the world around him we discern the analogical theological vision that underpins Williams' life and thought.[5]

## A communicative universe

The theme of 'communicative matter' is central to Williams' study of the operation of human language in *The Edge of Words*. There he sums up his perception of the material universe with the proposal that 'what we need is a metaphysics that thinks of matter itself as invariably and necessarily communicative.'[6] Drawing primarily on the evolutionary biological theory elaborated in Conor Cunningham's reinterpretation of Darwin,[7] Williams points to the 'negotiation systems' that operate across the whole material world: not only animals but also plants and inanimate objects are in a process of constant interactive adaptation. The cosmos is accordingly viewed as a vibrant flow of seemingly intentional energy, an ever-renewed 'seeking of form'.[8] He concludes that 'intelligence is literally the only phenomenon that makes sense of the overall direction of the material universe towards coherent, sustainable, innovative, adaptable forms.'[9] Here we discern the link that exists between intelligence and imagination in Williams' theological vision: imagination may be conceived as analogous to the 'intelligent' energy of divine desire.

Key to the intelligent, meaningful integration of the innumerable other systems in the universe is the phenomenon of human language, which displays a similar pattern of 'cooperative agency'. Through gesture and sign/word, language enables humans to symbolize their perceptions of the world around them, to communicate these perceptions, and so develop a shared understanding of their environment and their life together. Matter, for human beings, is thus never passive but is 'always already "saturated" with the workings of mind'.[10] What is perceived and apprehended is a shared world, already filled with meaning, but always under continuing negotiation and open to further transformation. The result is a conception of the 'material universe ... as an essentially *symbolic complex*'.[11]

Such a universe, says Williams, prompts reflection on 'the idea of an abundant or excessive reality engulfing our mental activities'.[12] From the notion of an all-encompassing intelligent reality, it is not a great leap to the Genesis 1 account of God speaking creation into being, thence to a concept of created matter as directly expressive of the divine, and from there to the Christian doctrine of the Incarnation, the *Word* made flesh.

Williams is, however, wary of making such a direct leap. His analysis of the relation between language, reality and God is far more nuanced, as is his understanding of the Incarnation. In the 1989 essay 'Beginning with the Incarnation', he points out the danger of the 'slippage into ideology' attendant on the Anglican enthusiasm for the so-called 'incarnational principle'.[13] The incarnation is not merely 'the spiritualizing of matter' such that matter is a straightforward revelation of God. What must be recognized is the difference between God and creation, between the infinite otherness of the divine and the finite materiality of created being.

Acknowledging that the infinite God is definitively revealed in Jesus Christ, the Word made flesh, Williams goes on to argue that we grasp the full significance of that revelation only when we recognize that Jesus' life, death and resurrection represent God's judgement of the world. It is a judgement on humanity's relation to the world and to its Creator.[14] The Incarnation is truly apprehended as gift only when we are ready to recognize the falsity of all human concepts of God.

A more nuanced conception of creation as 'sign' of the divine is developed in the 1989 essay 'Language, Reality and Desire in Augustine's *De Doctrina*',[15] an analysis of Augustine's insights into the relation between the incarnation, human language and finite reality. In that essay it is possible to discern the lineaments of the analogical metaphysic of symbolic realism underlying Williams' theological vision and which is developed more fully in *The Edge of Words* and *Christ the Heart of Creation*.

## Williams' analysis of Augustine's theory of language

Augustine's theory of signs[16] was discussed in Chapter 5 in relation to human desire. There, I set forth Williams' argument that the divine *res*, God, is the true focus of human desire. In this chapter I point to the significance he attributes to Augustine's *res/signum*, *uti/frui* distinction.[17] Williams' claim is that such a distinction offers insight into the relation between language and reality, a relation which he claims may be truly grasped only in the light of the Incarnation. As discussed above, Augustine asserts that a *res*/thing may function as a sign, pointing to, and thus assigning meaning to, another *res*. Since God is the ultimate context in which every *res* exists, God may be considered as the supreme *res* of which every created *res* is a sign, and from which each *res* derives its meaning. To this point, Augustine's thinking has its source in Greek semiotic theory.[18]

As Williams points out, Augustine diverges from classical tradition, first in his insistence that words function as signs,[19] second in his adoption of the *uti/frui* distinction,[20] and third in his recognition that signs must be interpreted, since signifying is a 'threefold not twofold' activity.[21] Signifying always involves a subject who attributes meaning to the sign. In a fallen world, created signs may accordingly be misinterpreted by human subjects and their true meaning misunderstood.

Further distortion occurs in respect of the *uti/frui* (use/enjoyment) of created things. In place of their proper function as signs to be used to point to God, created things become objects of enjoyment for their own sake.[22] Humans need 'purification' in order to learn to read and use signs rightly.[23] It was for that purpose that the divine Wisdom, the Word, became flesh, so as to be the true sign that points unerringly to God and which is to be 'used' for the purpose of humanity's healing and purification.[24]

At this juncture, Williams' distinctive emphases become apparent. As he acknowledges, his discussion of *De Doctrina* is aimed at bringing to the fore certain theological implications of Augustine's language theory.[25] The incarnation of the Word as fleshly sign makes it clear that created reality exists as sign of its Creator. All is *signum* pointing to the divine *res*. It may be concluded, says Williams, that 'the whole creation is uttered and "meant" by God, and therefore has no meaning in itself.'[26] Its meaning lies in being directed to God for God's 'use'. The consequence is that all earthly things are signs, words 'speaking' God, 'capable of opening out beyond themselves' to point to a 'wider context'.[27] Humans are thereby reminded that the ultimate purpose of human existence is not to be found within finite creation but only in the infinite and eternal love of God.[28]

The wider context opened by the incarnation means also that things and words are not restricted to a single meaning but possess a metaphorical resonance, signifying 'what [they] are not' in pointing beyond themselves to God.[29] Williams can therefore assert that 'we live in a world of restless fluidities in meaning.'[30] He cites Augustine's examples of ordinary objects, such as wood, stone and rams, resonating with a new depth of meaning as a result of their scriptural association with Moses, Jacob and Abraham.[31] According to Augustine, scripture, 'the supreme *signum* after Christ',[32] is intended to reveal to us how to 'read' the world around us, teaching us to discern the divine purpose for creation. The difficulties encountered in reading the scriptures serve to remind us that knowledge of God comes only from the purification of desire, the long process of learning *caritas*.[33]

In relation to the scriptural sign that is Jesus Christ, Williams' particular emphasis is on the difference it reveals about God. Drawing on Augustine's striking image, in the *Confessions*, of Christ as 'the weak God lying at our feet',[34] Williams follows his mentor in stressing that God is recognized in the brokenness of the crucified Christ only by those willing to emulate Christ's own humility and weakness.

Such humility is learned through the discipline of discipleship; it involves the arduous task of 'perfecting that unqualified and self-forgetting *caritas* which human beings are made for'.[35] Once again, we find reiterated Williams' contention that, whereas the 'incarnation manifests the essential quality of the world itself as "sign" or trace of its maker', the capacity to see the divine in ordinary matter is dependent upon conversion and the process of sanctification. This mode of seeing brings awareness that the true sign of God's transcendent presence within the created order is that of the weakness, failure and humiliation of the cross. To see created matter in this way is to realize that it is only through the finitude of temporal materiality that the infinite God may be known.[36]

Of particular significance for Williams are the 'restless fluidity' and metaphorical resonance he considers inherent in Augustine's theory of language. Reading Augustine through the lens of postmodern semiotic theory,[37] he highlights several features given prominence by more recent scholarship, with the aim of substantiating the relation detected by Augustine between language and divine desire. One such feature is the lack of closure of human language.

As Williams repeatedly stresses, no utterance is ever final.[38] Not only is there always more to be said but what is said is subject to modification, contradiction or clarification. To speak is to invite a response and all discourse is consequently dialogical, implying the presence of another to whom the speech is addressed. More significant still is the recognition that human language, with its infinite stock of possibilities and 'unfinishable nature', is suggestive of an infinite Other, an inexhaustible presence who is both the source of language and the one to whom linguistic signs are ultimately directed.[39] The very inexhaustibility of human language points to the possibility of the divine Other to whom humanity is inescapably connected.

Language's lack of closure means too that no utterance can be considered as definitive, since what is said is implicitly surrounded by all that is left unsaid. Absence and deferral are thus integral to all forms of discourse. The restlessness of language means that human knowledge can only ever be provisional since it is haunted by both the excess and the deferral of meaning adhering to every linguistic sign.

Augustine's argument, as developed by Williams, is that only one sign is identical with fullness of meaning. That sign is the Word incarnate, who is 'the central metaphor to which the whole world of signs can be related',[40] and who gives meaning to every other sign. The sign that is Christ crucified, risen and ascended is, however, a sign of 'absence and deferral'. He is the sign that informs us that the infinite God may be known only within 'the limit, incompletion, [and] absence' of mortal existence.[41] He is the sign of hope deferred, hope that depends on faith, hope that is ignited and sustained by desire.

Williams can therefore argue that 'the fact [of] absence and deferral are the means whereby God engages our desire so that it is freed from its own pull towards finishing, towards presence and possession.'[42] His conclusion is that the system of signs that is human language is interpreted correctly only when it is employed in the service of divine love. Impelled by desire, language, with its deferral of finality and its inexhaustible excess of meaning, is, rightly interpreted, a vehicle of love. Those who have learned to read the world as an expression of that love become themselves a text communicating God's unbounded love. For Williams, as for Augustine, 'The world of human discourse is ... extended between the love of God in creation and redemption, and the Beatific Vision.'[43]

Williams follows the Augustine scholar Carol Harrison in stressing the 'delight' to be evoked by 'good speech'.[44] As noted by Harrison, Augustine diverges from classical rhetorical practice to stress that the delight experienced by the listener lies less in the skill of the speaker than in the truth-bearing content of the material. Language that conveys divine truth, such as the language of scripture, is capable of arousing delight in the hearers, drawing them towards God. As is the case with artistic creations of beauty, truth-bearing language, whether scriptural or not, is a means whereby God is made known to fallen humanity. The implication is that delight is kindled by preaching that truthfully expresses the divine love revealed in Christ. A further implication, not made explicit by Williams at this point, is that the human use of language in literary art may arouse similar delight within the reader when it communicates truth.

We may conclude that, inspired largely by Augustine's reflections on language, Williams' vision of the communicative universe finds its theological grounding in Jesus Christ, the Word made flesh, whose life, death and resurrection enable the created order to be correctly read as signifying divine *eros*. The system of signs that is human language is the means whereby the divine meaning, to which created matter points, is apprehended and communicated by the beings created to know and respond to the kenotic, ecstatic love of God. Through language, humanity may grasp the metaphoric resonance of the created order, convey its beauty and significance to one another, and respond in grateful praise to the triune God, Creator, Word and Spirit. However, when language is divorced from awareness of the divine source of existence, it may all too readily degenerate into expressions of hostility, distrust, confusion and disbelief. Williams is adamant that we must *learn* to read the world correctly in the light of God's revelation in Christ.

Certain of these themes are developed at greater length in *The Edge of Words*. There, Williams studies the features of human language with a view to suggesting that the way language operates leads us to the 'edge' where human speech opens on to the ultimately 'unsayable ... sacred'.[45] As will be demonstrated in the section that follows, the features identified here are significant for the elucidation of the theology of imagination implicit in Williams' writings.

## *The Edge of Words*: Language and its operation

### *Language and symbol: Description and representation*

For those who see truly, the created order is imbued with divine significance. As we have seen, the concept that matter is 'always already "saturated" with ... mind'[46] underlies Williams' understanding of the symbolic nature of language and its descriptive and representational usages. While all language is symbolic in its sign-making function, Williams establishes a distinction between so-called literal descriptive language and language employed representationally.[47]

I discussed this distinction in the Introduction, where I observed that, in Williams' usage, 'description' presupposes a direct, unmediated relation between word and fact while 'representational' language carries with it a whole complex of associations and metaphorical resonances. The latter form of language seeks 'to embody, translate, make present or re-form what is perceived'[48] and thus express the multi-layered, interconnected, symbolic complexity of the human world.

In the Appendix to *The Edge of Words*, Williams draws attention to the further distinction established by Hegel in his discussion of *Darstellung* (depiction) and *Vorstellung* (representation).[49] According to Hegel, both types of language imply the 'fusion' of self and other.[50] They are both an investment of self in that which is other than the self in an attempt to portray the 'life' of the other, whether that other be a physical object or another person. The difference between the two usages lies in the outcome of that fusion. Unlike description (*Darstellung*), representation (*Vorstellung*) also involves *new insight* about self and the other gained from awareness of mutuality, the inextricable involvement of self with the otherness of the external world. In the case of representation, the fusion is 'a vehicle for self-understanding, for thought's recognition of itself'.[51]

Conceptualized in this way, the representational function of language is crucial to the formation of human thought processes and to the development of self-awareness. Representational language, the capacity to re-present in a new form the pulsating energy of the world, is indicative of the significant role Williams accords to imagination in the realization of our full potential as human beings. In offering an 'imaginative response to the world we inhabit', we 'collaborate' with the energy of that world itself[52] and thus act in accord with our true human vocation.

## Language as embodied practice

As noted in Chapter 1, the human body's neurological and sensorimotor systems have been shown to be involved in humanity's capacity for sign-making and are thus linked to the operation of imagination.[53] While Williams is keenly aware of the neurological substratum of language production[54] and of the inseparable connection between body, cognition and context,[55] his main interest is in the way our bodies act as agents of communication, enabling us to orient ourselves in both physical and social worlds. It is as we manoeuvre our bodies in various situations that we develop 'an internalized map and set of rules' derived from interaction with our environment and with the people around us.[56]

From this embodied experience comes speech as a form of practice, a way of responding appropriately to the situation. Language is accordingly not so much a means of passing on information as of engaging with other people within a shared world.[57] The fact of bodiliness means, however, that sharing can never be complete, as each body operates from a particular and unique perspective. Language as embodied practice accordingly carries an ethical imperative – no one embodied being may claim a total overview. Every perspective is meaningful and necessary as the unique intersection of insights gained from a particular set of relationships and experience.[58]

To recognize the association between language and the body should, claims Williams, lead us to an acknowledgement of the indispensability of the embodied other.⁵⁹ Such recognition involves an act of imagination, the capacity to place oneself imaginatively in another's place and see from another's perspective.

## Language as world-forming

'Worlds' are formed through the process of communicating with embodied others. Learned responses and shared perspectives give rise to world views, social imaginaries common to a community. This is explained by the very nature of human language: its open-endedness, its infinite variety of combinations, its freedom to represent not only what is present but also the past, the unreal, the possible and the impossible.⁶⁰

There is no such thing as a 'last word', notes Williams, because human speech is never finished. There is always something more to be said, a further response to every utterance. Language accordingly operates in time.⁶¹ It enables the past to be reviewed and revised, allowing learning to occur, mistakes to be identified, and alternative courses of action to be considered. It propels speakers and writers towards the future, towards what has not yet been thought or said.

The role played by imagination in such usage is made specific in an early article, 'The Nature of a Sacrament'.⁶² Recognizing that human beings have 'an insatiable desire for new perception and new possibilities of action', Williams states that 'Each effort to make the world "belong" to us ... puts a fresh question ... becomes a new puzzle or code in need of imaginative "reading" and re-ordering.'⁶³ Language is accordingly the means whereby problems and puzzling situations may be re-presented and interpreted afresh through the exercise of imagination, the human capacity to generate new and hitherto unforeseen possibilities. In this way, change occurs, both in the external world and in human understanding. Imagination and the possibility for transformative action are thus inseparably connected with the operation of language.

## Language as human-making

Through language, humans make and transform not only their world but also themselves. The self, argues Williams, is not an observable stable object but a 'narrative', a 'project', a 'body of experiences', a 'repertoire' and a 'lineage, family of representations'.⁶⁴ The self is formed and continuously reformed by our language as we, as 'speaking bodies', engage with, interpret and respond to the social and physical environment. At any one moment, our individual identity consists both in the narrative we have constructed from the history of our interactions and the repertoire of actions that lie within the range of possibility postulated by that narrative.

Identity is thus seen as a construct of the imagination. It is the 'project', the artwork that we each create for ourselves through the 'symbol-making activity' of human language.[65] Growth in self-awareness is dependent on the continuing and expanded exercise of imagination as we learn to engage first with the world of ordinary experience, the world in which 'there is always more otherness to encounter, the otherness of new perspectives and new requirements for "negotiation".'[66] Significantly too, it also involves engagement with the worlds of imagination available through literature, drama and ritual.[67] Finally, growth into a truly human self involves recognition of the finitude and contingency of the self thus constructed and of the need for a trust-filled dependence on that which language cannot contain, on the sacred which may be discerned at the 'edge of words'.[68]

## Paradox, irony, silence and religious language

The difficulties and aporias encountered in the use of language bring us to the edge where words no longer suffice or must be employed in a different register. That is the conclusion that Williams seeks to lead us to in these lectures. Language pushed to excess, in the forms of paradox, irony and poetry, forces us to question previous assumptions about the world and ourselves, to 'reshuffle the conceptual pack',[69] to rethink prevailing models of cause and effect; in short, to broaden our conceptual horizon so as to gain a wider vision of both the nature of reality and of ourselves. Such language serves to make the world *strange* for us so that we may be freed from habitual perception and thus acknowledge 'the always receding horizon of our knowing'.[70]

Silence goes even further in its questioning of the adequacy of language to convey fullness of meaning. Those moments when we fall silent in the face of intense emotion, whether it be horror, pain or joy, remind us of the limits of language. Silence at such moments tells us that 'there is something we have not captured (and are not likely to)',[71] that we are confronted by the limits of language when we attempt either to 'name the unnameable' or to express the inexhaustible plenitude of the universe. Silence in these circumstances is witness not to a void, says Williams, but to 'a plurality of meanings that cannot be mastered',[72] and is thus suggestive of a 'hinterland' of 'intelligible relations whose full scale is still obscure to us'.[73]

It is when language reaches this edge that the notion of God becomes intelligible as that towards which all language beckons but cannot encompass. So-called religious language is not comprehensible as straightforward description but only as language stretched beyond its usual currency to gesture towards what is ultimately *innominabile*. In acknowledging this, says Williams, we are confronted by our human limits, by the need to dispossess ourselves of our certainties, and to develop instead a 'deepened capacity for receptive stillness'.[74] When we come to this point, we finally begin to discover our true identity as human beings 'basically accountable' to that which is other, and 'engaged in growth, risk and love, shaping itself in relation to what is given'.[75]

The limit where language is found wanting is also the point where imagination comes into play. According to Williams, imagination has its source in the very 'incapacity' of human language to account for its own inexhaustibility, as there is always more to be said and known. The failure of language to find words for certain experiences is, he says, the 'source of its energy, its movement, its capacity for correction, innovation and imagination'.[76] Imagination, the capacity to leap from known to unknown, is thus seen by Williams to be integrally related to human language.

## Language and imagination

In *The Edge of Words* Williams does not set out to explicate the specific role played by imagination in the exercise of language. He nevertheless makes a number of statements which point to the interrelation of language and imagination. For instance:

> There are dimensions in what we encounter that require recognition in the imaginative world of our speaking, over and above whatever initial register we have found useful or 'natural'. The life of what we encounter is a many layered complex of invitations to that imagination.[77]

In this passage, imagination is conceptualized as responding to the generativity of the material world, which cannot be 'exhausted'[78] by its seemingly endless possibilities for new discovery. At the limit of what language may currently express, imagination takes a leap into the unknown in response to the invitation offered by the world. Imagination thus provides new possibilities for language.

In a second important passage, Williams argues that 'The conscious pushing of the boundaries of what we perceive in the exercise of the imagination is of a piece with all that we think of as the ordinary exercise of speech and significant gesture.'[79] The same impulse propels both speech and imagination. Both display an open-ended freedom, both have the capacity to represent perceptions in another register by the process of symbolization, both are involved in making us more fully human. Just as language is seen by Williams to be a response to the intelligible, communicative energy of the universe,[80] so imagination may be conceptualized as the inner human energy that impels such a response. Dependent on language's sign-making capacity, imagination is the energy that seeks to extend the limits of what language can encompass. Intentional and future-directed, it is the impulse towards the discovery of ever new patterns of possibility. It is, says Williams, of 'central theological importance'.[81]

In continuing the argument, Williams establishes the link between imagination and divine *eros*, the energy of love that permeates and activates the universe. He states that 'The imaginative response to the world we inhabit is, we could say, a collaboration with the energy of that world itself.'[82] Through the energy of imagination, humans have the capacity to perceive and identify the complex, vibrant plenitude of the universe we inhabit and to re-present it through the medium of language and other forms of symbolization.

The concept of imagination as 'a collaboration with the energy of the world' has significant implications for Williams' theology of imagination. These will be discussed more fully in the exploration of aesthetics, literature and art in the next chapters.

## Conclusion

In this chapter, I set out to discern the theological source of Williams' vision of a communicative universe and the place of human language in that universe. Building on Augustine's insights into the significance of the incarnation for understanding the relation between language and the created order, Williams concludes that human language is a truth-filled signifier of reality only in relation to Jesus Christ, the Word made flesh. The truth thus signified is that created matter is the expression of divine *caritas*, the love that is evidenced in the sacrificial gift of Christ crucified and risen. When oriented to Christ who is the Word of God, human words may also become gift, with the capacity to arouse delight and thus draw us towards the divine.

The second half of the chapter examined Williams' insights into the operation of language and the various ways language is shown to give expression to the energy of imagination that propels humanity's response to God. The theological implications of that insight will be further developed in Chapter 8, which will explore the phenomenon of human creativity in a discussion of Williams' aesthetical theory.

## Notes

1 Published as Rowan Williams, *The Edge of Words: God and the Habits of Language* (London: Bloomsbury, 2014).

2 The title of Williams' 1989 essay on Augustine's theory of language, 'Language, Reality and Desire: The Nature of Christian Formation' (in *On Augustine* (London: Bloomsbury, 2016), pp. 41–58) sums up the relation he discerns between created reality, language and divine desire.

3 This notion is also evident in Williams' reflection on Mark Jarman's 'Unholy Sonnets 17' in *A Century of Poetry*, where he asserts that 'God is the showing-through, in both physical and spiritual and imaginative life, of that initiative of invitation, embrace, the call to recognition, that is active in all that we encounter.' Williams, *A Century of Poetry: 100 Poems for Searching the Heart* (London: SPCK, 2022), p. 149.

4 For the notion of art as the 'willingness' to see things and people as the objects of the divine perspective, see Rowan Williams, 'Has Secularism Failed?' in *Faith in the Public Square* (London: Bloomsbury, 2012), p. 13.

5 Williams acknowledges the debt he owes to Balthasar in the development of his vision of divine love permeating creation in Todd Breyfogle, 'Time and Transformation: A Conversation with Rowan Williams', *Cross Currents* 45.3 (1995), p. 304.

6 Williams, *The Edge of Words*, p. xi. In her review, Catherine Pickstock suggests that Williams presents 'a theory of the nature of reality as itself linguistic'. Pickstock, 'Matter and Mattering: The Metaphysics of Rowan Williams', *Modern Theology* 31.4 (2015), p. 600. I contend that Williams' term 'communicative' is more appropriate, 'communicative' having a wider connotation than 'linguistic', with language as the supreme *human* form of communication, able to integrate and confer meaning on other communication systems.

7 Conor Cunningham, *Darwin's Pious Idea: Why the Ultra-Darwinists and Creationists both get it Wrong* (Grand Rapids, MI: William B. Eerdmans, 2010).

8 Williams, *The Edge of Words*, p. 124.

9 Williams, *The Edge of Words*, p. 102. See Williams' discussion of the Augustinian notion of the coherence and intelligibility of creation in *On Augustine*, pp. 59–78, and especially pp. 66–7. The 'intelligence' reference in the citation is to divine 'intelligence', which is broader than pure rationality and may be considered to encompass 'imagination'. See Williams, *On Augustine*, p. 136, where God is held to be 'endless awareness, intelligence and love'.

10 Williams, *The Edge of Words*, p. 101.

11 Williams, *The Edge of Words*, p. 102.

12 Williams, *The Edge of Words*, p. xii.

13 Rowan Williams, 'Beginning with the Incarnation' in *On Christian Theology: Challenges in Contemporary Theology* (Malden, MA: Blackwell, 2000), p. 85.

14 Williams, 'Beginning with the Incarnation', p. 85.

15 Rowan Williams, 'Language, Reality and Desire in Augustine's *De Doctrina*', *Literature and Theology* 3.2 (1989), pp. 138–50. This essay was reprinted unchanged in *On Augustine*, except for the final pages (pp. 56–8), which pick up Carol Harrison's thesis concerning the 'delight' aroused by 'truthful' language and Edward Morgan's argument that it is through the materiality of language that the infinitely different God is made known.

16 Augustine's semiotics have been studied extensively in relation to classical Greek rhetorical theory. See, for example, the article by R. A Markus, considered by Williams to be seminal, 'St Augustine on Signs', *Phronesis* 2.1 (1957), pp. 60–83. See also the collection of essays edited by Richard Leo Enos and Roger Thompson, *The Rhetoric of St Augustine of Hippo: De Doctrina Christiana and the Search for a Distinctly Christian Rhetoric* (Waco, TX: Baylor University Press, 2008). A study that examines the theological foundation of Augustine's language theory is Edward Morgan's *The Incarnation of the Word: The Theology of Language of Augustine of Hippo* (London: T&T Clark International, 2010).

17 Augustine, *On Christian Doctrine*, trans. J. F. Shaw (Mineola, NY: Dover, 2009), 1:3 and 1:4.

18 See, for example, Markus, 'St Augustine on Signs', p. 63.

19 Augustine, *On Christian Doctrine*, 1:2.

20 Williams, *On Augustine*, p. 43.

21 Williams, *On Augustine*. In this respect Augustine may be seen as anticipating the more recent 'science' of hermeneutics.

22 Augustine, *On Christian Doctrine*, 1:3, 1:4.

23 Augustine, *On Christian Doctrine*, 1:10.

24 Augustine, *On Christian Doctrine*, 1:12.

25 Williams, *On Augustine*, p. 42.

26 Williams, *On Augustine*, p. 45.

27 Williams, *On Augustine*, p. 46.

28 Williams, *On Augustine*, p. 49.

29 Williams, *On Augustine*, p. 46.

30 Williams, *On Augustine*, p. 46.

31 Williams, *On Augustine*, p. 46.

32 Williams, *On Augustine*, p. 46.

33 Williams, *On Augustine*, p. 47.

34 Williams, *On Augustine*, p. 49. The reference is to *Confessions*, VII.18.

35 Williams, *On Augustine*, pp. 47–8.

36 Williams, *On Augustine*, p. 50.

37 For Williams' familiarity with, and response to, postmodern treatments of language and difference, see for example, 'Hegel and the Gods of Postmodernity' and 'Balthasar and Difference' in Mike Higton, ed., *Wrestling with Angels: Conversations in Modern Theology* (Grand Rapids, MI: William B. Eerdmans, 2007).

38 See, for example, Williams, *The Edge of Words*, chs 5 and 6, and *On Augustine*, p. 53.

39 Williams notes (*On Augustine*, p. 55) that this implication has been reluctantly acknowledged by the literary critic Geoffrey Hartman.

40 Williams, *On Augustine*, p. 55.

41 Williams, *On Augustine*, p. 55.

42 Williams, *On Augustine*, p. 55.

43 Williams, *On Augustine*, p. 55.

44 Williams, *On Augustine*, p. 56.
45 Williams, *The Edge of Words*, p. 184.
46 In addition to the debt owed to Augustine, discussed above, Williams draws on the later work of Wittgenstein and the theology of language of the Russian Orthodox theologians Bulkakov, Florovsky and Losev.
47 See Williams, *The Edge of Words*, p. 186, where Williams acknowledges the variety of ways the term 'representation' is employed by different scholars.
48 Williams, *The Edge of Words*, p. 22.
49 Whereas many Hegel interpreters consider *Darstellung* and *Vorstellung* to signify successive stages in the movement of human consciousness towards the goal of absolute reason, Williams insists that Hegel holds that all thinking involves the mutual engagement of mind and matter. *The Edge of Words*, pp. 186–90.
50 Williams, *The Edge of Words*, p. 194. This conclusion is in line with the Thomist concept of the 'participatory' nature of human knowledge in view of the impact exercised on the 'knower' by the object of knowledge.
51 Williams, *The Edge of Words*, p. 194.
52 Williams, *The Edge of Words*, p. 124.
53 See, for example, *The Handbook of Cognitive Science: An Embodied Approach*, ed. P. Calvo and T. Gomila (Amsterdam: Elsevier, 2008).
54 Williams, *The Edge of Words*, p. 101.
55 Williams, *The Edge of Words*, pp. 98ff.
56 Williams, *The Edge of Words*, p. 98.
57 Williams, *The Edge of Words*, p. 114.
58 Williams, *The Edge of Words*, p. 117.
59 Williams, *The Edge of Words*, p. 116.
60 See Williams, *The Edge of Words*, chs 2 and 3.
61 Williams, *The Edge of Words*, p. 69.
62 Reproduced in Williams, *On Christian Theology*, pp. 197–208.
63 Williams, *On Christian Theology*, p. 198.
64 Williams, *The Edge of Words*, pp. 72–88.
65 Williams, *The Edge of Words*, p. 83.
66 Williams, *The Edge of Words*, p. 193.
67 Williams, *The Edge of Words*, pp. 83–5.
68 Williams, *The Edge of Words*, pp. 184–5.
69 Williams, *The Edge of Words*, p. 128.
70 Williams, *The Edge of Words*, p. 148.
71 Williams, *The Edge of Words*, p. 159.
72 Williams, *The Edge of Words*, p. 169.
73 Williams, *The Edge of Words*, p. 170.
74 Williams, *The Edge of Words*, p. 175.
75 Williams, *The Edge of Words*, p. 183.
76 Williams, *The Edge of Words*, p. 173.
77 Williams, *The Edge of Words*, p. 64.
78 Williams, *The Edge of Words*, p. 62.
79 Williams, *The Edge of Words*, pp. 123–4.
80 Williams, *The Edge of Words*, p. 124.
81 Williams, *The Edge of Words*, p. 124.
82 Williams, *The Edge of Words*, p. 124.

# 8

# *Poiesis* I: 'Making Other'

## Introduction

Chapter 7 presented us with an image of a communicative universe vibrating with the energy of divine love. It is a universe in which all that exists 'speaks' of its Creator who, in bringing a finite world into being, made it 'other'. In this chapter we explore the significance Williams attributes to the activity of *poiesis*, the human imaginative capacity for 'making other'.

Understood in its broadest sense, *poiesis* includes all forms of technological invention, as well as the skills involved in craftsmanship[1] and in literary, artistic and musical creation. Drawing on his own experience as a poet, and on the work of Hans Urs von Balthasar and Jacques Maritain, Williams argues that artistic creation, the act of 'making other', is the distinctive vocation of those beings who bear the image of the God who is Trinity of Otherness and the source of the otherness of finite creation. Created in God's image, humanity is called to use its capacity to 'make other' for the purpose of cooperating with God in bringing the created order to fulfilment.

Setting the scene for the chapter is a reflection on a poem that exemplifies the poetic vocation of 'making other'. The poem serves as the link between the Christological hermeneutic of language identified in Chapter 7 and the Thomist analogy of participation underpinning the aesthetical theology discussed in Chapter 8. It leads into an overview of the aesthetical theories of the neo-Thomist scholars Balthasar and Maritain, whose influence was significant for Williams' aesthetics. The chapter concludes with a discussion of Williams' distinctive contribution to aesthetical theology, giving further insight into the theological significance he attributes to imagination.

Chapter 8 thus serves as the theoretical springboard for the discussion of Williams' poetry and his views on tragedy and narrative that will be the subject of Chapter 9.

## Penrhys

The ground falls sharply: into the broken glass,
into the wasted mines, and turds are floating
in the well. Refuse.

May: but the wet, slapping wind is native here,
not fond of holidays. A dour council cleaner,
it lifts discarded

Cartons and condoms and a few stray sheets
of newspaper that the wind sticks
across his face –

The worn sub-Gothic infant, hanging awkwardly
around, glued to a thin mother.
Angelus Novus:

Backing into the granite future, wings spread,
head shaking at the recorded day,
no, he says, refuse,

Not here. Still, the wind drops sharply.
Thin teenage mothers by the bus stop
shake wet hair,

Light cigarettes. One day my bus will come, says one;
they laugh. More use 'n a bloody prince,
says someone else.

The news slips to the ground, the stone dries off,
smoke and steam drift uphill
and tentatively

Finger the leisure centre's tense walls and stairs.
the babies cry under the sun,
they and the thin girls

Comparing notes, silently on shared
unwritten stories of the bloody stubbornness
of getting someone born.

## POIESIS I: 'MAKING OTHER'

Presented here is the conjunction of infinite and finite, a conjunction which is transformative for finite reality. On the top of a hill in Wales stands a statue of Mary and Child, erected in 1953 to commemorate the site of a medieval Marian shrine, formerly a popular pilgrimage destination. Below is a bus stop where teenage mothers from the nearby council estate gather with their babies to wait for the bus. Linking the two is the 'wet, slapping wind' that blows the wretched 'refuse' of human occupation – 'cartons, condoms and a few stray sheets/of newspaper' – across the Child's face and down to the group below. The linking wind challenges the listener/reader to see the scenes above and below the hill in terms of each other. The Marian shrine on the hilltop, the one-time visible site of God's presence, is now desolate and desecrated, with turds floating in the holy well. All that remains is a 'sub-Gothic' stone statue standing as a reminder of the original statue, burned to ashes in 1538. We find ourselves asking whether God is present anywhere now, and if so, where?

The two middle stanzas evoke the pitiful, frail humanity of both the teenage mothers and the Child who is God in human flesh. Resembling Klee's *Angelus Novus*, the Child, glued 'awkwardly' to his 'thin' mother, yearns to fly away and so 'refuse' the squalid 'refuse' of human existence.[2] Yet it is the poignant stoicism of his gaunt human mother that holds him fast to the 'granite future' that is his destiny. In these verses is the answer to our question, since we see the infinite God represented in the only form by which the divine may be known, that of the finite frail humanity of Jesus of Nazareth.

Here too we have the context in which God's loving action is most fully made manifest: earthly reality at its dreariest. These stanzas disclose the only way in which we may apprehend the truth of God. In the group of thin, cigarette-smoking teenage mothers, holding their crying babies and dreaming of the 'bloody prince' who will rescue them from their life of squalor, we are given a glimpse of the infinite possibility opened up by the event represented by the statue. Ironically present in the form of the child is indeed the 'bloody prince' whose birth, death and resurrection have brought hope and renewal.

Just as these girls, like Mary, already have knowledge of 'the bloody stubbornness' of bringing new life to birth, so, with Mary, they may now share something of her responsive 'Yes' to the vocation of bearing God to the world. The babies they hold may now be brothers and sisters to the child borne by Mary. As depicted by the statue erected amid human misery, the conjunction of infinite and finite has definitively occurred. The event it represents has irrevocably changed the world and all within it. All mothers, all people, and all things may now be truly seen as *other* in the light of the transformation wrought by the Child, son of Mary, Son of God.

It is the capacity to bring out the otherness of the divine dimension present even within such mundane, desolate and seemingly hopeless situations that most powerfully characterizes Williams' imaginative vision. It is revealed not only in his poetry but also in his preaching and his reflections on art and literature, calling reader and listener to sense something of that energy of love that, in Williams' vision, holds the finite realm, even at its darkest, within the all-encompassing embrace of the infinite God.

The arts are accordingly regarded by Williams as of crucial importance for gaining insight into God's relation to the world. An early article, 'Poetic and Religious Imagination', published in 1977, sets out what is for him a fundamental purpose of the arts: 'to make an *option* about reality ... to struggle towards a vision of the contradictory world'.[3] Williams' *Grace and Necessity* draws on the thought of Maritain to provide the metaphysical scaffolding for his conception of art as manifesting the 'invisible substance' of the world as the free recipient of God's generative love.[4] Elsewhere Williams recognizes the debt owed to Balthasar, whose retrieval of the theological significance of Beauty helped to revive interest in aesthetics as a theological category.[5] The discussion of Williams' aesthetics therefore begins with an exploration of the influence of the Swiss theologian on the development of Williams' aesthetic theory.

## Balthasar and the analogy of beauty

Three aspects of Balthasar's theological aesthetics are particularly important for Williams. The first is the claim that God is initially encountered through the perception of a certain 'radiance' within created existence, the radiance that is the 'splendour of Being' itself.[6] Basic to this claim is Balthasar's reassertion of the inseparable interrelationship of the classical transcendental properties of Being: the Beautiful, the Good and the True. The premise is that the properties of Beauty, Goodness and Truth are integral to divine Being. Since everything that exists is derived from God, all being reflects something of that beauty, goodness and truth.

It is the beauty encountered in the created order that first draws us towards the divine Being. So Balthasar reminds us that 'God does not come primarily as teacher for us ("true") or as a useful "redeemer" for us ("good") but for *himself*, to display and radiate the splendour of his eternal triune life in that "disinterestedness" which true love has in common with true beauty.'[7]

Evident in this statement is the Balthasarian synthesis of classical philosophy and Christian theology: the philosophical transcendentals are revealed to be properties not of impartial Being but of the Being of the God revealed in Christ who is Love. Williams can therefore describe Balthasar's approach as that of 'coming to God through ... the bridge half-built from the human sense of the divine and the human sense of beauty'.[8] The bridge exists as the initiative of 'disinterested' divine desire, the love that, for Balthasar, is the essence of Trinitarian Being.[9] As the source of creation, that love impels, and seeks response from, the beings created in the divine image. The impulse for responsive love thus permeates the created order and is identified by Balthasar as the 'inner *eros*' of the world's reality which seeks its fulfilment in God.[10]

It is Jesus Christ who enables us to see the 'inner *eros*' of the finite world. Key to Balthasar's metaphysic is the Christological interpretation given to the Platonic concept of 'a unifying ideal form holding all things together, a pattern of divine rationality in and through which all specific intelligible forms are related to their divine source'.[11] In Christ Jesus, the 'ideal form' which 'hold[s] all things together' has taken human flesh within the conditions of finite materiality.[12] Manifest in the person of the incarnate Christ is not only the true relation between finite and infinite, but also very Form (*Gestalt*) of reality itself.

Through the events of Christ's life, death and resurrection, finite minds are also offered a glimpse of the nature of divine Being. They disclose the startling truth that infinite Being is revealed as kenotic and ecstatic love, freely giving life to that which is other than divine.[13] Finite reality, as the object of that love, is viewed by Balthasar as reproducing the same other-oriented movement of self-dispossessive love.[14] Possessing something of the mysterious 'inexhaustible quality' of its Creator, it is seen as moving towards 'being understood and delighted in'.[15] It is thus a limitless source of artistic creativity, giving rise to ever-new possibilities for representation.

The third aspect of Balthasar's aesthetic of significance for Williams is his treatment of analogy.[16] Balthasar stresses that analogy is to be understood only through the lens of Christology. It is not simply a matter of grasping the natural similarities between Creator and creation; more significant are the differences between them, and especially the immeasurable difference between the divine and human perspectives revealed in the 'dereliction of the cross and the silence of Holy Saturday'.[17]

So significant is the Holy Saturday silence for Balthasar that it becomes for him the foundation of his whole understanding of the divine purpose, leading him to assert that 'it is for the sake of this day that the Son became man.'[18] As Williams argues in the essay, 'Balthasar and the Trinity', the utter alienation from the Father which Christ experienced at his death not only highlights the depth of divine love but also brings into sharp relief the dimension of otherness that is constitutive of the divine life.[19]

The argument, as explicated by Williams, is that the dying Jesus' cry of abandonment on the cross and his separation from the Father in death reveal God as existing as the opposite of God, as not-God, as dead in the separation of hell. It is thereby concluded that 'God must be such as to make it possible for divine life to live in the heart of its own opposite.'[20] God's infinite life may be present even within the finite limits of sin and death.

The further conclusion follows that, since God remains God even in the state of being totally other than God (a dead human being), otherness/difference must be intrinsic to divine Being. Within the Godhead, the otherness of the Son consists in the eternal self-giving of the Father in an act of such utter kenosis that it is described by Bulgakov as 'self-devastation'.[21] It is a giving of divine life without remainder, such that the Father's identity is the total self-giving of outpoured love, while the identity of the Son is the complete self-gift of responsive love.[22]

The divine life is therefore one of infinite difference and thus of 'infinite *mutual freedom*'.[23] Summarizing Balthasar's Trinitarianism, Williams writes:

> The Father does not determine the Son, but rather gives the Son infinite space to be who he is. And in this free being-who-he-is, in free acceptance of the freedom the Father has given, the Son gives infinite space to the Father to be who *he* is; out of that free return of loving gift comes the Holy Spirit, given life in freedom by the Father and Son so that creatures may be brought into the Son's total response to the Father.[24]

The divine life of freely given interactive otherness allows for the possibility of authentic created freedom. Operating within the otherness of creation, such freedom finds its fulfilment when, following the model of divine freedom, it is realized as the kenotic, ecstatic giving-of-self in love. As Balthasar expresses it, the 'letting-go' of divine being allows what is not God to exist. Creation exists as other than God, having its own integrity of otherness, while remaining radically dependent on its divine source. As discussed in Chapter 3, Williams' position is that any theory of analogy faithful to Christian revelation must account for this otherness-in-continuity and for a conception of finite freedom which, in its kenotic 'letting-go of control for the sake of the other', allows for humanity's participation in divine Being.

Writing in the Foreword to John Saward's study of Balthasar, Williams sums up his appreciation of Balthasar's theological aesthetics:

[Balthasar] is ... interested in uncovering the kind of analogy or juxtaposition of Christian and non-Christian worlds that can fuse both in a transfiguring perception – a perception of the God who is able to be present, to be real, in all those places where he seems most signally absent. Such is the God who is with us as Jesus, crucified and descending into Hell.[25]

As already evidenced in the poem 'Penrhys', and as Chapter 9 will further argue, 'the God present ... in all those places where he seems most signally absent' is of crucial importance for Williams' own aesthetic theory and poetic practice.

## Maritain and poetry as ontology

Like Balthasar, Maritain sets out to construct a theological aesthetic on the foundation of a Thomist metaphysic of Being. He differs from Balthasar in the emphasis he places on the *process* of artistic creation, a process considered analogous to, and derived from, divine creativity. Maritain is concerned to uncover the intuitive, preconscious stirring of spirit which is the genesis of a work of art.

This stirring is aroused by an intuitive perception of the 'divine art' that is created reality. So Maritain declares that God is 'the First Poet', who, 'in an act of intellection which is His essence and His very Existence', freely creates from nothing.[26] God's act of creating is accordingly 'the supreme analogate of poetry',[27] the term 'poetry' being here understood as applying to all forms of 'inspired' creative expression.[28] As activity, 'poetry' is 'engaged in the free creativity of spirit',[29] and thus resembles divine creativity in that it too is an 'intellective act', arising from the poet's own spirit. Unlike God, however, the artist/poet can work only with matter already created, namely with the substance of finite reality. The resulting work thus becomes, as Williams declares, 'a claim about reality ... a metaphysical statement'.[30]

Maritain can therefore posit that art and metaphysics pursue the same aim: the discernment of the forms of divine creativity that constitute the matter of the universe. The two disciplines do so in different ways and by means of different kinds of knowledge. Metaphysics is a cognitive activity involving 'the conceptual, logical and discursive exercise of reason'.[31] By contrast, art/poetry is an activity of the practical intellect. It is concerned with 'making' rather than abstract intellection. Since it remains an intellective act, it produces knowledge, the kind of knowledge that Maritain calls 'connatural'[32] or 'poetic' knowledge.[33] Such knowledge emerges from preconsciousness, from the capacity of the human spirit to intuit the energy of divine creativity within the material world.[34] He argues that 'Of itself poetic intuition proceeds from the natural and supremely spontaneous movement of the soul which seeks itself by communicating with things in its capacity as a spirit endowed with senses as passions.'[35]

The resultant knowledge is 'connatural' in that it is a union of 'both the reality of the things of the world and the subjectivity of the poet'.[36] It is knowledge realized not in the form of concepts but as a work of creative expression, disclosing the artist's intuitive awareness of the spiritual dimension of created reality.[37] Art has therefore the capacity to reveal truth concerning reality: it 'will swarm with meanings, and will say more than it is, and will deliver to the mind at one stroke, the universe in a human countenance'.[38]

Evident here is the notion, dear to Williams, of a 'communicative universe'. So Maritain offers us a vision of a world in which:

> Things are not only what they are. They ceaselessly pass beyond themselves and give more than they have, because from all sides they are permeated by the activating influx of the Prime Cause. They are better and worse than themselves, because being superabounds and because nothingness attracts what comes from nothingness. Thus it is that they communicate with each other in an infinity of fashions and through an infinity of actions and contrasts, sympathies and ruptures ... This mutual communication in existence and in the spiritual flux from which existence proceeds, which is in things, as it were, the secret of creative sources, is perhaps in the last analysis what the poet receives and suffers, and grasps in the night of his own Self, or knows as unknown.[39]

Artists and poets thus have the vocation of making evident the metaphysical structure of created reality, permeated as it is by divine energy, and painfully grasped by the artist in 'an unpredictable experiential insight', which can be expressed only in the form of the resultant work.[40] The work thus created accordingly acts as a sign, indicative of the inner life both of the material world and of the artist.

As sign, it points to the intricate interconnectivity of the created order reflected in 'infinite mirrors of analogy',[41] and thus gives rise to a multitude of meanings. As work of art, through the uniting of the artist's subjectivity with the inner substance of a material object, it effects a new, hitherto undetected, expression of the finite world, thereby opening to the contemplative viewer/reader/listener a 'vision of reality-beyond-reality, an experience of the secret meaning of things'.[42] The work of art may thus be seen as a continuation of the work of God in the world, in the sense that it recombines finite matter into a previously unforeseen form. Unlike God's creation, however, the human artist's work is always imperfect, bearing as it does the mark of human finitude.

Maritain is concerned to maintain that art serves neither ideology nor self-revelation and is never mere imitation. True art is that which emerges from this process of disinterested poetic intuition, and it is only in such works that beauty is revealed. By 'beauty', he means not a work's outward appearance but its inner qualities of integrity, proportion and brilliance of form,[43] qualities that, according to Aquinas, are intuitively grasped by the intellect and which give delight to the senses.[44]

Clothed in the terminology and thought forms of Neo-Scholasticism, Maritain's aesthetic theology comes across as foreign to the contemporary mind. As pointed out by John Milbank,[45] Maritain's metaphysics focuses 'primarily upon being rather than God', as is evidenced by his use of terms such as the 'Illuminating Intellect' or 'First Cause'. Milbank further notes that Maritain's conception of analogy is limited to proper proportionality, with little account taken of attribution.[46] Absent from Milbank's discussion is the fact that Maritain's understanding of analogy fails to take adequate account of the otherness of God detected by Balthasar, the otherness that remains present even in the annihilation of death. Milbank's discussion of Maritain's aesthetic theory does, however, highlight the significance of the Thomist participatory conception of knowledge, which, 'elicited by desire',[47] both incorporates and respects the difference of the material other, thereby effecting the transformation of both self and other that is realized in a work of art.

## Williams and Maritain

Williams' early interest in the metaphysical foundation of Maritain's aesthetics is evidenced in the 1977 essay, 'Poetic and Religious Imagination'. In that essay he draws on Maritain's discussion of the ontological dimension of poetry. According to Maritain, the poet operates at the frontier of human knowledge,[48] with language as the medium for 'the "recomposition" of a world more real than the reality offered to the senses'.[49] Williams expands on Maritain's argument by stressing the *judgement* integral to poetic 'recomposition'. By adding to what already exists, poets point to the inadequacy of any conception of reality and of the language in which it is expressed.[50]

Poetry is thus essentially ironic in its recognition of the incompleteness of all attempts to give language to reality. Nevertheless, says Williams, the poet has the task of offering a 'recommitment to the world'. It is a recommitment undertaken at the cost of a journey into the 'dark night' of frustration and silence. Such a recommitment acknowledges that, while total understanding is impossible, the poetic work is an expression of hope, a hope-filled trust in the ultimate transformation of the world. Like the Christian believer, the poet wrestles with the as-yet-unknown, struggling at the frontier of knowledge to voice the glimpses of a reality infinitely greater than that which is accessible to the human senses.

Less anguished than the 1977 essay, and written almost 30 years later, *Grace and Necessity* takes up the same theme, with a more positive focus on the truth-telling potential of artistic creation as a product of the human imagination.[51] Primarily concerned with Maritain's insights into the whole process of artistic creation, Williams turns to recent psycho-analytic theory to seek support for Maritain's claim that poetic intuition is a form of intelligence that provides access to aspects of reality beyond the range of ordinary perception.[52] He concludes that art '"dispossesses" us of our habitual perception and restores to reality a dimension that necessarily escapes our conceptuality and our control'.[53] It puts us in touch with 'energies and activities that are wholly outside the scope of representation and instrumental reason' and is therefore related to the sacred.[54]

It is the capacity of art to convey to the human spirit something of the truth and energy of the sacred that is of greatest interest to Williams, serving as the basis for his aesthetic theology and for his analysis of the work of David Jones and Flannery O'Connor.

Entitled 'Material Words', Williams' chapter on the work of the Welsh artist and poet David Jones locates the key to Jones's work in Maritain's conception of 'poetry as ontology'.[55] Jones, says Williams, sees the universe as 'inextricably both material and significative, where things carry significance beyond what they tangibly are'.[56] In such a universe, with its complex interrelationships, material objects teem with a multitude of meanings, while the language expressing those meanings is inevitably drawn from the material world. In reference to Jones's thought, Williams can therefore state that: 'Words are material communication; things are material words.'[57] A painting is accordingly a form of language, while a poem expresses the materiality of the world.

Unsurprisingly then, Jones employs the same technique for both his painting and poetry. It is the technique of multiple layering of lines, perspectives, images, ideas, history, myth, all superimposed on each other to convey the multiple resonances of meaning and the intricate interconnectivity of material human existence. Holding together these 'chains of allusion and connection' is the central meaning which, for Jones, gives significance to all other meanings, the meaning displayed in the cross of

Christ.[58] So, in his paintings, the cross may often be discerned amid the tangle of overlapping lines and images, while, in his poetry, the horrors of war and suffering find expression in crucifixion imagery.

In the essay 'Art and Sacrament', Jones states that the human vocation is that of sign-making; it is the vocation which was fully realized in the Incarnation whereby Jesus became a 'material word', the word that gives all other signs their true meaning.[59] As sign-makers, artists and poets exemplify the calling of all human beings: to make of their lives signs that, like sacraments, point to the sacred reality that permeates and sustains the universe in sacrificial love.

Williams' interest in Flannery O'Connor lies in the way she uses narrative to bring awareness of the obscure and paradoxical movements of divine grace present even within the most destructive of human relationships. As O'Connor herself has claimed, her aim is 'to feel life from the standpoint of the central Christian mystery: that it has, for all its horror, been found by God to be worth dying for'.[60] To do this with integrity, she refuses to impose her own theological beliefs on the reader, but insists that, as in human existence itself, the possibility of divine grace must be shown to be consistent with developments of character and action, and thus emerge from 'the internal *necessity* of [the] work'.[61]

The fictional world created in this way is one which is true to human experience in its potential for horrific destructiveness, but is also open to the totally unexpected ways whereby the 'usually hidden otherness of God' is manifested within the visible materiality of the finite order.[62] In the course of the narrative, the otherness of divine grace is to be found in a character's action or gesture that is 'both totally right and totally unexpected ... both in character and beyond character [suggestive of] both time and eternity'.[63]

Such moments are occasions of intense irony, in that, while 'right', they are nevertheless contrary to what is foreseeable for the character. The irony offers the reader a glimpse of the excess of meaning that lies beyond finite perception. Williams's conclusion is that, in her awareness of the irony inherent in human existence, O'Connor sees more deeply than Maritain. She identifies the necessity integral to finite freedom with its necessary, and often horrific, consequences. At the same time, however, she recognizes that our finite necessity may be met by the excess of divine grace, bringing a realization of the utter 'strangeness of [God's] unconditional love'.[64]

## Williams' theological aesthetic

In the final chapter of *Grace and Necessity*, Williams reworks the insights of Maritain, Jones and O'Connor to articulate his own distinctive vision of art. For him, art is an expression of the human vocation of remaking the world through costly, self-dispossessive love, the love that echoes the kenotic, ecstatic character of divine love.[65] As in *The Edge of Words*, he presents a dynamic image of the material world, vibrating with energy and constantly evolving to generate new forms and new expressions of life.[66] Material existence is shown to be already suffused with meaning, not only with the meanings accorded by human language and culture but also with the meanings given by God, its Creator.

The artist's task is to be obedient to the reality he or she perceives, recognizing that reality is not static but a 'mobile pattern' in constant flux, somewhat akin to music.[67] The act of artistic perception is accordingly never complete; there is always more to see, uncover and know. Interactive and generative, perception involves an interrelationship between the perceiving subject with his or her complex of associations, and the excess of meanings already associated with the object perceived.

Following Aquinas, Hegel and Maritain, and supported by recent research into consciousness,[68] Williams attests to the participatory nature of knowledge gained from perception, stating that 'what is involved in knowing something is more like re-enacting a performance than labelling an object.'[69] Corresponding to Maritain's concept of 'poetic intuition', knowledge of this kind assumes that there is an analogous generative relation between the symbolic life of the object known and 'the symbolic structure of [the human] mind'.[70] Such knowledge involves awareness of the otherness of the object known, and of its life as both independent of, and existing within, the artist's mind.[71] Williams states that:

> Art is an acute case of knowledge in general. It is that form of intellectual life in which the generativity of the world we encounter and experience is allowed to work in ways that are free from many of the requirements of routine instrumental thinking.[72]

Significant for the argument of this study is the link subsequently developed between this form of knowledge and the activity of human imagination. Williams' exploration of the work of Dostoevsky and of Jones leads him to the conclusion that:

> Imagination produces not a self-contained mental construct but a vision that escapes control, that brings with it its shadow and its margins, its

absences and ellipses, a *dimensional* existence ... The degree to which art is 'obedient' ... is manifest in the degree to which the product has dimension outside its relation to the producer, the sense of alternative space around the image, of real time and contingency in narrative, of hinterland.[73]

When the above two quotations are read in conjunction with one another, the identity between the knowledge involved in artistic creativity and the activity labelled 'imagination' is highlighted. Both are a 'form of intellectual life' emerging from the preconscious, both deal with the reality of the finite world but in ways that escape the control of instrumental reason, both give rise to novel, unforeseen recompositions of the material world. The conclusion is that it is the operation of imagination which is signified by Maritain's references to poetic intuition and by Williams' discussion of the generative, participatory knowledge associated with a work of art. While the term 'imagination' is rarely used by either writer, the substance of their argument may be considered to apply to the way imagination functions as an indispensable means of accessing the invisible spiritual dimensions of finite reality beyond the reach of empirical investigation.

Accessed in this way by imagination, the knowledge gained by the artist is never private. A work of art, in whatever medium, exists as an independent phenomenon, having a presence of its own, the 'real presence' identified by George Steiner. It offers itself to be known by viewer, reader, spectator, listener as a medium whereby the artist's participatory knowledge becomes available as a new and challenging perspective to others. Williams' claim is that a work of art 'makes us present to ourselves in a fresh way, [engaging] us in dialogue with ourselves ... the object ... the artist and with what the artist is responding to'.[74] The knowledge produced by artistic creation serves as an essential complement to the perspectives provided by instrumental reason.

The work of artistic creation is therefore an immensely serious activity and, says Williams, has integrity only when it results from the labour of costly, self-dispossessive love.[75] The artist struggles not only to discern the excess of life of the phenomenon observed but also to reshape that life so as to convey its truth within another medium. In that process, the artist's own agenda and personal satisfaction take second place to the patient attentiveness required by the effort to uncover the truth of the phenomenon observed. That effort is ongoing, since finite reality is not static but is in a process of constant becoming.

Williams' conclusion is that 'The artist may be a "hunter of forms", but the life that the artist engages with is a shedder of forms, dispossessing itself of this or that shape so as to be understood and remade.'[76] As a consequence, the repeated process of understanding and representation undertaken by the artist is inseparably linked with the world's continual process of becoming.[77] In Williams' view, the critical significance of artistic creation accordingly lies in its contribution not merely to knowledge of reality but, more importantly, to the realization of what the created order is destined to become. He argues that 'the world's reality is always asymptotically approaching its fullness by means of the response of the imagination – the assumption of an "ideal" fullness of perception in which things reach their destiny.'[78]

Here we find a recapitulation of Williams' 1977 assertion of both the limits of human knowledge and the role of the poet/artist in continuing to find meaning within finite existence. In *Grace and Necessity*, however, the poet/artist's contribution is not only to enable awareness of a depth to the material universe beyond that which is observable but also, by the action of making, to '*facilitate* ... [the world's] generative capacity'.[79] In this role, the artist's responsibility is close to that of the priest, to draw out a creative response to the continuing generative energy of the world.[80]

By responding in this way to the generative excess of the material environment, the artist is actually obeying what Williams discerns as 'the constant pattern of "making other" that runs through ... reality'.[81] It is the impulse to 'make other' that, he claims, implies a certain consonance between the practice of art and the doctrine of the Trinity. As discussed in Chapter 4, God is seen by Williams as the eternal source of self-dispossessing love, ever generating the responsive Other, the Son, together with the Spirit, the Other, who, as 'the bearer of the inexhaustibl[e] divine life', makes otherness possible within creation.[82] The created order is accordingly both 'grounded in God' but also 'radically different from God'.[83]

The human capacity for 'making other', especially evidenced in artistic creativity, is not an imitation of divine creativity which, out of pure, gratuitous love, makes from nothing that which is essentially other than God. Human creativity, by contrast, is always *responsive* to what already exists. It is first a discovery of the otherness that is the densely textured, generative complexity of the material environment we inhabit. It is also an exploratory encounter with the mysterious otherness of the people we relate to daily. Finally, in the act of creation, the artist is forced to confront not only the external other but also the unsuspected inner other, namely the possibilities and impediments hidden within the self. Williams can therefore claim that 'the process of artistic production is a matter of self-discovery', 'the production of a self'.[84]

To 'make other', argues Williams, is to make space within the self for that other to be present.[85] It necessitates a process of inner 'withdrawal'[86] from any preconceived purpose for the other. It requires the artist to let go of the desire to control the outcome and instead to allow the other to reveal its own inner life. It is in this movement of letting go to give space to the other that human creativity comes closest to the essence of divine creation. Both involve an act of self-dispossession, the dispossession that does not seek to capture the object observed but rather to acknowledge and honour its existence as a 'radically independent reality'. It is a movement of love that gives of itself to allow the other to be truly itself, truly other. Such love, says Williams, is 'both the *gift* of self and the gift of *self*'.[87] In that self-giving it fulfils 'the human vocation to *caritas*' and is thus equivalent to holiness, the letting go in order to 'make other'.[88]

At this point, Williams' dense reasoning becomes even more gnomic. Into the argument, he introduces the term 'imagination', employed here in relation both to God and to humanity. He writes:

> A holiness ... that was seen simply as a static mirroring of God's perfection would in fact not be real holiness; God's life exercises its own perfection in the imagining of a world into life, so that the exercise of the artist's imagination fills out what must be the heart of holy life for human creatures. The artist imagines a world that is both new and secretly inscribed in all that is already seen ... and in so doing imagines himself, projects an identity that is fully in motion towards its now ungraspable completion. In this bestowing of life on self and the world, the artist uncovers the generative love that is at the centre of holiness. There is no 'godlikeness' without such bestowal, such 'imagining' into life.[89]

Here we find a rare specific reference to the theological significance of the phenomenon of imagination. In reference to God, imagination is here synonymous with divine generativity, the self-dispossessing kenotic generativity that is the essence of the divine being. In reference to humanity, imagination is associated with the exercise of that self-dispossessing love which cherishes all that is other and seeks to bring forth its truth in a new form. It is that generative, self-dispossessing love that enables growth into holiness, and thus into one's identity as image of God. Through the exercise of imaginative, life-giving love, human beings realize their vocation to cooperate with God in bringing the created order to its fulfilment. The creative labour of artists thus serves as an indispensable model for the whole of humanity.[90]

Williams' identification of 'godlikeness' with 'imagining into life' is perhaps his most explicit statement concerning the nature and purpose of the human capacity for imagination. The analogy between human and divine creativity is accordingly that of continuity-in-difference, being both similar and different. Human creativity resembles divine generativity in that it too is free to 'make other'. It involves a movement of self-dispossession in order to be fully available to the radical otherness of the object studied. It offers what Maritain calls 'connatural' knowledge, a term that assumes a metaphysic that views the world as a multi-dimensional complex of interconnected energy, the energy of divine *eros*. It reminds us that the God who remains present even within what is radically other than God, in death itself, makes it possible for human creators to do what would be otherwise beyond imagination, namely to discern divine grace even in the most horrific situations. That is why authors such as Flannery O'Connor can portray the paradox of grace through the vehicle of irony, as will be discussed more fully in Chapter 9.

## Conclusion

In this chapter, I have shown that Williams' conception of imagination encompasses the human creative capacity for 'making other'. With its source in the infinite generativity of divine *eros*, creative imagination requires a similar costly self-dispossessive movement of love towards the other. The resultant knowledge is participatory, giving access to dimensions of reality unavailable to empirical investigation and serving to further God's ultimate purposes for the created order.

The aesthetic theory elaborated in this chapter will be explored from a different angle in Chapter 9, where the emphasis is on the human imaginative capacity to 'make strange' and thus raise awareness of the inescapable otherness of our world and its inhabitants.

### Notes

1 See, for example, Rowan Williams, *Being Human: Bodies, Minds, Persons* (London: SPCK, 2018), p. 50.

2 Williams plays on the double meaning of the word 'refuse', which signifies both rubbish and rejection. The refuse swirling in the wind at the top of the hill is replicated at the bottom by the teenage mothers, often considered to be 'human refuse'. It is this human 'refuse' that the Child is tempted to reject in a 'refusal' of his mission.

3 Rowan Williams, 'Poetic and Religious Imagination', *Theology* 80.675 (1977), p. 179.

4 Rowan Williams, *Grace and Necessity: Reflections on Art and Love* (London: Morehouse, 2005), p. 18.

## POIESIS I: 'MAKING OTHER'

5 Todd Breyfogle, 'Time and Transformation: A Conversation with Rowan Williams', *Cross Currents* 45.3 (1995), pp. 304–5; Rupert Shortt, *God's Advocates: Christian Thinkers in Conversation* (Grand Rapids, MI: William B. Eerdmans, 2005), pp. 15–16. Williams was among the group who translated *The Glory of the Lord* into English, his involvement being with Volumes 3, 4 and 5.

6 Cited by Oliver Davies, 'The Theological Aesthetics', in *The Cambridge Companion to Hans Urs von Balthasar*, ed. Edward T. Oakes and David Moss (Cambridge: Cambridge University Press, 2004), p. 134.

7 Hans Urs von Balthasar, 'In Retrospect', in John Riches, ed., *The Analogy of Beauty* (Edinburgh: T&T Clark, 1982), p. 213.

8 Williams in Shortt, *God's Advocates*, p. 15.

9 See, for example, Hans Urs von Balthasar, *The Glory of the Lord, volume 1: Seeing the Form*, tr. Erasmo Leiva-Merikakis (Edinburgh: T&T Clark, 1982), p. 158.

10 Oliver Davies, 'The Theological Aesthetics', pp. 134–5.

11 Rowan Williams, 'Balthasar and the Trinity', in *The Cambridge Companion to Hans Urs Von Balthasar*, ed. Edward T. Oakes and David Moss (Cambridge: Cambridge University Press, 2004), p. 40.

12 Williams, 'Balthasar and the Trinity', p. 41.

13 Williams, 'Balthasar and the Trinity', p. 41.

14 Williams, 'Balthasar and the Trinity', p. 41.

15 Williams, 'Balthasar and the Trinity', p. 41.

16 The influence of Balthasar's teacher, Erich Przywara, is discernible in the treatment of the Thomist doctrine of the *analogia entis* with its insistence on the 'ever greater dissimilarity' between the infinite God and finite creation.

17 Williams, 'Balthasar and the Trinity', p. 37. Howsare argues that, for Balthasar, Jesus Christ is the key to a proper understanding of analogy, 'the difference between God and the world [being located] *within* the difference between the Trinitarian processions'. Rodney A. Howsare, *Balthasar: A Guide for the Perplexed* (London: T&T Clark, 2009), pp. 134–5.

18 Hans Urs von Balthasar, *Mysterium Paschale*, trans. Aidan Nichols, OP (Edinburgh: T&T Clark, 1990); 2nd corrected edn (Grand Rapids, MI: William B. Eerdmans, 1993), p. 49; cited by Williams, 'Balthasar and the Trinity', p. 37.

19 The notion of essential otherness within the Godhead is fundamental for Williams' understanding of both creation and human existence. For his further discussion of otherness in Balthasar's writings, see the essays 'Balthasar and Difference' and 'Balthasar, Rahner and the Apprehension of Being', in Mike Higton, ed., *Wrestling with Angels: Conversations in Modern Theology* (Grand Rapids, MI: William B. Eerdmans, 2007).

20 Williams, 'Balthasar and the Trinity', p. 38.

21 Williams, 'Balthasar and the Trinity', p. 38.

22 Williams, 'Balthasar and the Trinity', p. 39.

23 Williams, 'Balthasar and the Trinity', p. 41.

24 Williams, 'Balthasar and the Trinity', p. 41.

25 Rowan Williams, 'Foreword', in John Saward, *The Mysteries of March: Hans Urs von Balthasar on the Incarnation and Easter* (Washington: Catholic University of America Press, 1990), p. ix.

26 Jacques Maritain, *Creative Intuition in Art and Poetry: The A.W. Mellon Lectures in the Fine Arts* (New York: Meridian Books, 1955), p. 81.

27 Maritain, *Creative Intuition in Art and Poetry*, p. 81.

28 Maritain says that 'Poetry is akin to "*mousikè*, the secret life of all of the arts".' John G. Trapani Jr, *Poetry, Beauty, and Contemplation: The Complete Aesthetics of Jacques Maritain* (Washington: Catholic University of America Press, 2011), p. 164.

29 Maritain, *Creative Intuition in Art and Poetry*, p. 81.

30 Williams, *Grace and Necessity*, pp. 16, 17.

31 Maritain, *Creative Intuition in Art and Poetry*, p. 85.

32 Jacques Maritain, *Art and Scholasticism with Other Essays*, trans. J. F. Scanlan (London: Sheed & Ward, 1946), p. 75.

33 Maritain, *Creative Intuition in Art and Poetry*, p. 85.

34 Maritain, *Creative Intuition in Art and Poetry*, p. 92.

35 Maritain, *Creative Intuition in Art and Poetry*, p. 89.

36 Maritain, *Creative Intuition in Art and Poetry*, p. 89.

37 Maritain refers to 'the spiritual milieu ... activated by the diffuse light of the Illuminating Intellect ... which is the preconscious life of the intellect'. *Creative Intuition in Art and Poetry*, p. 203.

38 Maritain, *Creative Intuition in Art and Poetry*, p. 93.

39 Maritain, *Creative Intuition in Art and Poetry*, p. 92.

40 Maritain, *Creative Intuition in Art and Poetry*, p. 86.

41 Maritain, *Creative Intuition in Art and Poetry*, p. 94.

42 Jacques Maritain, *The Responsibility of the Artist* (New York: Charles Scribner's Sons, 1960), p. 85.

43 Maritain, *Art and Scholasticism*, pp. 22–3. By 'brilliance of form' is meant the inner being of the object which, in its own way, reflects something of the beauty of its divine Creator.

44 For a discussion of Maritain's Thomist conception of beauty, see Trapani, *Poetry, Beauty, and Contemplation*, ch. 10.

45 John Milbank, 'Scholasticism, Modernism and Modernity', *Modern Theology* 22.4 (2006), pp. 651–71.

46 Milbank, 'Scholasticism, Modernism and Modernity', p. 652.

47 Milbank, 'Scholasticism, Modernism and Modernity', p. 653.

48 The original title for Williams' article was borrowed from Maritain's essay, 'The Frontiers of Poetry' in *Art and Scholasticism*.

49 Williams, 'Poetic and Religious Imagination', p. 179.

50 Williams, 'Poetic and Religious Imagination', p. 178.

51 Williams, *Grace and Necessity*, p. x. The material in this book was delivered as the 2005 Clark Lectures with the title, 'Grace, Necessity and Imagination: Catholic Philosophy and the Twentieth Century Artist'.

52 Williams refers to the studies of preconscious thought undertaken by the clinical psychologist Michael Maltby, and the analytic theorist Ignacio Matte-Blanco, which lend support to Maritain's account of the operation of poetic intuition in the realm of the preconscious. *Grace and Necessity*, pp. 32–6.

53 Williams, *Grace and Necessity*, p. 37.

54 Williams, *Grace and Necessity*, p. 38.

55 Williams, *Grace and Necessity*, p. 75.

56 Williams, *Grace and Necessity*, p. 75.

57 Williams, *Grace and Necessity*, p. 75.

58 Williams, *Grace and Necessity*, p. 82.

59 Williams, *Grace and Necessity*, p. 82.
60 Flannery O'Connor, *Mystery and Manners: Occasional Prose* (London: Faber, 1972), p. 146, cited by Williams in *Grace and Necessity*, p. 94.
61 Williams, *Grace and Necessity*, p. 97.
62 Williams, *Grace and Necessity*, p. 103.
63 Williams, *Grace and Necessity*, p. 104.
64 Williams, *Grace and Necessity*, p. 131. Here we find the explanation for Williams' title.
65 Williams, *Grace and Necessity*, p. 165.
66 Williams, *Grace and Necessity*, pp. 154–5.
67 Williams, *Grace and Necessity*, p. 138. In *A Century of Poetry: 100 Poems for Searching the Heart* (London: SPCK, 2022), p. 232, Williams reflects that 'Music … provides … a compelling metaphor for God's presence in the world, the presence of rhythm within the music, neither something that can be abstracted from the actual sequence of sounds nor something that depends on the sounds themselves.'
68 Williams, *Grace and Necessity*, pp. 135–7. Here Williams draws on discussions of the nature of consciousness by the cognitive scientists Douglas R. Hofstadter and Daniel C. Dennett in *The Mind's Eye: Fantasies and Reflections on Self and Soul* (London: Penguin Books, 1981).
69 Williams, *Grace and Necessity*, p. 138.
70 Williams, *Grace and Necessity*, p. 140.
71 Williams, *Grace and Necessity*, pp. 141, 143.
72 Williams, *Grace and Necessity*, pp. 140–1.
73 Williams, *Grace and Necessity*, p. 147.
74 Williams, *Grace and Necessity*, p. 150.
75 Williams, *Grace and Necessity*, p. 151.
76 Williams, *Grace and Necessity*, p. 153.
77 Williams, *Grace and Necessity*, pp. 153–4.
78 Williams, *Grace and Necessity*, p. 154.
79 Williams, *Grace and Necessity*, pp. 154–5. The italics are mine.
80 Williams, *Grace and Necessity*, p. 155, notes the similarity between his concept of the world's 'gratuitous capacity' and Balthasar's notion of the material order permeated by divine energy.
81 Williams, *Grace and Necessity*, p. 157. Rejecting what he calls 'vulgarized Darwinism', Williams' view of evolution more closely resembles Meister Eckhart's concept of *ebullitio*, an overflowing of life and energy, which is a matter not merely of 'environmental adjustment' but also of 'exploration and reformation'.
82 Williams, *Grace and Necessity*, p. 159.
83 Williams, *Grace and Necessity*, p. 159.
84 Williams, *Grace and Necessity*, pp. 162–3.
85 Here Williams, like David Jones, grounds making space for the other within the self in the Trinitarian doctrine of the eternal begetting of the Son/Word from the Father which, in the finite temporal context, takes the form of the Incarnation. See Williams, *Grace and Necessity*, p. 164.
86 Williams, *Grace and Necessity*, p. 161.
87 Williams, *Grace and Necessity*, p. 164.
88 Williams, *Grace and Necessity*, pp. 165–6.
89 Williams, *Grace and Necessity*, p. 167.
90 Williams, *Grace and Necessity*, p. 166.

# 9

# *Poiesis* II: 'Making Strange'

## Introduction

Chapter 8 set out to explore Williams' understanding of creativity as the act of 'making other'. In Chapter 9, the focus shifts to a fuller consideration of the purpose of human creativity. Here I draw attention to Williams' concept of 'making strange'. To 'make strange' is to enlarge perception by bringing to the forefront of awareness the otherness of the world around us. It operates by disrupting conventional ways of perceiving reality, enabling the viewer/reader/listener to grasp a different way of experiencing human existence, thus enlarging the range of available options.

A poem that 'makes strange' the horror of war brings together the main themes to be explored in this chapter. It will lead into a discussion of Williams' reflections on 'excessive speech' in *The Edge of Words*, to be followed by a study of the excessive modes of speech employed in poetry, narrative and tragedy. From Williams' poetry we gain insight into the ways in which excessive language offers glimpses of the unexpected in ordinary phenomena. The role of narrative in bringing out the paradoxical strangeness of human existence will be examined through Williams' study of Dostoevsky's fiction and will serve as the springboard for his analysis of the importance of tragic drama for increasing awareness of both human finitude and the human capacity for hope.

### Arabic Class in the Refugee Camp (Islamabad 2006)[1]

One by one the marks join up:
easing their way through the broken soil,
the green strands bend, twine,
dip and curl and cast off little drops
of rain. Nine months ago,
the soil broke up, shouting,
crushing its fist on houses, lives,

crops and futures, opening its wordless mouth
to say No. And the green strands
stubbornly grow back. The broken bits
of a lost harvest still let
the precious wires push through
to bind the pain, to join with knots and curls
the small hurt worlds of each
small life, to say another no: no,
you are not abandoned. The rope of words
is handed on, let down from a sky
broken by God's voice, curling and wrapping
each small life into the lines of grace,
the new world of the text that maps
our losses and our longings, so
that we can read humanity again
in one another's eyes, and hear
that the broken soil is not all, after all,
as the signs join up.

The poem is a tender depiction of an outdoor class of refugee children learning to read, write and recite the Koran. Nine months earlier, the earth on which they now sit was torn apart by the 'wordless mouth' of a bomb, 'crushing its fist on houses, lives/crops and futures', bellowing its 'No' to all life. And yet over the period of those nine pregnant months, life has begun to appear again, its persistently stubborn strands of new green shoots replicating the 'knots and curls' of the Arabic script the children are striving to decipher. In growing back, those 'broken bits/ of a lost harvest' are a defiant 'no' to the annihilating 'No' of warfare.

Like the curling twists of the new growth, the script of the Koran becomes a 'rope of words' let down from a sky now broken open not by bombs but by 'God's voice'. Gently 'wrapped' in the words of the Koran, the 'small life' of each child becomes a new story of grace, giving meaning to both past loss and present longing, and acting as a sign that the final word is not that of destruction but is instead the promise of shared humanity.

Evident in the poem are several of the linguistic devices identified by Williams as the means whereby poets seek to bring 'a fresh perspective to birth'[2] and thus to make strange. The poem exemplifies 'the complicating of what seems normal in order to uncover what "normal" perception screens out'.[3] Here an unexpected connection is made between the new life emerging from the ground and the script of the Koran studied by the children. Both are evidence of life emerging as divine grace and are therefore signs of hope amid devastation, of reconciliation in the face of seemingly irreparable division.

Further unexpected connections are evoked by the imagery. The bombing becomes an animate being, 'crushing its fist' and shouting 'No' from a 'wordless mouth'. Contrasted with the bombs' destructive plunge from on high is the Koranic 'rope of words' let down by God, with its own 'no' to the bombs' attempts at annihilation. The 'knots and curls' of green shoot and Arabic script convey the image of lives being gently 'wrapped' by a divine hand. The pattern of lines and line breaks serves to reinforce the meaning of the words: the stubborn persistence of the new life growing back from destruction is conveyed by the carrying over of meaning from one line to the next, as 'the green strands bend, twine/dip and curl' and 'the precious wires push through/to bind the pain.'

Similarly, on two occasions contrasting meanings are juxtaposed and then explicated in the following line, forcing the listener to wait in hope for grace to be revealed. So the 'no' of the bombing is transformed into the 'no' of divine presence, and the 'all' of broken soil and lives is shown to be 'not all, after all', since, in Williams' vision of this scene, the koranic signs of healing hope 'join up' as the final word, thus recapitulating the joining up of the 'marks' of new green life at the end of the first line. The whole content of the poem is accordingly held within the 'lines of grace' which 'join up' horror with hope in human life.

By means of allusion, imagery, word and line patterning, the poem succeeds in communicating what normal perception may grasp only by faith, namely, the operation of divine grace. Mentioned only once, grace may be considered the real subject of the poem. Williams presents us with a vision of a world marred by sin and evil but also permeated by the presence of grace, a presence that enables life and hope to persist even amid devastation. The technical point he is making is that certain aspects of human existence, those that are not susceptible to empirical description, may be given expression only by means of what he calls 'excessive speech'. His analysis of this form of language is discussed in the section that follows.

## Excessive speech: Poetry

The importance accorded by Williams to language which diverges from conventional speech is evidenced by his devoting a whole chapter to it in *The Edge of Words*. Here he argues that it is by pushing language to extremes and putting pressure on it to create new tensions that advances are made in understanding the immeasurable complexity of what we call reality. The difficulties experienced in deciphering the eccentricities of extreme language become 'tool[s] of exploration and discovery' as new insights are gained, new connections discerned, new relationships established.

Referring to Margaret Masterman's work on metaphor, he claims that '"tense despair" precedes intellectual advance', thus inviting us 'to rethink our metaphysical principles'.[4] The work of poets, novelists and playwrights, who push language to extremes in a quest for truthful utterance, is indispensable for gaining insight into the intricate complexities of both the human psyche and the universe in which we are located.

It follows that, for Williams, poetry can never be a mere avocation, a relaxing respite from the serious business of ministry. Poetry, no less than ministry, is a way of realizing the human call to imagine and remake the world in accordance with the creative action of God. As he has written in *A Silent Action*:

[Poetry] require[s] from me, that most demanding of activities, the weaving in of my action, with the action, the act, that is at work around in the universe ... [It is] where *this* reality, me, my words, my perception, meet what is fundamental, God.[5]

The poetry that has come into being through the 'weaving' of Williams' action with the continuing process of divine creativity is a means of enabling the listener/reader to gain a deepened connection with the complex, multifaceted universe that is the exuberant utterance of divine creativity. It puts us in touch with dimensions of existence not readily perceptible and inaccessible to the superficial gaze. It helps us experience the world as strange and other, so that we may come to discern something of the inner truth of the object, landscape, person or situation described. It re-presents in new forms what has become so familiar that it is taken for granted and no longer truly seen.

So, for example, a landscape of drystone walls assumes the new form of a sheet of writing, inscribed with a 'spell' against the wind, and penned by craftsmen skilled at seeing the meaning and possibilities of scattered rock.[6] The human senses are re-presented as though experienced for the first time by an infant newly discovering the surrounding world through the exploration of the five senses, each sense opening a door on to the unknown.[7]

More enlightening still are the new forms given to well-known works of art. Bach's *St Matthew Passion* is transformed into a perilous sea voyage.[8] The *Resurrection* fresco of Piero della Francesca, as re-presented by the poet, forces us to experience the paralysing, time-stopped tension of the moment, just prior to the resurrection, when Christ, 'exhausted, hungry, death running off his limbs', pauses, before stepping once again into the finite world with its imperative demands.[9]

Even more powerful is the poet's re-production, through the medium of words, of the tormented, avoidant gaze of the Pantocrator depicted in the monastery at Daphni.[10] While the reader's inner eye is directed to the pain of the 'bulging eyes' and the 'knotted' arthritic hands of the Christ figure, the listener's ear is oppressed by the 'sweaty', 'leaden' 'heaviness' of the 'congealing galaxies of heat and weight' clogging the dying Saviour's blood. The anguished agony of ultimate divine self-dispossession is here presented to us in double form – the image of the fierce, tormented figure gazing down from the dome of the church is doubled by the heavy, relentless beat of the language as it inexorably moves towards its final gasp.

In all three of these re-presentations of other artists' works, the listener and reader are taken into a new and deeper awareness of the incommensurable pain of self-dispossession that is Christ's passion.

A persistent theme in Williams' work is the insurmountable barrier constituted by the otherness of another person. The medium of poetry, with its multiple associations and indirect allusions, obliges listeners and readers to experience for themselves the struggle involved in seeking to know another person, whose mysterious depths can never be fully plumbed. The opening poem of the 2002 collection gives us four perspectives of the artist Gwen John.[11] Overshadowed by her more famous brother and by her lover, Rodin, she, like St Thérèse of Lisieux, is seen only through her work – through her quiet, domesticated interiors and silent portraits of ordinary women. By means of a cluster of four different representations, Williams gently points to the unreachable inner life of this gifted woman, whose capacity to bring out the luminous quality of the ordinary has become her final 'absolution'. In 'Crossings',[12] the poet anguishes over the gap opened up between lovers, which can be bridged neither by silence nor by the flux of words. Trapped, helplessly inarticulate, yet also unable to remain silent, in the shared bed now turned to stone, the poet wonders whether there was ever a genuine connection between them, 'an assignation/Under the station clock? An intersection/Of complicated routes?' Or whether, like railway travellers, their lives had simply crossed, with no real possibility of mutual understanding.

Even more difficult than getting to know another person is the process of learning to know oneself. According to Williams, it is in the struggle of creative expression, in the effort of discerning and re-presenting the truth of what is seen and experienced, that the poet comes to a deepened knowledge of self. Several poems convey the pain of such knowledge. 'Indoors'[13] and 'Return Journey'[14] remind us that the wounds of the past remain 'fresh' and 'waiting to be collected' from the 'freezer' of memory.[15] 'First Thing'[16] and 'The Night Kitchen: Dreamwork'[17] communicate something of the heaviness of the dread that haunts the poet's mind, even in sleep. 'Alone at Last'[18] leaves us breathlessly counting off the myriad characters jostling just below the level of ordinary awareness, insisting that we can never be truly alone, by ourselves or with another person.

As Williams reminds us in his third collection, *The Other Mountain*, poetry may also be a form of protest, an assertion of the need to resist the forces of oppression and dehumanization.[19] The first poem, 'The Other Mountain: Riding Westward',[20] sets the tone of the collection. The ominously looming mountain of storm clouds that finally crashes down in lashing rain over the Welsh hills becomes for the poet the 'wave' of violence that, set off by unknown hands, repeatedly and mercilessly breaks over the world, sweeping away its helpless victims.

In this collection, a world's worth of atrocities is re-membered: past and present martyrdoms and exiles, the fall of ancient Jerusalem and of Constantinople, the Holocaust and the bombing of Hiroshima and Nagasaki. Significantly, the cry of resistance echoes from poem to poem: we discover the 'few green words' of the pacifist poet Waldo Williams, gaoled for refusing to pay taxes to fund a war;[21] Dylan Thomas, singing 'in his chains';[22] the Jesuit priest Don Pedro, ministering to the victims of Hiroshima;[23] the 'lifted' voice of the Patriarch's cantor in defeated Constantinople;[24] the flowing blood of the slave girl Felicity, rendering her 'sister' to her mistress Perpetua;[25] and the cursed yellow star defiantly worn by Mother Maria Skobstova.[26] These too are the fresh green strands of hope discernible amid death and destruction.

Keenly sensitive to the reiterated 'No' of bigotry and violence, Williams, in his poetry, offers his own form of resistance, his own 'no' to the life-denying 'No' of evil. His poems, like the Arabic of the Koran taught in the refugee camp, or like the dusty pollen 'brewed up [by bees] into food and firelight',[27] become both text and food for hope in a threatened world. As he reminds us, however, such hope comes at a cost. It is the cost displayed by the 'split wood' of an opened Bible that reveals both the pain of the human condition and of the One who bore that pain.[28] It is shown too in the tightly condensed 'Stations of the Gospel',[29] which place a sensitive finger on the pain associated with each of the 24 stations of Jesus' human existence, as portrayed by St John. As evidenced by the ever-renewed company of those who resist, it is a cost that cannot be avoided by all who, with Christ, defiantly hold out hope to a suffering world. It is a cost that, the poet, as a father, knows must be painfully learned anew by each generation when, 'baring skin to be scalded', young people begin to act out the roles imposed by adulthood.[30]

Key to Williams' poetry is the struggle with difficulty. That difficulty is certainly experienced by the listener/reader who, initially plunged into confusion, nevertheless finds that the effort to grasp the poet's vision suddenly sparks unexpected connections and a whole series of allusions that open up new and deepened insight into the phenomenon in question.

As Williams emphasizes, however, the difficulty is initially that of the poet himself, for whom 'poetry [is] a way of coming to terms with and exploring something that isn't yourself.'[31] It is the stubborn, alien otherness of what the poet is trying to grasp that makes the task of poetic creation so demanding. '[P]oets', says Williams, 'are at one level deeply humbled by the patterns in what they say – they don't know quite where it comes from or where it's going to, and they don't quite know whether they can manage what's coming through.'[32]

In *Christian Imagination in Poetry and Polity*, he refers to the poetic process as a kind of 'contemplative pragmatism', an 'attitude of time-taking, patient, absorbing awareness', which involves the 'willingness to look at ... apparently unpromising situations ... long enough and hard enough for God to come to light'.[33] Such patient attentiveness is a form of discipline comparable to spiritual disciplines, since God cannot be captured in words but 'comes to light' unexpectedly, in unforeseen ways and surprising situations.[34]

This tradition of patient, attentive, 'contemplative pragmatism' is, claims Williams, a distinctive contribution that Anglicanism has made not only to poetry but also to social action.[35] It was the willingness to engage attentively with life in all its difficult complexity that, he says, activated not only such public figures as Richard Hooker and William Temple, but also the poets George Herbert, Henry Vaughan, T. S. Eliot and R. S. Thomas. Each of those poets struggled to cling to a God 'whose presence is ... elusive ... dark and ... mysterious',[36] who is to be found 'not in religious places but in the stuff of human relation and in the stuff of the material world'.[37] For them, the dark night of God's absence was a very real experience, their faith being grounded in a theology of the cross.

The determination to represent not only divine presence but also the pain of loss and absence is, for Williams, the mark of authentic poetic attentiveness. He can thus assert that 'Poetry, when it is fully itself, enacts something of the cross and resurrection, abandoning its fluencies and successes in order to press further and further towards that "thin" texture through which truth may perhaps come.'[38]

While Williams rejects the designation of 'religious poet',[39] he considers his poetic writing to be 'religious' in the sense that it seeks to set aside ego in order to remain 'attune[d] to the doing of God' in the world.[40] The result is a 'transfiguring perception',[41] a kind of double vision: what is perceived is shown not only from a human perspective but also as though through God's eyes. The capacity to bring out the divine dimension in mundane, desolate and seemingly hopeless situations is perhaps the feature that most powerfully characterizes Williams' imaginative vision. It is revealed not only in his poetry but also in his preaching and social commentary, allowing reader and listener to sense something of that anguished energy of crucified love that, in Williams' vision, holds everything together.

## Excessive speech: Exaggeration and extremes in Dostoevsky's fiction

Williams is a voracious reader of fiction, as is evidenced by his discussion of a wide range of modern writers, including Iris Murdoch, Doris Lessing, Alan Garner, P. D. James, Ian McEwan, Philip Pullman, Marilynne Robinson, as well as such 'classic' authors as Dickens, Tolstoy and Dostoevsky. The importance of narrative fiction, in his view, lies in its capacity to create imaginary worlds peopled with characters whose stories make us strange to ourselves, thereby enabling us to see ourselves from a new perspective and to experiment with possible alternative approaches to living.[42]

Such fiction enlarges and challenges our understanding of self and the world and is 'a necessary tool of human maturity'.[43] It has an ethical dimension, 'dispossess[ing us] of the desire to hold everything inside [our] own head'.[44] In seeking to offer a truthful picture of humankind, it may resort to exaggeration, humour, irony and excess, as is the case with such writers as Charles Dickens[45] and Flannery O'Connor,[46] their exaggerations enabling us to identify 'the hell of concealment, deceit and self-deceit',[47] and thereby learn to 'expand into the space ... available for human beings to be what God meant them to be'.[48]

The expansion of space for authentic human life is identified by Williams as the principal intention of Fyodor Dostoevsky. In *Dostoevsky: Language, Faith and Fiction*, we have Williams' most extensive analysis of the significance of narrative fiction for human life and faith. Here he argues that a theology of narrative underlies Dostoevsky's creation of a fictional world that mirrors the moral uncertainty of the actual world. In that fictional world, the narrative strategies employed are analogous to God's dealings with the world,[49] offering insight into the operation of divine grace within finite reality.

## Dostoevsky's narrative world

'What else might be possible if we – characters and readers – saw the world in another light, the light provided by faith?' That is the question considered to be the essence of Dostoevsky's novelistic purpose.[50] A truthful response to that question, says Williams, requires the representation of an imaginative world corresponding as accurately as possible to the world of daily experience with its lack of a 'clear moral landscape'.[51] As is the case in contemporary Western society, Dostoevsky's fictional world was one in which God is hidden, faith is largely disregarded or mocked, and grace appears to be absent.

In that world a host of extreme characters embody various facets of evil,[52] from self-delusion and perverted notions of freedom to manipulation, deliberate destructiveness and murder.[53] Their stories alert us to the pernicious consequences of such actions: disconnection from self and others and from the openness of history. In the death-bound trajectory of their lives, we discover the ever-present power of the demonic within human experience.

The contrast is set up by the presence of characters whose lives give witness to genuine freedom, the freedom to love, to grow and to be transformed by their relations with others. These characters create awareness that the action of the novels takes place against a hinterland of 'plenitude'[54] in which the existence of order, generosity, grace and love is assumed.[55] They also remind us that we too are faced with choices similar to those of the novels. We can choose to pursue a trajectory that is death-bound, or to accept the unclear, always risky, openness to the future that is ultimately life-giving.

## Authorship and rejection of the omniscient narrator

In these novels, says Williams, the author's perspective remains opaque, obliging readers to draw their own conclusions. In this way a parallel is created between the authorship of a work of fiction and divine authorship. The novels show the characters in the process of formation, having the freedom to make choices, with their futures left open at the end of the novel. They parallel the real-life process of identity-formation in which we are each our own author, given freedom by the divine author to opt at any moment either for a trajectory that is life-bound or for one that is death-bound. This narrative technique not only offers insight into the authorship entailed in personal identity-formation but also enables the reader to glimpse something of the way God, the divine author, relates to creation.[56]

Mirroring the divine/human relationship is also the freedom given to Dostoevsky's characters. In these novels, various narrative techniques undermine the assumption of an omniscient narrator. Omissions in the narrative and the repeated interplay of alternative voices create for the reader a fictional world in which the future remains open to the as-yet-unforeseen choices of the various characters. Where the narrator speaks in the first person, the very style of speech makes his perspective questionable.[57] Williams argues that, by presenting us with narrators who do not have an overall grasp of the persons and events narrated, Dostoevsky replicates the real world in which, lacking a 'God's eye view', we cannot claim full understanding or control over other people or the context in which we live.

## Characterization

In Williams' analysis, history and time are significant elements in Dostoevsky's fiction. Each character has a history of choices which has brought him or her to the present situation, and out of which ongoing choices are made over the extended time of the novel. The reader is therefore witness to characters in process whose identity is constantly in formation and whose choices determine the positive or negative trajectory of their lives.[58] Having choice, they are free at any time to alter the course of that trajectory, and so to move in the direction of life rather than death.

That is the case with Raskolnikov in *Crime and Punishment* and Mitya in *The Brothers Karamazov*. They are free because, as Williams argues, their histories are not predetermined but are always open to the future.[59] Such freedom is evident at the end of these two novels, which leave both characters still in formation. In the face of an open future, they will continue to grow or diminish in their humanity according to choices yet to be made. In this way, their fictional depiction mirrors the real-life process by which human identity is formed. Having the freedom to choose, we human beings author our lives by the nature of our choices and are consequently always capable of change.[60]

Identity-formation does not take place in a vacuum. Williams emphasizes the dialogical nature of the process and, following Bakhtin, draws attention to the similarity of Dostoevsky's technique to ancient Menippean drama, which uses dialogue 'as the medium for the formation of persons'.[61] Dostoevsky's characters are experienced mainly through their dialogue whereby they not only make their identity known to each other but also, in that process, expose themselves to challenge and change.[62] So Williams can state that 'we are agents who are formed by the exchange of words'; we have the freedom to grow and develop since there is never a 'last word' to such dialogical exchange.[63] There is always a possible response and so the dialogue continues.[64] Those who refuse to expose themselves to dialogue are actually making a choice for the demonic since, in closing themselves off from others, they are closed to the possibility of change and growth. Such closure leads ultimately to diminishment and death.[65]

The person encountered in dialogue is also the other to whom one has responsibility. Williams notes that the Orthodox ritual of exchanging crosses symbolizes the assumption of responsibility for another's growth and flourishing.[66] Responsibility, in this context, involves a renunciation of egotistical control over other people, allowing them the freedom to clarify their options and make their own choices. It requires what Williams calls 'an imaginative penetration into what is other' to facilitate the accurate identification of needs and hopes waiting to be realized.[67] It is 'an invitation for others to be freely what they are'.[68]

In assisting in the formation of another person's identity, such egoless responsibility is a mode of authorship.[69] It replicates the process followed by Dostoevsky and others who portray characters who are free to develop as the action proceeds.[70] Significantly, it mirrors God's kenotic action in creation and in the incarnation. Not only is the created order allowed to be other but human nature is also enabled, through Jesus Christ, to be so 'drastically alter[ed]' that it acquires the freedom to realize its full potential.[71]

## Icons, images and grace

Icons are of major significance in Dostoevsky's imaginative world. They point to the presence of an excess of meaning beyond the purely instrumental.[72] Far from being 'faces on the wall'[73] to be looked at and forgotten, they are a form of narrative, conveying their Christian frame of reference.[74] As narrative, they invite dialogue. One does not look at an icon but is interrogated by it.[75] 'What the holy image represents', says Williams, 'is profoundly connected with the possibility of language itself, as a communal and dialogical reality, and as something that embodies the inextinguishable freedom to go beyond what is given.'[76]

The authority of icons is derived from the prototypical icon, Jesus Christ, the true image of God.[77] Their continuing credibility is determined by the holiness of life of those who have become iconic images of Christ.

As demonstrated by the characters of Tikhon and Zosima, such holiness is bought at the cost of repeated failure and repentance. It is only through an inner process of gradual transformation that they finally become a sign of divine presence within the secular world.[78]

Even defiled, icons continue to convey the fundamental truth that the mode of divine presence is that of self-dispossession. The 'narrative of vulnerability accepted' is, says Williams, the 'core narrative' of God's relation to the world as revealed in the life and death of Jesus. That is the one narrative that offers 'a possible future from within the nightmare of deformed and deforming human interaction'.[79] Just as Jesus was reviled and given over to destruction, no less a fate is to be expected for icons, both painted and human.

For the followers of Christ, the process of identity-formation involves the acceptance of vulnerability, limit and suffering in line with the pattern of his life and death.[80] Growth into one's true identity as 'icon/image' of Christ is a matter of losing oneself.[81] In the Dostoevskian world, characters such as Sonya, Alyosha and Mitya are shown in the process of growth into holiness. As such, they signal the way grace is experienced in human existence, namely as the persistence of belief in the 'imaginative possibilities' of an open future, despite the pressure to succumb to despair and death.[82]

Continuing belief in future imaginative possibilities is, for Williams, the key to interpreting the Grand Inquisitor narrative. For him, the kiss given by Christ to the Inquisitor is far from an empty gesture. It is a gratuitous act of love, expressive of the freedom to respond in unexpected ways to human power; it represents 'the reality of a freedom beyond the systems of the world'.[83] That reality is the hinterland of plenitude that he believes to be the foundation of Dostoevsky's imaginative world, and it is against that reality that the novelist offers his readers an opportunity to subject their choices and commitments to 'imaginative testing'.[84]

## Excessive speech: Tragedy

Williams' contention is that the 'imaginative testing' of choice is also one of the purposes of tragic drama. Both fiction and drama thus have a pedagogic role in helping us to reach maturity by teaching us to *learn to think* about the intransigent nature of human existence and the consequences of our choices in such a world.[85]

There is, however, a second related purpose to the enactment of tragedy. It challenges us to imagine a future that holds together both the reality of atrocity in an imperfect world and the possibility of going on speaking about it. The tragic, says Williams, is not ultimate, because we are able to re-present it in imagination and to speak about it in such a way that new learning may occur. Such re-presentation is all the more necessary in the current social climate with its avoidance of pain through resort to fantasy, cliché and sentimentality.[86] These interrelated purposes are explored in the 2016 study *The Tragic Imagination*, an analysis of the European tradition of tragedy.

## *The liturgical frame and access to knowledge*

Williams argues that part of the power of tragic representation is attributable to the frame within which it is held. With its origin in the Dionysian rites of the sixth and fifth centuries BCE,[87] tragedy, says Williams, is essentially a liturgical act that enables the spectators to confront the reality of their fragile existence while remaining safely held within the containing frame of the theatre.[88] Tragic drama is the collective, shared experience of viewing a course of action already familiar to the audience. While the characters are ignorant of their fate, the audience is aware of the inevitable tragic outcome. Spectators are thus encouraged to reflect on their own lack of control over the future, given the risks and uncertainties of contingent human existence.[89]

The theatre is therefore a learning experience. It is, says Williams, a vehicle for the impartation of knowledge about both self and society. The focus of ancient Greek tragedy was the fragility of the social order in which the rule of law was constantly threatened by the eruption of uncontrollable violence.[90] In the safety of the theatre, people could think through the danger, suffering and loss attendant on a failure of law,[91] and learn the difficult lesson that justice is 'the holding of tension, not a resolving into false simplicities'.[92] Such learning, says Williams, is as necessary in the modern world as in the past, since the personal and the civic are inseparable.[93]

A shift of focus occurs with Shakespearean drama.[94] Here, says Williams, the drama hinges on the inner consciousness of the protagonists rather than on an external threat; the characters' lack of knowledge of themselves becomes the impetus for tragedy, and thus for their own suffering and that of others. By contrast with the characters, the audience is 'immobilized',[95] unable to respond to the suffering represented on the stage. They learn not only the consequences of self-ignorance but also the important lesson that pain and weakness offer an opening to manipulation and exploitation.[96] Also to be learned is the realization that, while suffering is unique, it may nevertheless be spoken about, and may therefore become an occasion for becoming 'familiar' with 'what *can't* be, in the ordinary sense, learned'.[97] What we *may* learn is a way of responding to another's pain with empathy and compassion, recognizing it to be unique and yet able to be spoken of, and thus, in some measure, shared.[98]

Necessary though such learnings may be, they are not sufficient in themselves to effect a deep transformation of what Williams calls 'the solid and justified ego'.[99] What is required is the willingness to confront with painful honesty our self-delusions, self-justifications, fears and avoidances, 'those buried levels of awareness ... where our most significant human dysfunctions are rooted'.[100] The catharsis offered by tragedy is not a mere '*release* from tension',[101] but involves instead the 'dissolving' of the ego. It is a matter of being forced to explore hidden recesses within the self, a process which is not merely affective but requires, in Williams' view, 'a different mode of thinking'. He therefore turns to Hegel's discussion of tragedy[102] to clarify what this form of thinking entails.

## *Knowledge and the self: Hegelian 'thinking'*

Williams argues that Hegel viewed tragic representation as a necessary stimulus to 'thinking about thinking'.[103] In this interpretation, the Hegelian 'unfolding' of Spirit involves an increasing awareness of the ways in which humans construct self-images that conflict with the truth of 'mature interdependence, the recognition of self in the other towards which all human action and thought moves'.[104] According to this view, the suffering presented in tragic drama is the result of the protagonists' construction of a false self-image, an aesthetic image of themselves as an independent work of art.

Such images issue from identification of the self either with an idealized image of the divine, as occurred in ancient drama, or with an idealized view of personal authenticity, as in modern tragedy. They represent a conception of self as something already completed and therefore static, resistant to change. In both cases, the fixed image closes off the process of thought about self and others, since thinking about another requires not only a willingness to acknowledge the difference embodied in the other person but also the ever-present possibility of misunderstanding and error. In the process of observing the conflict and suffering that follow inevitably from such failures in thinking, spectators of tragedy are incited to think about their own thought processes and thus to change. Williams can thus conclude that 'tragedy exists to persuade us, repeatedly and diversely, to think better.'[105]

Better thinking means giving attention not simply to the protagonist's suffering but, more importantly, to the causes within ourselves of that suffering. It is intended, says Williams, to disrupt the spectator's complacency by precipitating a crisis of self-awareness, an acknowledgement of the social and individual dysfunction created by the false images we construct of self and others. Only as we think through and acknowledge the depth of our dysfunction can growth, change and healing occur.

Tragedy may thus serve to reconstitute us as moral beings, thoughtfully alert to the intricate complexity of our interdependent existence, keenly aware that becoming a self is a continuing process of dissolution and reconstitution: the dissolving of our constructed self-images through the crisis of confrontation with otherness, and the reconstitution effected by the thought-enabled recognition of our need for mutuality, compassion and the order provided by law.[106] It is knowledge of the inevitability of such challenges to our identity, while continuing to trust in the possibility of change, that constitutes what Williams calls 'the tragic imagination'.

## The tragic imagination

The irony at the core of Williams' conception of human imagination is made explicit in the final two chapters of *The Tragic Imagination*. Here the juxtaposition of the term 'tragic' with that of 'imagination' involves the holding together of both suffering and renewed meaning. Williams' argument is that the very presentation to an audience of an imaginary story of suffering is an act that contains the potential for change. To imagine suffering is to have the freedom to step back sufficiently to become aware of the temporal context in which suffering occurs. Time, says Williams, does not efface suffering but it brings the possibility of learning and change.

In reflecting on the human capacity to imagine and narrate tragedy, Williams acknowledges his debt to Donald MacKinnon. While accepting the validity of certain of the criticisms directed at MacKinnon, Williams agrees with his mentor that 'the tragic is intrinsic to Christian theology's workings.'[107] As MacKinnon argues, two basic truths about human existence are incontestable: its limitations and the irreversibility of time.[108] The full consequences of any human action are both unforeseeable and irreversible, and unanticipated harm is an inevitable possibility. Risk, loss and tragedy are thus unavoidable. Even the act of narrating past events is tragic, as the past cannot be relived or changed.[109] Suffering can never be made better by the events that follow. MacKinnon and Williams are therefore opposed to any Christian theology in which the reality of suffering is simply cancelled by the 'happy ending' of Christ's resurrection.

Williams insists, however, that recognition of the inescapability of loss need not lead to pessimism.[110] The experience of tragedy does not put a stop to time. The very continuation of the temporal process makes it possible to speak of past pain and thus find new meaning within that pain. While the narration of suffering does not change what has happened, it does allow for reflection on the past and thus for the possibility of 'relocating' loss within a wider context.[111]

Such is the ironic truth of the Christian gospel, an irony especially evident in John's Gospel. Here 'the one through whom all things were made' is shown as unrecognized and rejected by the very beings thus made. The crucifixion is the consequence of that ironic failure of recognition; it is the inevitable outcome of humanity's ignorance and misrecognition of the divine. The double irony lies in the fact that it is 'only in the working out of this misrecognition [that] recognition can occur'.[112] We only know the truth about God when we see God in the crucified Christ whose death reveals a truth hitherto incomprehensible to finite beings.

In an extremely condensed argument, reasoned more cogently elsewhere,[113] Williams reiterates Balthasar's contention that the dying Jesus' cry of abandonment signifies that even the greatest distance between God and humanity is held within the freedom of differentiated otherness that is the divine life. God remains God even across the 'radical ... rupture of the fabric of reality [that is] God alienated from God'.[114] The resurrection is not a 'deferred rescue operation' but witnesses to the divine freedom to encompass even the otherness of death within the divine life. 'Divine truth', says Williams, 'is torn apart in and by human history, and yet brings itself together and is not destroyed.'[115]

Re-presented in liturgical form, the irony at the heart of the Christian gospel is reprised week by week in the Eucharist. The re-enactment of the story of Jesus' betrayal and abandonment repeatedly contrasts divine faithfulness with continuing human ignorance and failure. While familiar with the events enacted, the participants are repeatedly challenged to discover what remains still unknown about the story and about themselves. In that process, repentance and mourning become possible, bringing solidarity with other believers and the possibility of new meaning. In Williams' view, the Eucharist is therefore the exemplary paradigm of tragic drama.[116] It confronts us with loss that is 'irremediable, beyond compensation', but it is a loss from which '*something emerges*'.[117]

## Tragedy, irony and imagination

The significance of Williams' concept of 'tragic imagination' is not to be underestimated. It is a concept that brings into focus the irony at the heart of finite reality and the function of irony as an imaginative device. The paradox of finite existence, that all beings are born to die, is essentially ironic. As an imaginative literary device, irony arises from a mind capable of holding together both an apparent state of affairs and its opposite. As Williams points out, the irony of tragedy lies in the fact that the audience, with the dramatist, is able to see the inevitable outcome to which the protagonist is blind, such irony serving as a reminder of the contingency of all human existence.

The Christian gospel takes irony to a deeper level. It reveals the contradiction at the core of finite reality, that the world created by God, in failing to recognize its Creator, effects its own downfall. Deeper still is the irony evidenced in the Christ story of incarnation/crucifixion/resurrection. Here, as Williams argues, God is revealed as other to God, remaining present even in the otherness of death. Otherness, that which is strange, different, even contradictory, is thus shown to be encompassed within divine being. We may conclude that God works through 'making strange', revealing to finite minds the ironic truth that life finds meaning only through its opposite, death, the death of Christ, who is the paradigm of dying to all that separates us from God. In this way, finite beings may begin to glimpse the God whose being holds together, and gives meaning to, the contradictions of finite reality.

Williams is therefore able to conclude that the very imagining of tragedy serves to provide insight not only into the paradoxical nature of finite reality but also into the incomparable ways of God who works through death to bring life. We may draw the further conclusion that our human desire to seek an alternative future beyond the limits of the present has its source in God's desire for the response of otherness, thereby giving rise to an infinite expansion of creative possibilities. Once again, we find evidence of the analogy between our human imagination and the energy of divine desire reaching out in embrace of the created other.

The claims made by Williams concerning the pedagogic value of fiction and tragedy have been disputed by several of his reviewers.[118] Similarly questionable is his assertion that artistic activity is essentially an act of self-dispossession. The validity of such criticisms does not, however, nullify the theological significance of his argument concerning the consciousness-expanding value of art and literature. The claim that the world is made 'strange' to us through its imaginative re-presentation is not a unique insight, but what is distinctive in Williams' notion is the emphasis he places on artistic re-presentation as the finite expression of the energy of divine *eros* permeating the created order. Through the arts we experience something of the ecstatic kenotic energy that, in Williams' vision, vibrates throughout all existence. Consciousness is thus expanded to glimpse the transcendent in the finite, and grace, beauty and truth within ugliness, misery and tragedy. Offered to us is knowledge that is connatural and relational, bringing a sense of the inner life of the object and its creator, both the human creator and the divine. In this way the listener/viewer/reader develops a capacity for double vision: the ability to see dimensions of existence beyond the finite and to glimpse possible futures beyond what is humanly foreseeable.

## Conclusion

In this chapter, I have explored the various ways in which the excessive language of poetry, narrative and drama makes strange our normal way of seeing, subverting unexamined assumptions and habits, and forcing us to see ourselves, our world and God in a new and surprising light. Significant for the study of imagination is what such language reveals about the human capacity to identify otherness and strangeness within finite existence.

As has been shown in Williams' reflections on these three literary genres, it is by means of imagination that we are able to hold in ironic tension the contradictions of loss and hope, of past trauma and future possibility. Through imagination, learning takes place in relation to personal identity and authenticity. Finally, the capacity to see not only the contradictions of the finite universe but also its multiple connections and infinitely varied forms enables human beings, in imitation of their maker, to take the 'stuff' of the material world and make of it something surprisingly new.

Contrasted with the transformative potential of human imagination is the damage wrought by what Williams calls 'fantasy', the misdirected and unredeemed expressions of desirous imagination. In this respect, the role of parody and irony is held to be crucial in raising awareness of the dehumanizing destructiveness of much contemporary Western culture. Acutely aware of the damage inflicted by fantasy, Williams accords supreme importance to the attentiveness required to see with 'double vision' God in the finite and Truth within the confusion of our world.

## Notes

1 Rowan Williams, *The Other Mountain* (Manchester: Carcanet, 2014), p. 51.
2 Rowan Williams, *The Edge of Words: God and the Habits of Language* (London: Bloomsbury, 2014), p. 132.
3 Williams, *The Edge of Words*, p. 134.
4 Williams, *The Edge of Words*, pp. 129–30.
5 Williams, *A Silent Action: Engagements with Thomas Merton* (London: SPCK, 2013), p. 47.
6 Rowan Williams, 'Drystone' in *The Poems of Rowan Williams* (Oxford: Perpetua Press, 2002), p. 12.
7 Rowan Williams, 'Senses' in *Headwaters* (Oxford: Perpetua Press, 2008), p. 31.
8 Williams, 'Matthäuspassion' in *Headwaters*, p. 23.
9 Williams, 'Resurrection' in *Headwaters*, p. 26.
10 Williams, 'Pantocrator: Daphni' in *The Poems of Rowan Williams*, p. 31.
11 Williams, 'Gwen John in Paris' in *The Poems of Rowan Williams*, pp. 9–11.
12 Williams, 'Crossings' in *The Poems of Rowan Williams*, pp. 17–20.
13 Williams, 'Indoors' in *The Poems of Rowan Williams*, p. 34.
14 Williams, 'Return Journey' in *The Poems of Rowan Williams*, p. 16.
15 Williams, 'Return Journey', p. 16.
16 Williams, 'First Thing' in *The Poems of Rowan Williams*, p. 46.
17 Williams, 'The Night Kitchen: Dreamwork' in *Headwaters*, pp. 18–20.
18 Williams, 'Alone at Last' in *The Poems of Rowan Williams*, p. 35.
19 See the Preface to *The Other Mountain*, p. 9.
20 Williams, 'The Other Mountain: Riding Westward' in *The Other Mountain*, p. 15.
21 Williams, 'From Carn Ingli' in *The Other Mountain*, p. 17.
22 Williams, 'Swansea Bay: Dylan at 100' in *The Other Mountain*, p. 25.
23 Williams, 'Nagasaki: Midori's Rosary' in *The Other Mountain*, p. 37.
24 Williams, 'To the City' in *The Other Mountain*, p. 40.
25 Williams, 'Felicity' in *The Other Mountain*, p. 43.
26 Williams, 'Yellow Star' in *The Other Mountain*, p. 44.
27 Williams, 'Hive' in *The Other Mountain*, p. 55.
28 Williams, 'Door' in *The Other Mountain*, p. 31.
29 Williams, 'Stations of the Gospel' in *The Other Mountain*, pp. 33–6.
30 Williams, 'Unsealings: School Play' in *The Other Mountain*, p. 59.
31 Interview with Alodie Fielding, 'Rowan Williams Through the Narrow Gate', *Monk*, May 2019, Monk.gallery/interviews/rowan-williams-interview/, accessed 24.09.2020.
32 'Rowan Williams on Poetry', http://rowanwilliams.archbishopofcanterbury.org/articles.php/1752/rowan-williams-on-poetry.html, accessed 27.07.2024.
33 'Rowan Williams on Poetry'. See also Rowan Williams, *Anglican Identities* (London: Darton, Longman & Todd, 2004), pp. 24–39, for a fuller discussion of the concept of 'contemplative pragmatism'.
34 Fielding, 'Rowan Williams Through the Narrow Gate', p. 7.
35 Williams, *Anglican Identities*, pp. 57–72, offers an account of George Herbert's anguished struggle for 'perseverance' amid God's 'absence'.

36 Rowan Williams, *Christian Imagination in Poetry and Polity: Some Anglican Voices from Temple to Herbert* (Oxford: SLG Press, 2004), p. 37.

37 Williams, *Christian Imagination*, p. 41. In *A Century of Poetry: 100 Poems for Searching the Heart* (London: SPCK, 2022), p. 177, he speaks of 'the poet's obligation to refresh the springs of vision'.

38 Rowan Williams, Sermon to commemorate the 400th anniversary of the birth of the poet John Milton, http://rowanwilliams.archbishopofcanterbury.org/articles.php/1222/archbishop-preaches-about-poet-john-milton-at-st-giles-cripplegate.html, accessed 5/07/2024.

39 See, for example, David Middleton, 'The Poems of Rowan Williams', *Anglican Theological Review* 88.3 (2006), p. 479.

40 Williams, *Silent Action*, pp. 47–8.

41 Rowan Williams, 'Foreword' to John Saward, *The Mysteries of March: Hans Urs von Balthasar on the Incarnation and Easter* (Washington: Catholic University of America Press, 1990), p. ix.

42 Williams, *The Edge of Words*, pp. 135ff.

43 Williams, *The Edge of Words*, p. 152. See also Rowan Williams and Greg Garrett, *In Conversation* (New York: Church Publishing, 2019), pp. 55–6.

44 Williams, *Grace and Necessity: Reflections on Art and Love* (London: Morehouse, 2005), p. 126.

45 Rowan Williams, *Luminaries: Twenty Lives that Illuminate the Christian Way* (London: SPCK, 2019), pp. 89–94.

46 Williams, *Grace and Necessity*, pp. 130–1.

47 Williams, 'Charles Dickens' in *Luminaries*, p. 91.

48 Williams, *Luminaries*, p. 90.

49 Williams, *Luminaries*, p. 234.

50 In reaching this conclusion, Williams acknowledges a debt to Mikhail Bakhtin's work on Dostoevsky. Rowan Williams, *Dostoevsky: Language, Faith and Fiction* (London: Bloomsbury, 2008), p. xii.

51 Williams, *Dostoevsky*, p. 1.

52 Williams, *Dostoevsky*, p. 67. Williams states that 'while Dostoevsky emphatically believed in the objective reality of the demonic, it is an objective reality that cannot be separated from human agents' (p. 99).

53 Williams, *Dostoevsky*, p. 85.

54 Williams, *Dostoevsky*, p. 143.

55 Williams, *Dostoevsky*, pp. 222–3.

56 Williams, *Dostoevsky*, p. 234. Williams' claim is that 'we best read Dostoevsky as working through th[e] analogy between writing and divine creation.'

57 Williams, *Dostoevsky*, pp. 136–7.

58 Williams, *Dostoevsky*, pp. 145–6.

59 Williams, *Dostoevsky*, p. 12.

60 Williams, *Dostoevsky*, pp. 110, 138–9.

61 Williams, *Dostoevsky*, p. 114.

62 Williams, *Dostoevsky*, pp. 117, 132.

63 Williams, *Dostoevsky*, p. 113, and ch. 3, 'The Last Word? Dialogue and Recognition'.

64 Williams, *Dostoevsky*, pp. 133–4.

65 Williams, *Dostoevsky*, p. 117. Williams cites the example of Stavrogin, who seemingly makes himself visible in his confession but does it in such a way that

his 'self-description [is] calculated to forestall dialogue' and thus aims to forestall exposure of the truth of his being.

66 Williams, *Dostoevsky*, pp. 151ff.
67 Williams, *Dostoevsky*, p. 171.
68 Williams, *Dostoevsky*, p. 169.
69 Williams, *Dostoevsky*, p. 172.
70 Williams, *Dostoevsky*, pp. 172, 187.
71 Williams, *Dostoevsky*, p. 174.
72 See Williams, *Dostoevsky*, pp. 190–200.
73 Williams, *Dostoevsky*, p. 125.
74 Williams, *Dostoevsky*, p. 200.
75 Williams, *Dostoevsky*, p. 207.
76 Williams, *Dostoevsky*, pp. 220–1.
77 Williams, *Dostoevsky*, p. 207.
78 Williams, *Dostoevsky*, p. 223.
79 Williams, *Dostoevsky*, pp. 213–14.
80 Williams, *Dostoevsky*, pp. 210–11.
81 Williams, *Dostoevsky*, p. 214.
82 Williams, *Dostoevsky*, p. 242.
83 Williams, *Dostoevsky*, p. 31.
84 Williams, *Dostoevsky*, p. 242.
85 Williams' claim that tragedy teaches us to think is rejected by David Bentley Hart, who argues that tragic drama's representation of suffering protects us from thought by veiling brute reality in 'shimmering ... beauty'. David Bentley Hart, 'The Gospel according to Melpomene: Reflections on Rowan Williams's *The Tragic Imagination*', *Modern Theology* 34.2 (2018), p. 226. Williams' reply to Hart's criticism is found in 'Not Cured, not Forgetful, not Paralysed: A Response to Comments on *The Tragic Imagination*', *Modern Theology* 34.2 (2018).
86 Rowan Williams, *The Tragic Imagination* (Oxford: Oxford University Press, 2016), pp. 1–2.
87 Williams insists that he is referring to a 'literary practice' developed within the European social and historical context and not to the problem of suffering in general or to forms of tragic drama practised in other cultures. See Williams, *The Tragic Imagination*, p. 137.
88 Williams, *The Tragic Imagination*, p. 18. Williams' claim concerning the 'Attic' origin and purpose of tragedy is disputed by Hart, who holds it to be a 'literary' treatment of texts abstracted from the specificity of cultural context. *Contra* Williams, Hart's claim is that tragedy 'consoles ... as much as it disenchants'. Hart, 'The Gospel according to Melpomene', pp. 223, 227, 230. Edith Hall points out factual errors in his discussion of Greek tragedy. *Prospect* (17 November 2016, https://www.prospectmagazine.co.uk/magazine/rowan-williamss-tragic-mistake, accessed 26.06.2024.
89 Williams, *The Tragic Imagination*, p. 10.
90 Williams, *The Tragic Imagination*, p. 6.
91 Williams, *The Tragic Imagination*, p. 24.
92 Williams, *The Tragic Imagination*, p. 14.
93 Williams, *The Tragic Imagination*, p. 25.
94 Williams' fascination with Shakespeare lies in the Bard's skill in exploring the subtle intricacies of the human psyche. In a play, *Shakeshafte*, Williams imagi-

nes the young Shakeshafte/speare 'want[ing] to be inside people ... to hear where [they] speak from' (Scene IV), and he has other characters say of him that he longs to 'jump into the dark inside you and everyone else' (Scene XI). See *Critical Survey* 25.3 (2013), pp. 61, 85.

95 Williams, *The Tragic Imagination*, pp. 35ff. Williams draws here on Stanley Cavell's thesis of the 'immobilised audience' in Stanley Cavell, *Disowning Knowledge in Seven Plays of Shakespeare*, updated edn (Cambridge: Cambridge University Press, 2003).

96 Williams, *The Tragic Imagination*, pp. 45–8.

97 Williams, *The Tragic Imagination*, p. 42.

98 Williams, *The Tragic Imagination*, p. 43.

99 Williams, *The Tragic Imagination*, p. 53.

100 Williams, *The Tragic Imagination*, p. 52.

101 Williams, *The Tragic Imagination*, p. 52. Williams' reference is to Walter Davis's analysis of catharsis in *Deracination: Historicity, Hiroshima and the Tragic Imperative* (Albany, NY: SUNY Press, 2001).

102 In his discussion of Hegel's views on tragedy, Williams' draws on the collection of Hegel's lectures, *Hegel on Tragedy*, edited by Ann and Henry Paolucci (Westport, CT and London: Greenwood Press, 1987).

103 Williams, *The Tragic Imagination*, p. 69. Williams' analysis of Hegel's views on tragedy differs from that of many other Hegel interpreters who argue that Hegel saw tragedy as exemplifying the dialectic of Spirit whereby opposing positions are reconciled within history. See, for example, Joel C. Daniels, 'Against Innocence, against Evasion: Rowan Williams on Thinking and Speaking Tragedy', *Anglican Theological Review* 100.2 (2018), pp. 391–2. Daniels considers Williams' position to be 'innovative' but expounded too briefly to be fully convincing.

104 Williams, *The Tragic Imagination*, p. 74.

105 Williams, *The Tragic Imagination*, p. 70.

106 Williams, *The Tragic Imagination*, pp. 78–9.

107 Williams, *The Tragic Imagination*, p. 108. For an extended discussion of MacKinnon's construction of the 'tragic' and its influence on Williams, see Khegan Delport, 'Of Danger and Difficulty: Rowan Williams and *the Tragic Imagination*', *The Heythrop Journal* 61.3 (2017), pp. 505–20.

108 Williams, *The Tragic Imagination*, p. 112.

109 Williams, *The Tragic Imagination*, p. 113.

110 Williams rejects George Steiner's conception of 'absolute tragedy' and the notion of an essentially tragic world view.

111 Williams, *The Tragic Imagination*, p. 115.

112 Williams, *The Tragic Imagination*, p. 121.

113 Rowan Williams, 'Balthasar and the Trinity' in *The Cambridge Companion to Hans Urs Von Balthasar*, ed. Edward T. Oakes and David Moss (Cambridge: Cambridge University Press, 2004), pp. 37–50, p. 41.

114 Williams, *The Tragic Imagination*, p. 123.

115 Williams, *The Tragic Imagination*, p. 124.

116 Williams, *The Tragic Imagination*, p. 143.

117 Williams, *The Tragic Imagination*, pp. 126, 127.

118 See, for example, Khegan Delport, 'Of Danger and Difficulty', p. 12, and David Bentley Hart, 'The Gospel according to Melpomene', p. 226.

# 10

# Rowan Williams' Theology of Imagination

## Introduction

'The idea of imagination as a road to truth and to a true envisaging of Christianity ... is a very powerful Anglican tradition that Rowan continues ... If you unleash the imagination, you grasp much wider dimensions to truth, and you're open to the kind of truths that religions are talking about.'[1] Such was John Milbank's assessment of Rowan Williams' potential contribution to the life and thought of the Anglican Church on the occasion of Williams' enthronement as Archbishop of Canterbury in 2003. It is an assessment that is supported by my exploration of his writings on language, aesthetics and literature.

Notable, however, is the absence from Williams' writings of any systematic attempt to develop a theology of imagination, an absence that is consistent with his reluctance to confine the complex diversity of human experience within the limits of any one system. As I will demonstrate, it is nevertheless possible to discern a coherent theology of imagination in the many references he makes to the operation and importance of human imagination.

That is the purpose of this final chapter. Beginning with an examination of Williams' use of the term 'imagination', I identify the lineaments of the theology of imagination implicit in his writings.

## Williams' use of the term 'imagination'

The word 'imagination' is employed by Williams without explanation or definition, the assumption being that readers and listeners will be familiar with its meaning. So we are told that 'Advent pulls the imagination in two directions',[2] that 'the intellectual community needs to give place to the imagination,'[3] and that history is a 'quest ... for the imagination to find out the lost perspective of the victim'.[4] The implication of such usage is that imagination is an integral feature of human mental activity. This conclusion is supported by Williams' tendency to employ the term 'imagination' in conjunction with other aspects of a person's inner life: intellect, emotion, memory, spirit. He writes:

We have intelligence and love and imagination.[5]

Responding ... to ... the Gospel requires of us a transforming of our whole self, our feelings and thoughts and imaginings.[6]

A counsellor [must] learn the inner shape, the grammar of someone else's mind and imagination.[7]

The desert as experienced is the size of your own heart and mind and imagination.[8]

We have to find somewhere dark enough for memory and imagination to join hands.[9]

Something has happened to the heart and imagination [of the New Testament writers].[10]

[The Gospel accounts are] reflections on what the raising of the crucified and rejected Jesus *does* to the human spirit and imagination.[11]

Imagination, for Williams, is inseparably associated with human language. Recognizing that all language is a process of sign-making that draws on the synthesizing function of imagination, he argues that, contrasted with instrumental and analytical language, the language that 'matters' and 'makes style, pattern and beauty out of our biological existence' is 'the language of transformation, imagination'.[12] Christian faith is accordingly 'interwoven' with imagination,[13] its development being dependent on both imagination and language being 'reshaped' by Christ.[14] All of these references attest to the significance he accords to the human capacity for imagination and its interrelationship with other mental processes.

While Williams would not claim to offer an adequate account of the neurological basis of imagination, he does draw on the work of others to further his insight into its role in human cognition. He cites the work of the palaeontologist Jill Cook, whose study of Ice-Age lion-men figurines led her to the conclusion that such works signal the pre-frontal cortex activity of the 'modern mind', which is 'capable of imagining new concepts rather than simply reproducing [existing] forms'.[15] From the psychiatrist

Iain McGilchrist he learns that 'There is always a range of operations in the brain making the connections that allow larger pictures to be seen, allowing us to know, by imagining, not simply by registering.'[16]

Imagination is accordingly considered to be an indispensable form of knowledge, necessary for gaining a more comprehensive picture of a situation by connecting disparate aspects of experience. Drawing on the observations of the cognitive scientist Douglas Hofstadter, he conceives of the mind as 'a spiral of self-extending symbolic activity', sparking off multiple associations within the perceiving subject, such that 'knowing something is more like re-enacting a performance than labelling an object.'[17]

Knowledge of this kind involves the whole person – senses, affect, intellect and imagination. It is an interrelationship between perceiving subject and object and is consequently participatory, a type of connatural knowledge. With David Jones, Williams deplores the impoverishment of the 'modern' imagination,[18] which he considers lacking in 'the sense of ontological depth to metaphor, the awareness of participatory patterns under the surface of appearance [making] thinking itself ... always allusive and (in every sense) involved'.[19] It may be concluded that Williams would concur with those theorists discussed in Chapter 1 who hold imagination to be an indispensable mode of cognition.

As a form of knowledge, imagination is associated by Williams with the capacity to see more and differently. It is the capacity for vision, insight and discovery. As such, it is the freedom to detach from the immediate to explore the realm of the unseen and unforeseen, as noted in Chapter 1. So, for example, he regards the exercise of imagination as 'the conscious pushing of the boundaries of what we perceive'.[20] In a conversation with Marilynne Robinson, he asserts that 'there's an element of real discovery in the work of the imagination', and draws the conclusion that 'the imagination really is a faculty in us which uncovers something.'[21] His references to imagination use images of 'opening',[22] 'expansion',[23] 'leap'[24] and 'escape from control',[25] such images being dynamic, evocative of the 'energy'[26] considered by Williams to propel the imaginative 'impulse'.[27]

What is uncovered, moreover, is not merely the new, surprising and exceptional. With Seamus Heaney, Williams contends that imaginative vision is open to seeing 'the radiance of ... ordinary things'.[28] He believes George Herbert's imagination to be particularly 'meaningful', even as it 'gallops off in a direction that can be very, very, very, very troubling'.[29] He argues that imaginative Christian witness must draw attention to 'the crack, the wound' underlying alienated social relations.[30] There is accordingly an ethical responsibility attached to the act of imagining, a responsibility that is especially important for Christians.

Closely linked with the freedom to detach from immediacy is the capacity of imagination to transcend the limits of finite reality. So Williams tells us that Christian faith involves a 'leap of imagination'[31] and that imagination which 'opens itself' discovers the 'new world' of revelation.[32] As T. S. Eliot and R. S. Thomas have both suggested, imaginative awareness is equated with a 'willingness to see things or other persons as the objects of another sensibility' than that of humanity, to look at them 'as though [God] had looked/At them too'.[33] To the VIII International Liturgical Conference, Williams wrote that 'exposure to the life of the imagination in its fullness is always a step towards exposure to the maker of all things.'[34] In line with John Milbank, he argues that 'the exploration of possible imagined alternatives is ... an attempt to penetrate into possibilities of healing that the present situation does not realise but are still in some way intuited as potential in the world we inhabit.'[35]

Enabled by grace, human imagination is thus a source of hope, discerning possibilities for divine healing and transformation within even the bleakest of situations. As exemplified by the series of conversations with Greg Garrett, that hope may be sustained by the discovery of a 'shared world of imagination and spirit ... the space into which the mystery of God invites us ... the Reign of God ... where transformation happens'.[36] It may be concluded that it is imagination, renewed by divine grace and enlightened by scripture, that enables us to discern God's unseen transformative activity within the world and to catch a glimpse of God's ultimate purpose for creation.

The capacity of the human imagination to create new forms was discussed extensively in Chapters 8 and 9. There it became evident that Williams associates creativity with the capacity to make connections among disparate aspects of experience so as to effect a new synthesis. Artists are those who, by their focused attention to the interconnected complexity of the material world, are able to 'dismantle the world of fixed concepts and self-enclosed objects' in order to explore 'possibilities, counterfactuals and imagined worlds' and thus enlarge the scope of human awareness.[37] Citing both the writer Annie Dillard and a Desert Father,[38] Williams asserts that creativity involves not only attention to the external world but also the laborious, and sometimes painful, inner work of memory, the conjunction of the two suggestive of the Zittoun and Gillespie diagram depicting the loop of imagination from present reality to future possibility through access to memory.[39]

The painful vulnerability of the creative artist is powerfully imaged in one of Williams' conversations with Greg Garrett. There, creativity is linked with 'the brokenness of great joy and great grief' which open 'the fountains of the deep', allowing God's grace to 'well up', enabling 'something [to] appear slowly, quietly, into the light and brightness'.[40] With that image we are given insight into the divine source of human creativity as well as into the cost involved in the creative process, a cost that will be shown in the next section to be the finite analogue of the kenotic *ekstasis* of the divine act of creation *ex nihilo*.

From the above examination of Williams' use of the term 'imagination', it may be concluded that, in scope and range of application, he conceives of imagination in terms of the five interrelated capacities noted in Chapter 1, namely the capacities for freedom, connection, synthesis, transcendence and creativity. Such is the significance of imagination for Williams that he holds its development to be necessary for growth into mature selfhood. Maturity is a matter of *learning* how to imagine 'truly', exposure to the imaginative worlds of narrative, drama and ritual being important for learning how 'to *imagine oneself* – to go on projecting possible futures of acting and speaking'.[41] The development of a 'moral imagination' is dependent on such exposure, bringing a necessary familiarity with the fact of suffering.[42] He is, however, all too aware of the attraction of fantasy, the temptation to escape into misleading and delusory visions of reality as a retreat from the vulnerability of an imagination open to both the beauty and ugliness of finite existence.

A final consideration in this exploration of Williams' use of the term 'imagination' is its frequent modification by such descriptors as 'secular', 'moral', 'religious', 'tragic' or 'Christian'. These modifiers are of particular interest in that they refer not to the operation of imagination but rather to world views and interpretations of existence. As social imaginaries, they bring together a range of beliefs, assumptions, ideas, practices, which are often the taken-for-granted and unexamined perspectives of whole communities.

Williams' purpose in much of his communicative theology – his meditations, homilies, lectures and addresses – is to present the Christian social imaginary in such a way that it offers his audience a coherent, intelligible and highly desirable world view, one that will draw them by its beauty into its way of life and is 'expansive' enough to 'cope with the seriousness of the world'.[43] He argues that 'God-talk ... sets the *whole* business of our knowing and perceiving against the measure of an all-inclusive vision and an all-inclusive affirmation ... a coming to see the world-as-a-whole.'[44]

The urgent need for the Christian Church to communicate that vision was the subject of an address delivered at Lambeth Palace in 2004. Entitled 'Changing the Myths We Live By', it is a call to the Church to take proper account of its 'dreaming' by resisting the 'paralysing' myth of *homo economicus* that currently holds the Western world 'captive', and offering instead the imaginative vision of *homo eucharisticus*, a way of being human 'defined by communion rather than consumption'.[45] It is his vision of restored humanity living in proper relation to God, to each other and to creation that impels Williams' thinking and teaching. As he said in his enthronement sermon, his prayer for the Christian Church is 'an imagination set on fire by the vision of God, the Holy Trinity'.[46]

## Williams' theology of imagination

In a message to the 2010 Liturgical Conference on Liturgy and Art, Williams wrote that 'To meet Christ and to participate in the liturgy of the Church ... is to be taken into the divine "imagination", the eternal purpose of God in creating and redeeming the world.'[47] The aim of this section is to explicate that statement, drawing out its implications for an integrated account of Williams' theology of imagination.

As I have argued, Williams is impelled by a powerful vision of the energy of divine love, *eros*, permeating, sustaining and renewing the whole created order. That vision imbues his whole oeuvre, his academic theology, his poetry and his spiritual reflections. It finds expression in a striking image in a meditation on an icon of the Virgin:

> The utter strangeness of God ... waits at the heart of what is familiar – as if the world were always on the edge of some total revolution, pregnant with a different kind of life, and we were always trying to catch the blinding light of its changing.[48]

A world 'pregnant with a different kind of life', a life that is 'utterly strange' and 'blinding' in its transformational power – those are the features of the vision that informs Williams' theology. Here are held together both the immeasurable difference between God and the material world, and God's presence as pulsating possibility within the very fabric of creation.[49] Encapsulated by that viscerally experienced image is the concept of the *analogia entis*, which underpins Williams' metaphysical theology.

As discussed in Chapter 3, Williams follows Przywara in conceiving of the relation between the infinite God and finite creation as analogical, the relation of in-and-beyond, of continuity-in-ever-greater-difference. Thus, in line with Austin Farrer, Williams argues that God is always present and active within the world as the energy of creative transformation, that creative energy finding expression through the medium of created matter 'not by displacing but by intensifying from within the capacity of created agency'.[50]

Permeating creation, the divine energy is the energy of relationality; it is the dynamic energy of the other-oriented relationships that constitute the life of the Holy Trinity. As relational and directed towards the different other, it gives rise to the intricate network of complex interrelated activity that is the created order and accounts for the excess discerned in finite matter.[51] In Williams' view, it is the excess of divine transformative energy which provides 'the sense of ontological depth to metaphor, the awareness of participatory patterns under the surface of appearance'.[52] I argue that it also accounts for the significant role accorded to imagination in Williams' writings and has its theological rationale in the analogical in-and-beyond relation of infinite God and finite creation. My further argument is that it provides a sound metaphysical foundation for the theories of imagination and symbolization discussed in Chapters 1 and 2.

Integral to the analogical in-and-beyond relation implicit in the image of a 'pregnant' world is the notion of an initial act of conception, the bringing into being of new life. As discussed in Chapter 4, the divine act of creation *ex nihilo* is seen by Williams to be the overflow of the Trinitarian relationships of infinite self-dispossessive love. Conceptualized as an eternal movement of inexhaustible desire/*eros* for the bliss of the other, the divine life is revealed as unlimited gift of kenotic/self-dispossessive, ecstatic/other-oriented love.

That love is accordingly infinitely creative, desirous of generating forms of otherness capable of responding to and sharing the divine bliss. The created order in its profusion, diversity and capacity for transformation is thus a manifestation of the infinite generativity of divine love which gives rise to newness and difference. In an illuminating address to an Alpha group, as reported by Rupert Shortt, Williams establishes a connection between love, creativity and imagination, and between imagination and belief in God:

> It's not just about mind, it's about love. Mind on its own – powerful intelligence – is never creative just by itself ... It's not intelligence alone – it's absorption, commitment, love, and *the leak of imagination that goes with real love*. Only love can make something completely different and rejoice in its difference ... God is a God of loving intelligence, who loves what is different ... there is a leap of faith involved [in believing in God] – or what I would rather call a 'leap of the imagination'.[53]

The conclusion is that Williams conceives of imagination as participating in the orientation towards otherness that is the essence of divine love.

The created order is also seen by Williams to be a vehicle of divine communication. It is a means whereby God becomes known to finite beings, such that 'what we perceive is a facet of eternal activity, unconditioned "energy", the divine Logos.'[54] Here the Greek-influenced late-Judaic notion of the 'Logos' is treated by Williams as the active principle of creation which has not only brought the world into being but also holds it together in meaningful unity. As a result, finite reality is intended as an intelligible expression of the life of the eternal Logos.[55] Williams can therefore assert that 'every reality is a communication of God, and everything exists therefore in virtue of God's communicating act.'[56]

A similar idea is evident in Augustine's theory of language discussed in Chapter 7. According to Augustine, all earthly things are signs, words speaking God, and capable of opening out beyond themselves to point to the divine context in which they exist. The material world is thus a form of divine communication and, being activated by divine energy, is in a process of continuing transformation, generating ever-new possibilities of representation, the most significant of which is human language.[57] By means of language, human beings make sense of the coherence of the world while also giving imaginative expression to hitherto unrealized 'configurations' of divine energy. Williams therefore concludes:

> The fact that the world ceaselessly prompts new configurations may be a brute fact about experience, or it may point us to an apprehension of unconditioned act, a fundamental energy in response to which all finite agency or movement is constituted as the flow of searching for ('desiring'... ) self-renewing, self-diversifying form ... we cannot make sense of our linguistic life without reflecting on the diverse ways in which speech opens on to an ever-receding horizon.[58]

His further conclusion is that human imagination, in employing language which 'push[es] the boundaries of what we perceive', is 'a collaboration with the energy of the world itself' and is accordingly of 'central theological importance'.[59]

An example of language pushed to the boundaries of perception is the image claimed in this chapter to be central to Williams' theology of imagination. The notion of a world pregnant with revolutionary transformation has multiple associations. It points, for example, to a world in transition, a world as yet imperfect and incomplete. Chapter 9 noted Williams' insistence on employing 'tragic' in conjunction with 'Christian' imagination. His contention is that the Christian tragic imagination is the capacity to hold together in faith and hope both the destructive aspects of finite existence and the vision of God's ultimate eschatological purpose. Described by Williams as 'that desperate creativity which comes from the brokenness of great joy and great grief',[60] imagination is the capacity to see divine presence in even the most horrific of situations, the capacity exemplified by Christ in his Gethsemane submission to the cross.

Such a capacity is further indication of the analogical nature of finite existence in which, as Przywara points out, existence/being does not coincide with essence but is instead a process of becoming. As recognized by St Paul, 'we groan [in this earthly tent] longing to be clothed with our heavenly dwelling ... so that what is mortal may be swallowed up by life.'[61] The world as it is, with its imperfections and tragedies, is not yet what God has created it to be. In his extensive social commentary, Williams attests to the Western world's captivity to the dehumanizing gods of materialism and consumerism and to the human capacity for seemingly inconceivable atrocities.[62] His message is that human transformation is possible only when it is renewed in Christ and enabled by the Spirit.[63] Only then will human 'becoming' be gradually transformed into its true essence as a 'new creation' formed into 'the image of Christ'.[64] Never completed within our lifetime, that transformation remains the vision of hope that sustains the Christian imagination in times of tragedy and daily struggle. Christians are those who are 'pregnant' with the possibilities of God's future for creation.

In a further elaboration on the image of a 'pregnant' universe, we turn to the account of the pregnancy of Mary of Nazareth. Hers was a pregnancy that was brought to its fulfilment in the birth of the One who, in Williams' words, is 'the heart of creation'.[65] As Williams argues in his work on Christology, the gospel narratives of the life, death and resurrection of Christ provide us with 'a world to live in', a 'credible environment for action and imagination'.[66] They do so by putting us in touch with Jesus Christ who is 'God the Son on earth ... a fullness of holy life within the limit of mortality'.[67] Fully divine and fully human, he is the embodiment of the proper relation between finite humanity and the infinite God, a relation expressed as a human life lived as the response of ecstatic, kenotic, filial love to the eternal Father. In his words and actions, in his submission in faith to the divine purpose at every moment, even the moment of death, he enacts the perfect human relation of trusting dependence on the God whose purpose is love.

The event of his crucifixion is the paradoxical revelation that the very Being of God is nothing less than 'absolute ... gift', that excess of self-dispossessive, other-focused love freely poured out for the sake of the other that is the life of the Holy Trinity.[68] The crucified Christ is thus the incarnation of the *analogia entis*. His crucified body is both the finite coincidence of essence and existence, being and becoming, and the disclosure to finite beings of the infinite depth of the ecstatic, kenotic divine love that gave rise to, sustains and redeems the whole created order. In a particularly vivid image from an Easter Day sermon, Williams awakens us to the divine significance of the crucifixion in declaring that 'Jesus has made himself translucent, the burning glass through which God's light comes to set the world on fire; he has made an empty space in the world for God to come in.'[69]

The insistent pressure of the divine desire for humanity's filial response was examined in Part Two of this book. There it was argued that Williams locates the source of all human desire in God's passionate desire for humanity to share the ecstatic bliss that is the divine life. Throughout his writings we find recurring imagery expressive of the importunate tenacity of divine desire in seeking humanity's response. An early image portrays 'God pull[ing] taut the slack thread of human desire binding it to himself'.[70] In a discussion of Welsh poetry, he refers to 'the sense of sheer agency', 'the whistle at an infinite distance' of 'the shepherd's call' to the poet.[71] Divine grace is described as 'that underlying pressure, the fountains of the great deep, which underlies our human experience and is always pushing to be through'.[72] The history of the Jewish people is interpreted as 'God's Spirit ... pressing this people toward a complete openness, receptivity and vulnerability that will "clear a space" for renewing grace to flow freely'.[73] The image of the 'sparkle from the coal' captures the insistent lure of divine grace sparking a response of yearning love from the compressed matter of finite existence.

As was noted in Chapter 5, Williams argues that the human reaction to the intensity of divine desire is frequently terror, resulting in either resistance or avoidance. Seeking its terminus in such finite goals as power, fame or sexual satisfaction in place of God, resistant desire accounts for the devastating history of human destructiveness. Avoidant desire takes refuge in fantasy, as evidenced by such contemporary phenomena as the cult of celebrity, fascination with the apocalyptic and addiction to gaming and other forms of escapism. Only when human desire is aligned with divine desire in the form of self-dispossessive love is true satisfaction to be found, such alignment being the increasingly realized outcome of lives renewed in Christ through the power of the Spirit. So with Maximus the Confessor, Williams concludes: 'Our alignment with [Christ's] humanity by incorporation into his sacramental Body makes possible our own *kenosis* and *ekstasis*, our self-emptying and self-transcending in love.'[74] Within the Body of Christ, the Church, human desire is gradually purified, and its imaginative energy redirected towards its true terminus in the life of the Holy Trinity.

Williams thus grants the Christian Church the task of cooperating with divine grace in the purification of desire, a process involving the re-alignment of the energy and goal of human imagination. Renewed in baptism as 'those who have disappeared under the surface of Christ's love and reappeared as different people', Christians are regularly 'fed by [Christ's] love and power' in the Eucharist and are consequently 'touched with the glory of the end of all things'.[75]

Such language may seem extravagant, and yet it expresses what is for Williams an incontrovertible fact, that the Christian life is a renewal of the whole person, a renewal of which the sacraments are not mere symbols but are the means of radical transformation. The transformation is not instantaneous but gradual, the action of the Holy Spirit enabling the development of faithful habits of prayer, eucharistic observance, worship, witness and service. Especially transformative is the practice of contemplation, a practice that, according to Williams, results in the 'dismantling of the imagination and its reconstructing by the gift of God in darkness'.[76] Involving a 'kind of costly openness', a 'refusal of the comforts of memory and ... fantasy', contemplation is described thus:

> The process of growth into God's fullness ... a total restructuring of our inner life. Memory, understanding and will are transformed into faith and hope and love. The renewed self or heart or imagination ... becomes *hopeful* ... open to God's future ... *faithful* ... trustful in what it can't perceive or control [and] *lovingly attentive to truth*.[77]

Linked in this way to the 'reconstruction' of human imagination, the regular practice of contemplation is, says Williams, not only 'the key to the essence of a renewed humanity', but also 'deeply revolutionary', 'the only ultimate answer to the unreal and insane world that our financial systems and our advertising culture and our chaotic and unexamined emotions encourage us to inhabit'.[78] In contemplation, ego-driven passions are gradually transformed by the divine action of grace, such that 'the face we ... show to the world is the face of a humanity in endless growth towards love.'[79] Christians thus become acclimatized to 'joy in the sheer reality of God', which is the experience of eternity.[80] Far from distancing its practitioners from the world, the kenotic, ecstatic practice of contemplation serves to clarify finite vision, enabling a more accurate perception of people and events[81] and leading to action in line with the divine mission of eternal self-dispossession for the sake of the world.[82]

Christian mission is thus integrally linked with the clarity of imaginative vision associated with the self-dispossessive, other-oriented practice of personal holiness. The saints feature prominently in Williams' thought and imagination, serving as exemplars of the kind of holy life that is the vocation of all Christians.[83] Such people, says Williams, are 'words from God to us'.[84] They change our perspective, enabling us to see the world and ourselves in a new light;[85] they 'produce ... a kind of longing in us';[86] they 'make us look not at *them*, but at the wellsprings of their life in Christ and Christ's in God the Father'.[87] People whose lives mirror something of the beauty of Christ draw others to them and so 'become a place in the world where the act of God can come alive'.[88]

Holiness is thus the mission of every Christian but, according to Williams, it is a mission defined by the crucifixion, 'the supremely holy thing'.[89] To become holy is a matter of sacrificial dispossession; it is 'the radically other-directed life of God lived in finite and vulnerable subjects'.[90] It means going, like Jesus, 'right into the middle of the mess and the suffering' of humanity.[91] As with Jesus, such radical involvement is dependent on the power of the Holy Spirit.[92] In situations where Christians have learned the self-dispossessing habits of contemplative attentiveness and expectancy towards God, 'God-shaped change can take place around [them].'[93] Holiness is thus life-changing.

Change occurs not only in the life of the holy person but, significantly, in the lives of others.[94] In the presence of holy people, as in the sharing of the Eucharist, the new creation begins to appear. Williams' claim is that, while the eschaton lies in 'a future we cannot but call God's because we have no secure human way of planning it or thematizing it',[95] experiences of holiness make the Kingdom of God a present reality. Like the life of Jesus of Nazareth, holy lives are thus a manifestation of 'the divine "imagination", the eternal purpose of God in creating and redeeming the world'.[96]

Similar transformative power is attributed by Williams to the process and product of artistic creation. Asserting that 'exposure to the life of the imagination in its fullness is always a step towards exposure to the maker of all things,'[97] he considers artists to be especially attuned to the activity of divine creativity within the finite order.[98] As was discussed in Chapter 8, humanity, in Williams' view, shares something of the creativity of its Creator. Possessing the capacity for representation, human beings are sign-makers with seemingly inexhaustible power to give new forms to the matter of the world through the developments of technology, science and social organization, as well as of art, literature and music.[99]

All such developments are expressions of human creativity and reflect, to a greater or lesser extent, something of the generativity of the divine Creator. Williams' claim is that artists are distinguished by their depth of sensitivity to the creative energy permeating finite matter. Like the saints, they see more than the surface appearance, discerning the excess inherent in the material order. Whether or not they are consciously alert to the divine presence, they are nevertheless responsive to the intractable otherness of the world around them, seeking to create a space within themselves for the observed object to make itself known in all its distinctiveness. Their relation to the world is thus that of self-dispossessive love, ecstatic in its movement towards the object, kenotic in its self-forgetfulness.[100]

Having access in this way to knowledge, which is participatory and relational, they produce work capable of revealing aspects of finite reality inaccessible to instrumental reason. Williams accordingly concludes that not only do artists contribute to humanity's knowledge of the world but that they also participate in the creative energy that is continually drawing the world towards its fulfilment. It is, says Williams, 'by means of the response of the imagination [that] the world's reality is always asymptotically approaching its fullness'.[101]

The creative activity of the artist is thus an indispensable model for the whole of humanity in accomplishing the human vocation of cooperating with God in the realization of God's purposes. Self-dispossessive and other-oriented, the artist's generative love of created matter shares something of the holiness of the saint, the holiness that, says Williams, participates in divine perfection in its 'bestowing of life ... on the world'. Humanity may be considered 'godlike' to the extent that it is life-bestowing in its response of imaginative creativity.[102]

## Notes

1 John Milbank, 'Extended Interview', *Religion and Ethics Newsweekly* (21 February 2003), https://www.pbs.org/wnet/religionandethics/2003/02/21/february-21-2003-john-milbank-extended-interview/12980, accessed 05.12.2019. 'Truth' in this statement, and as employed in this chapter, refers to the conception of truth discussed in the Introduction (p. 9), namely, 'truth conceived as ever-greater openness to that which is beyond representation'.

2 Williams, *Ray of Darkness* (Lanham, MD: Cowley, 1995), p. 3.

3 Williams, *Ray of Darkness*, p. 202.

4 Williams, *Ray of Darkness*, p. 207.

5 Rowan Williams, *Holy Living: The Christian Tradition for Today* (London: Bloomsbury, 2017), p. 27.

6 Williams, *Holy Living*, p. 97.

7 Rowan Williams, *The Truce of God* (London: Fount Paperbacks, 1983), p. 107.

8 Rowan Williams, *Silence and Honey Cakes: The Wisdom of the Desert* (Oxford: Lion, 2003), p. 80.

9 Williams, *Silence and Honey Cakes*, p. 96.

10 Rowan Williams, *Tokens of Trust: An Introduction to Christian Belief* (Louisville, KY: Westminster John Knox Press, 2007), p. 63.

11 Rowan Williams, *Resurrection: Interpreting the Easter Gospel*, 2nd edn (London: Darton, Longman & Todd, 2002), p. vii.

12 Rowan Williams, *Lost Icons* (Harrisburg, PA: Morehouse, 2000), p. 73.

13 Rowan Williams and Greg Garrett, *In Conversation* (New York: Church Publishing, 2019), p. 9.

14 Rowan Williams, *Christ on Trial: How the Gospel Unsettles our Judgement* (Grand Rapids, MI: Zondervan, 2000), p. 8.

15 Rowan Williams, *The Edge of Words: God and the Habits of Language* (London: Bloomsbury, 2014), p. 25. The work referred to is Jill Cook's *Ice Age Art: The Arrival of the Modern Mind* (London: British Museum Press, 2013).

16 Rowan Williams, *Being Human: Bodies, Minds, Persons* (London: SPCK, 2018), p. 13. The reference is to Iain McGilchrist, *The Master and his Emissary: The Divided Brain and the Making of the Western World* (New Haven, CT: Yale University Press, 2005).

17 Rowan Williams, *Grace and Necessity: Reflections on Art and Love* (London: Morehouse, 2005), pp. 135–8. Hofstadter's claims are to be found in Douglas R. Hofstadter and Daniel C. Dennett, *The Mind's Eye: Fantasies and Reflections on Self and Soul* (London: Penguin Books, 1981).

18 'Modern' imagination in this context is a reference to the 'secular' imagination of Western modernity with its emphasis on functionalism and rejection of 'reference to agencies or presences beyond the tangible'. Rowan Williams, *Faith in the Public Square* (London: Bloomsbury, 2012), p. 12.

19 Williams, *Grace and Necessity*, p. 76.

20 Williams, *The Edge of Words*, p. 123.

21 'A Conversation between Marilynne Robinson and Rowan Williams', in *Balm in Gilead: A Theological Dialogue with Marilynne Robinson*, ed. Timothy Larsen and Keith L. Johnson (Downers Grove, IL: IVP Academic, 2019), p. 181.

22 Rowan Williams, *On Christian Theology: Challenges in Contemporary Theology* (Malden, MA: Blackwell, 2000), p. 147; Williams and Robinson, 'A Conversation between Marilynne Robinson and Rowan Williams', in Larsen and Johnson, eds, *Balm in Gilead*, p. 189.

23 Williams, *The Edge of Words*, p. 122.

24 Rupert Shortt, *Rowan's Rule: The Biography of the Archbishop* (London: Hodder & Stoughton, 2008), p. 18.

25 Williams, *Grace and Necessity*, p. 147.

26 Williams, *Faith in the Public Square*, p. 184.

27 Williams, *The Edge of Words*, p. 122.

28 Williams and Robinson, 'A Conversation between Marilynne Robinson and Rowan Williams', in Larsen and Johnson (eds), *Balm in Gilead*, p. 191.

29 Williams and Robinson, 'A Conversation between Marilynne Robinson and Rowan Williams', in Larsen and Johnson (eds), *Balm in Gilead*, p. 183.

30 Rowan Williams, 'Beyond Goodness: *Gilead* and the Discovery of the Connections of Grace', in Larsen and Johnson, eds, *Balm in Gilead*, p. 165.

31 Shortt, *Rowan's Rule*, p. 18.

32 Williams, *On Christian Theology*, p. 147.

33 Williams, *Faith in the Public Square*, p. 13.

34 Message to the VIII International Liturgical Conference on Liturgy and Art, Monastery of Bose, 2010, http://www.monasterodibose.it/en/hospitality/conferences/liturgy/1095-2010-liturgy-art/5008-message-rowan-williams-2010-liturgy-art?, accessed 27.11.2019.

35 Williams, *The Edge of Words*, p. 123.

36 Williams and Garrett, *In Conversation*, pp. 123–4. See also p. 84, where God's energy permeating creation is described as 'that More than You Thought'.
37 Williams, *The Edge of Words*, p. 122.
38 Williams, *Silence and Honey Cakes*, pp. 87–8.
39 See Williams, *Silence and Honey Cakes*, p. 42.
40 Williams and Garrett, *In Conversation*, pp. 84–5.
41 Williams, *The Edge of Words*, pp. 85–6.
42 See Rowan Williams, *Resurrection: Interpreting the Easter Gospel*, 2nd edn (London: Darton, Longman & Todd, 2002), p. 61.
43 Williams, *On Christian Theology*, p. 40.
44 Mike Higton, ed., *Wrestling with Angels: Conversations in Modern Theology* (Grand Rapids, MI: William B. Eerdmans, 2007), p. 243.
45 Williams, *Faith in the Public Square*, pp. 183–4.
46 Rowan Williams, 'Enthronement Sermon', Canterbury Cathedral, 27 February 2003, http://rowanwilliams.archbishopofcanterbury.org/articles.php/1624/enthronement-sermon.html, accessed 5.07.2024.
47 Message to the VIII International Liturgical Conference. The italics are mine.
48 Rowan Williams, *Ponder These Things: Praying with Icons of the Virgin* (Mulgrave, Vic: John Garrett, 2002), p. xvii.
49 A similar image is found in Williams and Garrett, *In Conversation*, pp. 84–5, where Williams refers to 'the divine energy ... throbbing in every moment' within creation, as the action of grace 'always pushing to be through'.
50 Rowan Williams, *Christ the Heart of Creation* (London: Bloomsbury Continuum, 2018), p. 70.
51 Williams, *Christ the Heart of Creation*, p. 252.
52 Williams, *Grace and Necessity*, p. 76.
53 Shortt, *Rowan's Rule*, pp. 17–18. The italics are mine.
54 Williams, *The Edge of Words*, p. 122.
55 Williams, *Christ the Heart of Creation*, p. 104. Here Williams is drawing on the thought of Maximus the Confessor. See also Rowan Williams, *Choose Life: Christmas and Easter Sermons in Canterbury Cathedral* (London: Bloomsbury, 2013), p. 89; *Why Study the Past? The Quest for the Historical Church* (London: Darton, Longman & Todd, 2005), p. 44.
56 Rowan Williams, *A Silent Action: Engagements with Thomas Merton* (London: SPCK, 2013), p. 77.
57 Williams, *The Edge of Words*, pp. 122–4.
58 Williams, *The Edge of Words*, p. 124.
59 Williams, *The Edge of Words*, pp. 123–4.
60 Williams and Garrett, *In Conversation*, p. 84.
61 2 Corinthians 5.2, 4.
62 See, for example, *Faith in the Public Square* and *The Truce of God*.
63 See, for instance, Williams, 'Enthronement Sermon'.
64 Rowan Williams, *Meeting God in Paul* (London: SPCK, 2015), pp. 79ff.
65 See Williams, *Christ the Heart of Creation*.
66 Williams, *Christ the Heart of Creation*, p. xi.
67 The quotation is from Austin Farrer, 'Very God and Very Man', cited by Williams in *Christ the Heart of Creation*, p. 252.
68 Williams, *Christ the Heart of Creation*, p. 253.
69 Williams, *Ray of Darkness*, p. 58.

70 Rowan Williams, *The Wound of Knowledge: Christian Spirituality from the New Testament to St John of the Cross*, 2nd rev. edn (London: Darton Longman & Todd, 1990), p. 84.
71 Williams and Garrett, *In Conversation*, p. 16.
72 Williams and Garrett, *In Conversation*, pp. 84–5.
73 Williams and Garrett, *In Conversation*, p. 18.
74 Williams, *Christ the Heart of Creation*, p. 106.
75 Williams, *Tokens of Trust*, pp. 112, 120.
76 Williams, *A Silent Action*, p. 48.
77 Williams, *A Silent Action*, p. 48.
78 Williams, *Holy Living*, pp. 96–7.
79 Williams, *Holy Living*, p. 95.
80 Williams, *Tokens of Trust*, p. 155.
81 Williams, *Holy Living*, p. 96.
82 Williams, *Holy Living*, p. 99; *Ray of Darkness*, p. 225.
83 See, for example, Williams' study of Teresa of Avila, and his reflections on St John of the Cross (*The Wound of Knowledge*) and Julian of Norwich (*Holy Living*, pp. 169–86).
84 Williams, *A Silent Action*, p. 50.
85 Rowan Williams, *Being Disciples: Essentials of the Christian Life* (London: SPCK, 2016), pp. 51–2.
86 Williams, *Ray of Darkness*, p. 132.
87 Williams, *Ray of Darkness*, p. 132.
88 Williams, *Being Disciples*, p. 18.
89 Williams, *Being Disciples*, p. 47.
90 Williams, *Ray of Darkness*, p. 232.
91 Williams, *Being Disciples*, pp. 47–8.
92 Rowan Williams, *Why Study the Past? The Quest for the Historical Church*, 2nd edn (London: Darton, Longman & Todd, 2014), p. 46.
93 Williams, *Being Disciples*, p. 18.
94 Williams, *Choose Life*, pp. 105–6, 149, 176; *Tokens of Trust*, pp. 21–2.
95 Williams, *On Christian Theology*, p. 58.
96 Message to the VIII International Liturgical Conference.
97 Message to the VIII International Liturgical Conference.
98 See, for example, Williams, *On Christian Theology*, pp. 200–1.
99 Williams, *On Christian Theology*, pp. 200–1.
100 Rowan Williams, 'Creation, Creativity and Creatureliness: The Wisdom of Finite Existence', http://rowanwilliams.archbishopofcanterbury.org/articles.php/2106/creation-creativity-and-creatureliness-the-wisdom-of-finite-existence.html, accessed 5.07.2024.
101 Williams, *Grace and Necessity*, p. 154.
102 Williams, *Grace and Necessity*, p. 167.

# Conclusion

Rowan Williams began his tenure as Archbishop of Canterbury with the desire to present his readers and audiences with an imaginative vision sufficiently captivating to engage and sustain hope and trust in the face of the inhospitable climate of Western modernity. In sermons and addresses, theological works, social commentary and poetry, his consistent purpose has been to articulate a hope-filled vision of a 'world to live in' and a 'way of living' that allows human beings to flourish. In this study I have pointed to the source of that vision, his conception of a 'communicative' universe charged with the energy of divine *eros*.

As evidenced by his social commentary, the urgency of communicating the vision derives from his assessment of the 'cultural bereavement'[1] of modern Western societies. Indicative of that bereavement are two seemingly conflicting features of contemporary Western culture: first, the atrophying of imagination resulting from a predominantly instrumentalist concept of reason;[2] and second, the distortions of imagination expressed as escapist fantasies or as the fiction of 'self-creation' focused on the satisfaction of individual desires and the realization of finite goals.[3]

By contrast, the vision offered by Williams is founded on a theological metaphysic that provides an expansive understanding of finite reality as gift of divine love, of knowledge as participation in that love, and relationship as the infinitely multiplied expression of self-dispossessive, other-oriented love. The world to live in is one in which acute awareness of the fact of suffering and evil is held in tension with hope-filled trust in the inexhaustibility of love and its ultimate eschatological consummation. The way of living is that exemplified by religious devotion and artistic creation. Focused on the otherness of the universe, its inhabitants and its Creator, religious practice and artistic craftsmanship develop the habit of attentiveness to that which escapes human control: the infinite reality of interconnected ecstatic, kenotic relationality, known through participation.

Evident from the above account is the exalted transformative significance Williams attributes to grace-enabled human imagination. It may be argued that Williams' claims concerning imagination are subject to the same criticism of unrealistic idealism that has been directed towards his ecclesiology and his political and social vision.[4]

Countering that criticism is the fact that Williams' vision of Christian discipleship is far from idealistic. At the centre of that vision is the cross, a cross shared by all who seek to remain true to Christ in the outworking of their faith. As recognized by certain of his commentators, the gospel he preaches is a 'difficult gospel',[5] the Christ it portrays is a 'stranger' to human understanding,[6] and the vision he offers his listeners and readers requires the development of a 'tragic imagination'. Balancing the idealism evident in certain of his writings is the insistence on the ironic nature of human existence, as discussed in Chapter 9.

A poem written following the death of his father captures his own experience of the tragic dimension of human existence. It offers insight into the struggle involved in maintaining the tension between the pain of loss and continuing trust in God's unknowable future.

### Ceibr: Cliffs

*For Aneurin Williams: September 1999*

The quilt of willowherb muffles
the stream before it drops
invisible to the beach;
the moist whisper thinned
in its straight seaward fall,
its shore sound coming back up, dry
as two palms rubbing steadily
close to your ear, or pages
fingered through, or a hand
stroking an unshaved cheek, hard;
or a thick old fabric, tearing
very slowly. Sea on stone
never settles for good if this
is a story of meeting or
an endless creeping scission:
a palmer's kiss, book skimmed
for the familiar quote, touching
the distant face against
hospital pillows, or
slow surgery, faded cloth
pulled and surrendering

> every breath unstitching
> something. Whatever,
> the hoarse bass echo
> doesn't change: just the one
> voice, touching or tearing.[7]

As we read the poem, its meaning only gradually becomes clear. Like a palimpsest underlying the image of the stream's clifftop fall into the sea, the picture of a son sitting at the bedside of his dying father is slowly revealed through the references to the 'distant face against/hospital pillows' and the 'slow surgery' of dying whereby life is 'unstitched' at every breath. Encapsulated here is the essence of Williams' tragic imagination. Finite human existence finds its true end in the sea of the Creator's all-embracing love. And yet grief remains. The 'tearing' sense of loss is not diminished. It remains in tension with the eschatological hope that sustains the Christian believer.

The poem draws together the various lines of argument pursued in this book. It demonstrates the five interrelated capacities of imagination identified in Chapter 1: the freedom to detach from the immediate situation to stand back for a more holistic perspective; the ability to connect the different experiences of watching the sea and waiting beside a deathbed; the power to synthesize the two into a new symbol; the sensing of the transcendent in-and-beyond the immanent; and the bringing into being of a hitherto unforeseen perspective to be shared with others.

As discussed in Chapter 2, the imaginative language of metaphor and symbol has the power to communicate more than a literal meaning. Carried by that language are emotions, and multiple, complex resonances of meaning. The 'palmer's kiss' evokes both pilgrimage to holy shrines and the doomed love of Romeo and Juliet. The 'quilt of willowherb' is not only a groundcover beside a stream but also the dying man's bedding. The knowledge gained by the listener/reader is more than factual; it is the 'connatural' knowledge of empathic insight into another's experience, knowledge which cannot be adequately conveyed through purely 'factual' language.

Of especial significance is the metaphysical underpinning of the poem, which is an example of the analogical relation of finite to infinite as discussed in Chapter 3. For the poet, the relation between life and death is the in-and-beyond relation of the *analogia entis*. It is the relation of similarity-in-ever-greater-difference, a relation that cannot be held within a single frame of reference but is experienced as an oscillating movement between seen and unseen, meeting and parting, closeness and distance, finite and infinite.

Desire, the subject of Part Two, is not explicitly mentioned in this description of the slow process of dying. It is nevertheless captured by the image whereby the son's touch of his father's face becomes a 'palmer's kiss', a touching of holiness. Similarly, the sound of the dying man's breathing is heard as a meeting with, and 'surrender' to, the eternal presence which brought all things into being. Listening to that laboured breathing, the poet hears it as 'the one voice' of (the oceanic) God, 'touching' him in this moment of 'tearing' from the father he loves. Evidenced in this poem of loss is Williams' conception of the kenotic, ecstatic nature of love, divine and human, which, in moving out from self towards the other, involves an act of costly self-dispossession. In the conditions of finite existence, love, for Williams, inevitably brings pain as well as joy.

Evident also are the effects of the poet's habit of patient attentiveness as discussed in Chapter 6. The heightened sensitivity manifest in the aural associations with breath is the outcome of years spent in attentive listening and observing. As Williams has stated, it is through the discipline involved in the practice of such attentiveness to the otherness of the world and its inhabitants that human imaginations become attuned to discerning the holy Otherness of God, the ever-present energy of divine desire which permeates the universe.

The aesthetic theory discussed in Part Three is vividly illustrated by the poem. In the symbol of finite existence as a stream dropping into an infinite sea, we find an example of Williams' notion of the communicative universe, discussed in Chapter 7. While the symbol of the stream of life is banal in most contexts, here its significance lies in the memories it evokes for the poet, familiar as he is with the Welsh coastline of his youth. In the watch by his father's bed, it is to a specific landscape that his mind is directed, a landscape communicative of emotional associations. The language employed in that symbol allows us to glimpse Williams' vision of the interrelatedness of creation, animate and inanimate. The role of the artistic creator, says Williams, is to raise our awareness of the divine depth of meaning present in every aspect of finite existence, the ugly and painful as well as the beautiful.

The symbol of the stream's clifftop fall is also an example of Williams' notion that artistic creation involves 'making other' and 'making strange', as discussed in Chapters 8 and 9. In the first lines of the poem, the reader's imagination is sparked by the image of a stream winding its course through a meadow of willowherb before its sudden drop to the sea. As the poem progresses, however, the stream image is made more and more strange by various aural associations. Only in the final third of the poem does the actual significance of the symbol become clear. The reader's experience thus follows the process whereby the familiar was increasingly made strange for the poet as he waited by his dying father's bedside.

As shown in this poem, it is through the imaginative expansion of vision provided by religion and artistic creativity that we gain access to dimensions of existence unavailable to instrumental reason. Here, in the poet's struggle to hold in tension the grief of loss and the hope of his Christian faith, we encounter the action of divine grace, unseen and yet evidenced in the poet's seeking to find language that will give meaning to his loss. In this way, we sense something of the mystery of divine presence amid human pain. It is a presence unaccounted for by rationality but known through love, the love that allows hope to persist and imagination to flourish even in the face of an impenetrable future. It is the love that, by the gift of grace, persists as the 'sparkle from the coal' of finite human existence.

## Notes

1 This is the subtitle of Williams' book *Lost Icons* (Harrisburg, PA: Morehouse, 2000).

2 Rowan Williams, 'Has Secularism Failed?' in *Faith in the Public Square* (London: Bloomsbury, 2012), pp. 13ff.

3 Williams, *Faith in the Public Square*, p. 64.

4 Rupert Shortt, *Rowan's Rule: The Biography of the Archbishop* (London: Hodder & Stoughton, 2008), pp. 172 and 175, where Williams is judged to be a 'theological fox' skilled in nuanced theological analysis, but a 'hedgehog' in respect of the practical outworking of that theology.

5 Mike Higton, *Difficult Gospel: The Theology of Rowan Williams* (London: SCM Press, 2004).

6 Benjamin Myers, *Christ the Stranger: The Theology of Rowan Williams* (Edinburgh: T&T Clark, 2012).

7 Rowan Williams, *The Poems of Rowan Williams* (Oxford: Perpetua Press, 2002), p. 71.

# Afterword
# The Sparkle from the Coal

This book had its origin in a 1992 sermon expressed as poetry. It is fitting that it should conclude with Williams' more recent reflection on the origins of poetry and on the transformation effected by Christ to all faithful realizations of our human imagination.

### Felin Uchaf: Poetry in the Roundhouse

The wall leaves a gap, a grinning letterbox
before the thatch starts: steady light
pours smooth into the long mould, sets
in a beam, pivoting on the sill, tilting
by inches, slowly, as the thirsty darkness on the far
side of the wooded rise hauls it down
and pulls the bucket up out of the wide
fire's well. It hauls the smoke into the glowing
mould, packing it firm; sparks, scraps of ash
blazing like snowflakes, the smoke's column
a blizzard of sharp stars. The writers
round the fire feel their way, by inches,
hauled to their feet by the rising dark,
their words spat fast out of the whirl
of charred debris. Poems blaze in the glowing bar
of smoke, and disappear, grey in the roof.
And they sit again, the poets, sink
into the cooling cauldron. Hard to believe
that what they mixed, kneaded, moulded,
boiled is so quickly eaten in the shadows:
a short shining in the bright moulded smoke,
then the grey drift into evening. The poets
wonder, shrinking again to their benches,

# AFTERWORD

> how is it anyone believes where it all
> started, before the long patibulum
> lifted them up and out.

The setting is the Storytelling Roundhouse in the Felin Uchaf Centre near Aberdaron in Wales. Here, in a replica of the dwelling places of our prehistoric forebears, groups gather once again to listen to the stirrings of the human spirit expressed as poetry and story. As the sun gradually sets behind the nearby hill, those huddled inside watch as the long beam of solid light from the 'letterbox' window moves slowly across the interior of the round 'mould' of cob and thatch until it is finally consumed by 'thirsty darkness'. Like a bucket from a well, the central smoking fire is drawn up by the now pervasive darkness, shedding 'snowflakes' of white ash and a 'blizzard' of sparks over the group sitting tightly packed together in that smoke-filled enclosure. Now is the time for the poets, drawn to their feet by the darkness, to 'spit' out their poems in a blaze of words, before they and their poems 'sink' and disappear into the 'cooling cauldron' of creative energy. Poet after poet rises and sits again, while their poems, mixed, moulded, 'kneaded' out of their life's energy, are consumed by the all-pervading dark.

But all is not consumed. The poets are left with a wondering. It was around such fires that language, poetry, story had their beginning. So now they wonder, how is it that words, 'spat' out into the darkness and quickly 'eaten' in those shadows, have been lifted 'up and out' of the smoke-filled cauldron of those primitive mould houses? The answer is 'the long patibulum', that beam of wood anticipated by the 'steady' beam of light poured daily into the dark mould of human experience. The patibulum, borne by Jesus along the path to the cross, is the site on which his nailed body was lifted up and out of the imprisoning deathly darkness of this finite world. The lifting of that crossbeam with its burden has become the means by which language is set free to convey lasting meaning, so that poetry, story, art and song may 'lift' finite beings up and out of confining darkness into the all-pervasive light of God's presence. Freed from ignorance, human imagination may now raise our eyes to the source of infinite, ultimate meaning.

Skilfully employed by the poet are a number of literary devices – repetition, alliteration, assonance, repeated enjambment. These help to create the stifling oppressive atmosphere experienced by the audience crammed together inside the Roundhouse. The darkness is experienced as animate, 'thirstily' drinking the light, and hungrily 'eating' the poets' blazing words. Its effortful power is conveyed by the thrice-repeated verb 'hauls'. The sounds made by the crackling fire are echoed by the repetition of 's' sounds: 'sparks', 'scraps', 'snowflakes', 'sharp stars'. Vivid imagery conveys the 'blaze' and 'short shining' of the poems, while the poets 'sit ... sink ... and shrink', their significance quickly forgotten in the 'cooling cauldron' of memory and history. The enjambment of the long lines conveys the breathlessness both of the poets as they 'spit' out their verses and of the audience waiting in anticipation for the promised words. Only once does a new line convey a new idea, the let-down feeling of the poets as, having 'spat' out their lines, they now sink again into the shadows of oblivion. One line stands out in its brevity – the final line in which the impact of the death endured on the patibulum sets humanity, its language, and its imagination free.

Encapsulated in this poem is the significance of human imagination as it finds expression as language, poetry and story. Here, the 'sparkle from the coal', that 'sharp dart of longing love' that is the source of poetry and all artistic effort, is given its true meaning. Freed from the darkness of unknowing, the human longing for God is raised, with Christ's patibulum, out of our clumsy inarticulate ignorance to give lasting form and language to the manifold communication of divine love that is the finite world.

Human words and all signs – poetic, scientific, mathematical – are now lifted out of futility and may henceforth convey Truth, the Truth of the Word, the Logos that is 'God's own identity-in-difference', the source of the analogical identity-in-difference that is the 'coal' of created existence.

# Bibliography

## Primary works by Rowan Williams

### Books

*Anglican Identities*, London: Darton, Longman & Todd, 2004.
*Arius: Heresy and Tradition*, London: Darton, Longman & Todd, 1987.
*Being Christian: Baptism, Bible, Eucharist, Prayer*, London: SPCK, 2014.
*Being Disciples: Essentials of the Christian Life*, London: SPCK, 2016.
*Being Human: Bodies, Minds, Persons*, London: SPCK, 2018.
*Candles in the Dark: Faith, Hope and Love in a Time of Pandemic*, London: SPCK, 2020.
*A Century of Poetry: 100 Poems for Searching the Heart*, London: SPCK, 2022.
*Choose Life: Christmas and Easter Sermons in Canterbury Cathedral*, London: Bloomsbury, 2013.
*Christ on Trial: How the Gospel Unsettles our Judgement*, Grand Rapids, MI: Zondervan, 2000.
*Christ the Heart of Creation*, London: Bloomsbury Continuum, 2018.
*Christian Imagination in Poetry and Polity: Some Anglican Voices from Temple to Herbert*, Oxford: SLG Press, 2004.
*Collected Poems*, Manchester: Carcanet, 2021.
*Dostoevsky: Language, Faith and Fiction*, London: Bloomsbury, 2008.
*The Dwelling of the Light: Praying with Icons of Christ*, Mulgrave, Vic: John Garratt, 2003.
*The Edge of Words: God and the Habits of Language*, London: Bloomsbury, 2014.
*Faith in the Public Square*, London: Bloomsbury, 2012.
*God with Us: The Meaning of the Cross and Resurrection – Then and Now*, London: SPCK, 2017.
*Grace and Necessity: Reflections on Art and Love*, Harrisburg, PA: Morehouse Publishing, 2005.
*Headwaters*, Oxford: Perpetua Press, 2008.
*Holy Living: The Christian Tradition for Today*, London: Bloomsbury, 2017.
*The Lion's World: A Journey into the Heart of Narnia*, London: SPCK, 2012.
*Looking East in Winter: Contemporary Thought and the Eastern Christian Tradition*, London: Bloomsbury, 2021.
*Lost Icons: Reflections on Cultural Bereavement*, London: Morehouse, 2000.
*Luminaries: Twenty Lives that Illuminate the Christian Way*, London: SPCK, 2019.
*Meeting God in Mark*, London: SPCK, 2014.
*Meeting God in Paul*, London: SPCK, 2015.

*On Augustine*, London: Bloomsbury, 2016.
*On Christian Theology: Challenges in Contemporary Theology*, Oxford: Blackwell, 2000.
*The Other Mountain*, Manchester: Carcanet, 2014.
*The Poems of Rowan Williams*, Oxford: Perpetua Press, 2002.
*Ponder These Things: Praying with Icons of the Virgin*, Mulgrave, Vic: John Garratt, 2002.
*A Ray of Darkness: Sermons and Reflections*, Cambridge, MA: Cowley Publications, 1995.
*Resurrection: Interpreting the Easter Gospel*, 2nd edn, London: Darton, Longman & Todd, 2002.
*Silence and Honey Cakes: The Wisdom of the Desert*, Oxford: Lion Publishing, 2003.
*A Silent Action: Engagements with Thomas Merton*, London: SPCK, 2013.
*Teresa of Avila*, Harrisburg, PA: Morehouse Publishing, 1991.
*The Tragic Imagination*, Oxford: Oxford University Press, 2016.
*The Truce of God: Peacemaking in Troubled Times*, 2nd edn, Norwich: Canterbury Press, 2005.
*Tokens of Trust: An Introduction to Christian Belief*, Louisville, KY: Westminster, John Knox Press, 2007.
*The Way of St Benedict*, London: Bloomsbury Continuum, 2020.
*Where God Happens: Discovering Christ in One Another*, Boston: New Seeds, 2005.
*Why Study the Past? The Quest for the Historical Church*, 2nd edn, London: Darton, Longman & Todd, 2014.
*The Wound of Knowledge: Christian Spirituality from the New Testament to St John of the Cross*, 2nd rev. edn, London: Darton, Longman & Todd, 1990.
*Wrestling with Angels: Conversations in Modern Theology*, ed. Mike Higton, Grand Rapids, MI: William B. Eerdmans, 2007.
*Writing in the Dust: After September 11*, Grand Rapids, MI: William B. Eerdmans, 2002.

## Co-authored books

Cotter, Jim, Martyn Percy, Sylvia Sands, W. H. Vanstone and Rowan Williams, *Darkness Yielding: Liturgies, Prayers and Reflections for Christmas, Holy Week and Easter*, rev. edn, Norwich: Canterbury Press, 2009.
Rowell, Geoffrey, Kenneth Stevenson and Rowan Williams, *Love's Redeeming Work: The Anglican Quest for Holiness*, Oxford: Oxford University Press, 2003.
Williams, Rowan, and Joan Chittister, *For All That Has Been, Thanks: Growing a Sense of Gratitude*, Norwich: Canterbury Press, 2010.
Williams, Rowan, and Greg Garrett, *In Conversation*, New York: Church Publishing, 2019.
Williams, Rowan, and Larry Elliott, *Crisis and Recovery: Ethics, Economics and Justice*, Basingstoke and New York: Palgrave Macmillan, 2010.

# BIBLIOGRAPHY

## Articles, book chapters, essays and lectures

'Absence of Mind: The Dispelling of Inwardness from the Modern Myth of the Self by Marilynne Robinson', book review, *Telegraph* (28 May 2010).

'Address to the World Council of Churches Plenary on Christian Identity and Religious Plurality', 2006, https://www.oikoumene.org/resources/documents/rowan-williams-presentation.

'Afterword', in *The Blackwell Companion to Christian Ethics*, ed. Stanley Hauerwas and Samuel Wells, Oxford: Blackwell, 2004.

'Alderlet: For Alan Garner', *New Statesman* (6 May 2016).

'An address by the Archbishop of Canterbury given to a meeting of the Alcuin Club at Lambeth Palace', http://rowanwilliams.archbishopofcanterbury.org/articles.php/812/an-address-by-the-archbishop-of-canterbury-given-to-a-meeting-of-the-alcuin-club-at-lambeth-palace.html, accessed 5.07.2024.

'Archbishop's Liverpool Lecture: Europe, Faith and Culture', 2008, http://rowanwilliams.archbishopofcanterbury.org/articles.php/1164/archbishops-liverpool-lecture-europe-faith-and-culture.html, accessed 5.07.2024.

'The Art and Life of Josef Herman', book review in *Art and Christianity* 63 (2010), p. 12.

'Authority Deferred: A Christian Comment', *Studies in Christian Ethics* 29.2 (2016), pp. 213–17.

'The Authority of the Church', *Modern Believing* 46.1 (2005), pp. 16–28.

'Balthasar and the Trinity', in *The Cambridge Companion to Hans Urs von Balthasar*, ed. Edward T. Oakes and David Moss, Cambridge: Cambridge University Press, 2004, pp. 37–50.

'Beyond Goodness: Gilead and the Discovery of the Connections of Grace', in *Balm in Gilead: A Theological Dialogue with Marilynne Robinson*, ed. Timothy Larsen and Keith L. Johnson, Downers Grove, IL: IVP Academic, 2019, pp. 157–67.

'The Body's Grace', in *Our Selves, Our Souls, Our Bodies: Sexuality and the Household of God*, ed. Charles Hefling, Cambridge, MA: Cowley Publications, 1996, pp. 58–68.

'Christian Identity and Religious Plurality', *The Ecumenical Review* 58.1 (2006), pp. 69–75.

'The Church as Sacrament', *International Journal for the Study of the Christian Church* 10.1 (2010), pp. 6–12.

'The Church: God's Pilot Project', Address to a Clergy Synod, Chelmsford, 5 April 2006, http://rowanwilliams.archbishopofcanterbury.org/articles.php/1779/the-church-gods-pilot-project.html, accessed 5.07.2024.

'A Conversation between Marilynne Robinson and Rowan Williams', in *Balm in Gilead: A Theological Dialogue with Marilynne Robinson*, ed. Timothy Larsen and Keith L. Johnson, Downers Grove, IL: IVP Academic, 2019, pp. 180–98.

'Creation, Creativity and Creatureliness: The Wisdom of Finite Existence', Lecture delivered at a Study Day Organised by the St Theosevia Centre for Christian Spirituality, Oxford, 2005, http://rowanwilliams.archbishopofcanterbury.org/articles.php/2106/creation-creativity-and-creatureliness-the-wisdom-of-finite-existence.html, accessed 5.07.2024.

'The Deflections of Desire: Negative Theology in Trinitarian Disclosure', in *Silence and the Word: Negative Theology and Incarnation*, ed. Oliver Davies and Denys Turner, Cambridge: Cambridge University Press, 2002, pp. 115–35.

'Dialectic and Analogy', in *The Impact of Idealism: The Legacy of Post-Kantian German Thought*, Volume IV, ed. Nicholas Adams, Cambridge: Cambridge University Press, 2013, pp. 274–92.

'Eastern Orthodox Theology', in *The Modern Theologians: An Introduction to Christian Theology in the Twentieth Century*, 2nd edn, ed. David F. Ford, Malden, MA: Blackwell, 1997, pp. 499–512.

'Enthronement Sermon', Canterbury Cathedral, 27 February 2003, http://rowanwilliams.archbishopofcanterbury.org/articles.php/1624/enthronement-sermon.html, accessed 5.07.2024.

'Everything is Illuminated: Haunted by his Time in the Trenches and Disturbed by the Modern Marketplace, Jones Formed a World-View Full of Symbols and Connections', *New Statesman* 146.5359 (2017).

'Faith and Image: Rowan Williams and Neil McGregor Discuss the Significance of Images in the Lives of the Faithful', *Art and Christianity* 75 (Autumn 2013), pp. 2–5.

'Foreword', in John Saward, *The Mysteries of March: Hans Urs von Balthasar on the Incarnation and Easter*, Washington: Catholic University of America Press, 1990.

'Foreword', in Nicholas Afanasiev, *The Church of the Holy Spirit*, trans. Vitaly Permiakov, edited with an Introduction by Michael Pleban, Notre Dame, IN: University of Notre Dame Press, 2007.

'Foreword', in Christopher Irvine, *The Cross and Creation in Christian Liturgy and Art*, London: SPCK, 2013.

'Foreword', in *Animating Liturgy: The Dynamics of Worship and the Human Community*, ed. Stephen Platten, Durham: Sacristy Press, 2017.

'Imagining Christ in Literature', in *The Oxford Handbook of Christology*, ed. Francesca Ann Murphy, Oxford: Oxford University Press, 2015, pp. 488–505.

'Interiority and Epiphany: A Reading in New Testament Ethics', *Modern Theology* 13.1 (1997), pp. 29–51.

'It is Not a Crime to Hold Traditional Values', *Times Higher Education Supplement* 1772 (2006), pp. 16–17.

'It's intelligence all the way down', interview by Theos Think Tank, http://www.theosthinktank.co.uk/comment/2014/10/20/its-intelligence-all-the-way-down, accessed 26.06.2024.

'"Know Thyself": What Kind of an Injunction?', in *Philosophy, Religion and the Spiritual Life*, ed. Michael McGhee, Cambridge: Cambridge University Press, 2010, pp. 211–27.

'Liturgical Humanism: Orthodoxy and the Transformation of Culture', Fordham University, 30 September 2014, https://www.fordham.edu/info/23004/orthodoxy_in_america_lecture_series, accessed 26.06.2024.

'Making it Strange: Theology in Other(s') Words', in *Sounding the Depths: Theology Through the Arts*, ed. Jeremy Begbie, London: SCM Press, 2002.

'Making Moral Decisions', in *The Cambridge Companion to Christian Ethics*, ed. Robin Gill, Cambridge: Cambridge University Press, 2001, pp. 3–15.

'Message to the VIII International Liturgical Conference on Liturgy and Art, Monastery of Bose, 2010', http://www.monasterodibose.it/en/hospitality/conferences/liturgy/1094-2012-liturgy-art/5008-message-rowan-williams-2010-liturgy-art, accessed 24.06.2024.

'Native Speakers: Identity, Grace, and Homecoming', *Christianity and Literature* 61.1 (2011), pp. 6–18.
'No More Happy Endings: We need Fairy Tales Now more than Ever', *New Statesman* (19 December 2014/8 January 2015).
'Not Cured, not Forgetful, not Paralysed: A Response to Comments on *The Tragic Imagination*', *Modern Theology* 34.2 (2018), pp. 280–8.
'On Being a Human Body', *Sewanee Theological Review* 42.4 (1999), pp. 403–13.
'One Hope, One Church', *Internationale Kirchliche Zeitschrift* 96.4 (2006), pp. 207–16.
'Pardon is the Word: Shakespeare, Edmund Campion and the Grace of Forgiveness', *America* (1 March 2010), pp. 18–20.
'Poetic and Religious Imagination', *Theology* 80.675 (1977), pp. 178–87.
'Politics and the Soul: A Reading of the *City of God*', *Milltown Studies* 19–20 (1987), pp. 55–72.
'Recognition of the Sacred: Religious Conviction and Human Rights', *ABC Religion and Ethics Report*, 10 December 2012, http://www.abc.net.au/religion/articles/2012/12/10/3651192.htm.
'A Response', in *Essays on Eucharistic Sacrifice in the Early Church – a Sequel to Liturgical Study No 31: Eucharistic Sacrifice, The Roots of a Metaphor: Group Liturgical Study*, ed. Colin Buchanan, Bramcote, Notts: Grove Books, 1984, pp. 34–7.
'Response to Kerr, Hedley, Pickstock, Ward and Soskice', *Modern Theology* 31.4 (2015), pp. 630–6.
'Review of *R. S. Thomas: Poet of the Hidden God. Meaning and Mediation in the Poetry of R. S. Thomas*, by D. Z. Phillips', *Journal of Theological Studies* 39.2 (1988), pp. 653–5.
'Rome Lecture: Secularism, Faith and Freedom', Pontifical Academy of Social Sciences, Rome, 2006.
'Rowan Williams on Poetry', http://rowanwilliams.archbishopofcanterbury.org/articles.php/1752/rowan-williams-on-poetry.html, accessed 27.07.2024.
'Sacramental Living', *St Peter's Public Lectures*, Melbourne: Trinity Papers, 2002.
'"The Sadness of the King": Gillian Rose, Hegel and the Pathos of Reason', *Telos* 173 (Winter 2015), pp. 21–36.
'Sermon to commemorate the 400th anniversary of the birth of the poet John Milton', http://rowanwilliams.archbishopofcanterbury.org/articles.php/1222/archbishop-preaches-about-poet-john-milton-at-st-giles-cripplegate.html, accessed 6.07.2024.
'Theological Doubt and Institutional Certainty: An Anglican Paradox', *Studies in Church History* 52 (2016), pp. 250–65.
'The Theology of Personhood: A Study of the Thought of Christos Yannaras', *Sobornost: The Journal of the Fellowship of St Alban and St Sergius* 6 (1972), pp. 415–30.
'To Stand Where Christ Stands', in *An Introduction to Christian Spirituality*, ed. Ralph Walker and Benedicta Ward, London: SPCK, 1999, pp. 1–13.
'What do Atheists mean When they Talk about Religion?', *ABC Religion and Ethics Report*, 13 April 2012, https://www.abc.net.au/religion/what-do-atheists-mean-when-they-talk-about-religion/10100626, accessed 6.07.2024.
'What Does Love Know? St Thomas on the Trinity', *New Blackfriars* 82.964 (2001), pp. 260–72.

'Worship Makes our Lives Bigger and Better', *Catholic Herald*, 27 September 2014, https://catholicherald.co.uk/worship-makes-our-lives-bigger-and-better/, accessed 6.07.2024.

## Secondary literature

Alison, James, *Raising Abel: The Recovery of the Eschatological Imagination*, New York: Crossroad, 1996.

Allison, Dale C., Jr, *Night Comes: Death, Imagination and the Last Things*, Grand Rapids, MI: William B. Eerdmans, 2016.

Asma, Stephen T., *The Evolution of Imagination*, Chicago, IL: University of Chicago Press, 2017.

Augustine, *Confessions*, translated with Introduction and Notes by Henry Chadwick, Oxford: Oxford University Press, 1998.

———, *On Christian Doctrine*, translated by J. F. Shaw, Mineola, NY: Dover, 2009.

Austin, Michael, *Explorations in Art, Theology and Imagination*, London: Equinox, 2005.

Avis, Paul, *God and the Creative Imagination: Metaphor, Symbol and Myth in Religion and Theology*, London: Routledge, 1999.

Bachelard, Gaston, *La Poétique de l'Espace*, Paris: Presses Universitaires de France, 1957.

Bachelard, Sarah, *Resurrection and the Moral Imagination*, Farnham: Ashgate, 2014.

Bailer-Jones, Daniela M., 'Models, Metaphors and Analogies', in *The Blackwell Guide to the Philosophy of Science*, edited by Peter Machamer and Michael Silberstein, Malden, MA: Blackwell, 2002, pp. 108–27.

Balthasar, Hans Urs von, *The Glory of the Lord, Vol. 1, Seeing the Form*, translated by Erasmo Leiva-Merikakis, Edinburgh: T&T Clark, 1982.

———, 'In Retrospect', in *The Analogy of Beauty: The Theology of Hans Urs von Balthasar*, edited by John Riches, Edinburgh: T&T Clark, 1986, pp. 194–221.

Barbour, Ian, *Myths, Models and Paradigms*, London: SCM Press, 1974.

Barker, Sebastian, 'On the Aesthetics of Art in the Theology of Rowan Williams', in *Rowan Williams' Theology of Art and Other Essays*, Lewiston, NY: Edwin Mellen Press, 2009, pp. 7–17.

Barth, J. Robert, *The Symbolic Imagination: Coleridge and the Romantic Tradition*, New York: Fordham University Press, 2001.

Baumgaertner, Jill Pelaez, 'Review of *The Poems of Rowan Williams*', *Christian Century* 122.21 (18 October 2005), pp. 61–5.

Begbie, Jeremy, ed., *Beholding the Glory: Incarnation through the Arts*, Grand Rapids, MI: Baker Books, 2000.

Berth, J. Robert, *The Symbolic Imagination: Coleridge and the Romantic Tradition*, New York: Fordham University Press, 2001.

Betz, John R., 'The *Analogia Entis* as a Standard of Catholic Engagement: Erich Przywara's Critique of Phenomenology and Dialectical Theology', *Modern Theology* 35.1 (2019), pp. 81–102.

———, 'Beyond the Sublime: The Aesthetics of the Analogy of Being (Part Two)', *Modern Theology* 22.1 (2006), pp. 1–50.

Black, Max, *Models and Metaphors*, Ithaca, NY: Cornell University Press, 1962.

# BIBLIOGRAPHY

Blundell, Boyd, *Paul Ricoeur between Theology and Philosophy: Detour and Return*, Bloomington, IN: Indiana University Press, 2010.

Boothby, Richard, *Death and Desire: Psychoanalytic Theory in Lacan's Return to Freud*, London and New York: Routledge, 1991.

Braunstein, Néstor A., 'Desire and Jouissance in the Teachings of Lacan', in *The Cambridge Companion to Lacan*, edited by Jean-Michel Rabaté, Cambridge: Cambridge University Press, 2003, pp. 102–15.

Breyfogle, Todd, 'Time and Transformation: A Conversation with Rowan Williams', *Cross Currents* 45.3 (Fall 1995), pp. 293–311.

Brown, David, *God and Mystery in Words: Experience through Metaphor and Drama*, Oxford: Oxford University Press, 2008.

———, *Tradition and Imagination: Revelation and Change*, Oxford: Oxford University Press, 1999.

Brueggemann, Walter, *Hopeful Imagination: Prophetic Voices in Exile*, Philadelphia, PA: Fortress Press, 1986.

———, *The Prophetic Imagination*, 2nd edn, Minneapolis, MN: Fortress Press, 2001.

———, *The Practice of Prophetic Imagination: Preaching on Emancipating Word*, Minneapolis, MN: Fortress Press, 2012.

Bryant, David J., *Faith and the Play of Imagination: On the Role of Imagination in Religion*, Macon, GA: Mercer University Press, 1989.

Calvo, P., and T. Gomila, eds, *The Handbook of Cognitive Science: An Embodied Approach*, Amsterdam: Elsevier, 2008.

Cary, Phillip, *Outward Signs: The Powerlessness of External Things in Augustine's Thought*, Oxford: Oxford University Press, 2008.

Casey, Edward S., *Imagining: A Phenomenological Study*, Bloomington, IN: Indiana University Press, 1976.

Cavell, Stanley, *Disowning Knowledge in Seven Plays of Shakespeare*, updated edition, Cambridge: Cambridge University Press, 2003.

Cazeaux, Clive, *Metaphor and Continental Philosophy: From Kant to Derrida*, New York: Routledge, 2007.

Coleridge, Samuel Taylor, *Biographia Literaria, 1*, edited by J. Engell and W. Jackson Bate, Princeton, 1983.

———, *The Statesman's Manual or The Bible the Best Guide to Political Skill and Foresight: A Lay Sermon Addressed to the Higher Classes of Society, with an Appendix containing Comments and Essays connected with the Study of the Inspired Writings*, London: Gale and Fenner, 1816, Open Library, openlibrary.org/books/OL23340184M/the_stateman%27s_manual, accessed 6.07.2024.

Cowdell, Scott, Chris Fleming and Joel Hodge, eds, *Violence, Desire and the Sacred: Girard's Mimetic Theory across the Disciplines*, New York: Continuum International, 2012.

Cox, D. Michael, 'Grammar and Glory: Eastern Orthodoxy, the "Resolute" Wittgenstein, and the Theology of Rowan Williams', PhD Diss., University of Dayton, Dayton, Ohio, 2015, https://ecommons.udayton.edu/graduate_theses/799/, accessed 6.07.2024.

Cunningham, Conor, *Darwin's Pious Idea: Why the Ultra-Darwinists and Creationists both get it Wrong*, Grand Rapids, MI: William B. Eerdmans, 2010.

Cunningham, David S., 'Living the Questions: The Converging Worlds of Rowan Williams', *The Christian Century* 119.9 (2002), https://www.christiancentury.org/article/living-questions, accessed 6.07.2024.

Daniels, Joel C., 'Against Innocence, against Evasion: Rowan Williams on Thinking and Speaking Tragedy', *Anglican Theological Review* 100.2 (2018), pp. 385–95.

Davies, Oliver, 'The Theological Aesthetics', in *The Cambridge Companion to Hans Urs von Balthasar*, edited by Edward T. Oakes and David Moss, Cambridge: Cambridge University Press, 2004, pp. 131–42.

Davies, Oliver, and Denys Turner, eds, *Silence and the Word: Negative Theology and Incarnation*, Cambridge: Cambridge University Press, 2002.

Delport, Khegan, 'Of Danger and Difficulty: Rowan Williams and *the Tragic Imagination*', *The Heythrop Journal* 61.3 (2017), pp. 505–20.

——, 'Towards a Visionary and Historical Consciousness: Rowan Williams's *Four Quartet* Lectures (1974–1975)', *Studia Historiae Ecclesiasticae* 43.3 (2017), https://doi.org/10.25159/2412-4265/3388.

——, '*Interior Intimi Meo*: Rowan Williams on the Self', *Stellenbosch Theological Journal* 4.2 (2018), pp. 471–504.

Dor, Daniel, *The Instruction of Imagination: Language as Social Communication Technology*, Oxford: Oxford University Press, 2015.

Dorsch, Fabian, 'Hume', in *The Routledge Handbook of Philosophy of Imagination*, edited by Amy Kind, London: Routledge, 2016, pp. 40–54.

D'Souza, Mario O., and Jonathan R. Seiling, eds, *Being in the World: A Quotable Maritain Reader*, Notre Dame, IN: University of Notre Dame Press, 2014.

Eilers, Kent, 'Rowan Williams and Christian Language: Mystery, Disruption, and Rebirth', *Christianity and Literature* 61.1 (2011), pp. 19–32.

Enos, Richard Leo, Roger Thompson et al., eds, *The Rhetoric of St Augustine of Hippo: De Doctrina Christiana and the Search for a Distinctly Christian Rhetoric*, Waco, TX: Baylor University Press, 2008.

Farrer, Austin, *The Glass of Vision*, in *Scripture, Metaphysics, and Poetry: Austin Farrer's* The Glass of Vision *with Critical Commentary*, edited by Robert MacSwain, Farnham: Ashgate, 2013, Kindle locations 312–2888.

Fennell, Rob, ed., *Both Sides of the Wardrobe: C. S. Lewis, Theological Imagination, and Everyday Discipleship*, Eugene, OR: Resource Publications, 2015.

Fielding, Alodie, 'Rowan Williams through the Narrow Gate', *Monk* (2019), Monk.gallery/interviews/rowan-williams-interview, accessed 27.06.2024.

Fodor, James, *Christian Hermeneutics: Paul Ricoeur and the Refiguring of Theology*, Oxford: Clarendon Press, 1995.

Fodor, Luke, 'The Occasional Theology and Constant Spirituality of Rowan Williams', *Anglican Theological Review* 94.2 (2012), pp. 263–79.

Fraser, Giles, 'Faith to Faith: Dialectical Anglicanism has many problems, foremost among them the damage to its champion – Rowan Williams', *The Guardian* (17 June 2006).

Fuentes, Agustin, *The Creative Spark: How Imagination Made Humans Exceptional*, New York: Dutton, 2017.

Gentner, Dedre, Keith J. Holyoak and Boicho N. Kokinov, eds, *The Analogical Mind: Perspectives from Cognitive Science*, Cambridge, MA: The MIT Press, 2001.

Gibbs, Raymond W., ed., *The Cambridge Handbook of Metaphor and Thought*, Cambridge: Cambridge University Press, 2008.

Gioia, Luigi, *The Theological Epistemology of Augustine's De Trinitate*, Oxford: Oxford University Press, 2008.

Girard, René, *Violence and the Sacred*, translated by Patrick Gregory, Baltimore, MD: Johns Hopkins University Press, 1977.

Goddard, Andrew, *Rowan Williams: His Legacy*, Oxford: Lion Hudson, 2013.
Gonzales, Philip, *Reimagining the Analogia Entis: The Future of Erich Przywara's Christian Vision*, Grand Rapids, MI: William B. Eerdmans, 2019.
Gray, Brett, *Jesus in the Theology of Rowan Williams*, London: Bloomsbury, 2016.
Green, Garrett, *Imagining God: Theology and the Religious Imagination*, Grand Rapids, MI: William B. Eerdmans, 1989.
——, *Theology, Hermeneutics, and Imagination: The Crisis of Interpretation at the End of Modernity*, Cambridge: Cambridge University Press, 2000.
Griffiths, Dominic, 'The Poet as "Worldmaker": T. S. Eliot and the Religious Imagination', in *Poetry and the Religious Imagination: The Power of the Word*, edited by Francesca Bugliani Knox and David Lonsdale, Farnham: Ashgate, 2015.
Guite, Malcolm, *Faith, Hope and Poetry*, Farnham: Ashgate, 2010.
——, 'Keeping Alive the Head in the Heart: Poetic Imagination as a Way of Knowing', in *Head and Heart: Perspectives from Religion and Psychology*, edited by Fraser Watts and Geoff Dumbreck, West Conshohocken, PA: Templeton Press, 2013, pp. 49–70.
Hankey, Wayne J., 'Self-Knowledge and God as Other in Augustine: Problems for a Postmodern Retrieval', *Bochumer Philosophisches Jahrbuch für Antike und Mittelalter* 4.1 (1999), pp. 83–123.
——, '*Theoria versus Poesis*: Neoplatonism and Trinitarian Difference in Aquinas, John Milbank, Jean-Luc Marion and John Zizioulas', *Modern Theology* 15.4 (1999), pp. 387–415.
Hart, David Bentley, *The Beauty of the Infinite: The Aesthetics of Christian Truth*, Grand Rapids, MI: William B. Eerdmans, 2003.
——, 'The Gospel according to Melpomene: Reflection on Rowan Williams's *The Tragic Imagination*', *Modern Theology* 34.2 (2018), pp. 220–34.
Hart, Trevor, Gavin Hopps and Jeremy Begbie, eds, *Art, Imagination and Christian Hope: Patterns of Promise*, Farnham: Ashgate, 2012.
Hart, Trevor, *Between the Image and the Word: Theological Engagements with Imagination, Language and Literature*, Farnham: Ashgate, 2013.
Heaney, Seamus, *The Redress of Poetry*, New York: Farrar, Straus & Giroux, 1995.
Hedley, Douglas, *Living Forms of the Imagination*, London: T&T Clark International, 2008.
——, *The Iconic Imagination*, New York: Bloomsbury Academic, 2016.
Heidegger, Martin, *Basic Writings*, edited by David F. Krell, San Francisco, CA: HarperCollins, 1993.
Henriksen, Jan-Olav, *Desire, Gift, and Recognition: Christology and Postmodern Philosophy*, Grand Rapids, MI: William B. Eerdmans, 2009.
Higton, Mike, *Difficult Gospel: The Theology of Rowan Williams*, New York: Church Publishing, 2004.
Hobson, Theo, *Anarchy, Church and Utopia: Rowan Williams on Church*, London: Darton, Longman & Todd, 2005.
——, 'The Policing of Signs: Sacramentalism and Authority in Rowan Williams' Theology', *Scottish Journal of Theology* 61.4 (2008), pp. 381–95.
——, 'Rowan Williams got it right about Ritual', *The Guardian* (31 October 2012).
Hofstadter, Douglas, and Daniel C. Dennet, *In the Mind's Eye: Fantasies and Reflections on Self and Soul*, London: Penguin Books, 1981.
Hofstadter, Douglas, and Emmanuel Sander, *Surfaces and Essences: Analogy as the Fuel and Fire of Thinking*, New York: Basic Books, 2013.

Holyoak, Keith J., and Paul Thagard, 'The Analogical Mind', *American Psychologist* 52.1 (1997), pp. 35–44.
Hopkins, Robert, 'Sartre', in *The Routledge Handbook of Philosophy of Imagination*, edited by Amy Kind, London: Routledge, 2016, pp. 82–93.
Howes, Rebekah, 'In the Shadow of Gillian Rose: Truth as Education in the Hegelian Philosophy of Rowan Williams', *Political Theology* 19.1 (2018), pp. 20–34.
Howsare, Rodney A., *Balthasar: A Guide for the Perplexed*, London: T&T Clark, 2009.
Hurford, James R., *The Origins of Language: A Slim Guide*, Oxford: Oxford University Press, 2014.
Imbelli, Robert P., 'The Heart of the Matter', *America* 220.7 (2019), p. 44.
Irving, Alexander J. D., 'The Eucharist and the Church in the Thought of Henri De Lubac and Rowan Williams: Sacramental Ecclesiology and the Place of the Church in the World', *Anglican Theological Review* 100.2 (2018), pp. 267–89.
Jameson, Jonathan, 'Erotic Absence and Sacramental Hope: Rowan Williams on Augustinian Desire', *Anglican Theological Review* 102.4 (2020), pp. 575–95.
Jenkins, Scott, 'Hegel's Concept of Desire', *Journal of the History of Philosophy* 47.1 (2009), pp. 103–30.
Johnson, Mark, *The Body in the Mind: The Bodily Basis of Meaning, Imagination, and Reason*, Chicago, IL: University of Chicago Press, 1990.
———, *Moral Imagination: Implications of Cognitive Science for Ethics*, Chicago, IL: University of Chicago Press, 1993.
———, 'Moral Imagination', in *The Routledge Handbook of Philosophy of Imagination*, edited by Amy Kind, London: Routledge, 2016, pp. 355–67.
Jørgensen, Dorthe, 'The Philosophy of Imagination', in *Handbook of Imagination and Culture*, edited by Tania Zittoun and Vlad Glăveanu, Oxford: Oxford University Press, 2018, pp. 19–45.
Kant, Immanuel, *Critique of Judgement*, 2nd edn revised, translated with Introduction and Notes by J. H. Bernard, London: Macmillan, 1914. Kindle.
Kaplan, Jonathan, and Robert Williamson, Jr, eds, *Imagination, Ideology and Inspiration: Echoes of Brueggemann in a New Generation*, Sheffield: Sheffield Phoenix Press, 2015.
Kaufman, Gordon, *Theological Imagination: Constructing the Concept of God*, Louisville, KY: Westminster John Knox Press, 1981.
Keane, Philip S., *Christian Ethics and Imagination: A Theological Inquiry*, Mahwah, NJ: Paulist Press, 1984.
Kearney, Richard, *The Wake of Imagination: Ideas of Creativity in Western Culture*, London: Hutchinson Education, 1988.
———, *Poetics of Imagining: Modern to Post-Modern*, Edinburgh: Edinburgh University Press, 1998.
———, *On Paul Ricoeur: The Owl of Minerva*, Aldershot: Ashgate, 2004.
———, ed., *Paul Ricoeur: The Hermeneutics of Action*, London: Sage, 1996.
———, 'Exploring Imagination with Paul Ricoeur', in *Stretching the Limits of Productive Imagination: Studies in Kantianism, Phenomenology, and Hermeneutics*, edited by Saulius Geniusas, Lanham, MD: Rowman and Littlefield, 2018, pp. 187–204.
Kerr, Fergus, *Theology after Wittgenstein*, Oxford: Basil Blackwell, 1986.
Kind, Amy, ed., *The Routledge Handbook of Philosophy of Imagination*, Abingdon: Routledge, 2016.

# BIBLIOGRAPHY

Kind, Amy, and Peter Kung, eds, *Knowledge Through Imagination*, Oxford: Oxford University Press, 2016.
Knox, Francesca Bugliani, and David Lonsdale, eds, *Poetry and the Religious Imagination: The Power of the Word*, Farnham: Ashgate, 2015.
Lacan, Jacques, *Écrits: A Selection*, translated by Alan Sheridan, London: Tavistock, 1977.
Lachman, Gary, *Lost Knowledge of the Imagination*, Edinburgh: Floris Books, 2018.
Lakoff, George, and Mark Johnson, *Metaphors We Live By*, Chicago, IL: University of Chicago Press, 1980.
———, *Philosophy in the Flesh: The Embodied Mind and its Challenge to Western Thought*, New York: Basic Books, 1999.
Lodziak, Conrad, *The Myth of Consumerism*, London: Pluto Press, 2002.
Long, Steven A., *Analogia Entis: On the Analogy of Being, Metaphysics and the Act of Faith*, Notre Dame, IN: University of Notre Dame Press, 2011.
Lossky, Vladimir, *The Mystical Theology of the Eastern Church*, translated by members of the Fellowship of St Alban and St Sergius, London: James Clark, 1957.
———, *In the Image and Likeness of God*, Introduction by John Meyendorff and a Bibliography by Thomas E. Bird, Crestwood, NY: St Vladimir's Seminary Press, 1974.
Mackey, James P., ed, *Religious Imagination*, Edinburgh: Edinburgh University Press, 1986.
MacMurray, John, *The Self as Agent*, London: Faber & Faber, 1957.
MacSwain, Robert, *Scripture, Metaphysics, and Poetry: Austin Farrer's* The Glass of Vision *with Critical Commentary*, edited by Robert MacSwain, Farnham: Ashgate, 2013, Kindle.
Marcus, Nancy du Bois, *Vico and Plato*, New York: Peter Lang, 2001.
Marcus, R. A., 'St Augustine on Signs', *Phronesis* 2.1 (1957), pp. 60–83.
Maritain, Jacques, *Art and Scholasticism with Other Essays*, translated by J. F. Scanlan, London: Sheed & Ward, 1946.
———, *Creative Intuition in Art and Poetry: The A.W. Mellon Lectures in the Fine Arts*, New York: Meridian Books, 1955.
———, *The Responsibility of the Artist*, New York: Charles Scribner's Sons, 1960.
Matherne, Samantha, 'Kant's Theory of the Imagination', in *The Routledge Handbook of Philosophy of Imagination*, edited by Amy Kind, London: Routledge, 2016, pp. 55–68.
McCurry, Jeffrey, 'Towards a Poetics of Theological Creativity: Rowan Williams Reads Augustine's *De Doctrina Christiana* after Derrida', *Modern Theology* 23.3 (2007), pp. 415–32.
McGowan, Andrew, 'Conversations with Rowan Williams', *Eureka Street* (22 March 2012), https://www.eurekastreet.com.au/article/conversations-with-rowan-williams, accessed 27.06.2024.
McInerny, Ralph, *Aquinas and Analogy*, Washington: Catholic University of America Press, 1996.
McIntosh, Mark A., *Mystical Theology: The Integrity of Spirituality and Theology*, Malden, MA: Blackwell, 1998.
McIntyre, John, 'Analogy', *Scottish Journal of Theology* 12.3 (1959), pp. 1–20.
———, *Faith, Theology and Imagination*, Edinburgh: Handsel Press, 1987.

McKinlay, B., 'Ludwig Wittgenstein in Rowan Williams' Theological Account of Language', *New Blackfriars* 98.1075 (2017), pp. 327–41.
Middleton, David, 'The Poems of Rowan Williams', *Anglican Theological Review* 88.3 (2006), pp. 479–81.
Midgley, Mary, *Science and Poetry*, London: Routledge, 2001.
——, *The Myths We Live By*, London: Routledge, 2004.
Milbank, John, 'Extended Interview', *Religion and Ethics Newsweekly*, 21 February 2003, https://www.pbs.org/wnet/religionandethics/2003/02/21/february-21-2003-john-milbank-extended-interview/12980, accessed 27.06.2024.
——, 'Scholasticism, Modernism and Modernity', *Modern Theology* 22.4 (2006), pp. 651–71.
Miles, Margaret R., *Desire and Delight: A New Reading of Augustine's Confessions*, New York: Crossroad, 1992.
Mithin, Stephen, *The Pre-History of the Mind: The Cognitive Origins of Art, Religion and Science*, London: Thames & Hudson, 1996.
Modell, Arnold H., *Imagination and the Meaningful Brain*, Cambridge, MA: MIT Press, 2006.
Modrak, Deborah K. W., 'Aristotle on *Phantasia*', in *The Routledge Handbook of Philosophy of Imagination*, edited by Amy Kind, London: Routledge, 2016, pp. 15–26.
Moody, Andrew, 'The Hidden Center: Trinity and Incarnation in the Negative (and Positive) Theology of Rowan Williams', in *On Rowan Williams: Critical Essays*, edited by Matheson Russell, Eugene, OR: Cascade Books, 2009, pp. 25–46.
Morgan, Edward, *The Incarnation of the Word: The Theology of Language of Augustine of Hippo*, London: T&T Clark International, 2010.
Moseley, Carys, 'Persons in Community in the Theology of Rowan Williams: Issues Arising with the Use of Sociology in Christian Reasoning', *Studies in Christian Ethics* 21.2 (2008), pp. 250–68.
Mudge, Lewis S., ed., *Paul Ricoeur: Essays on Biblical Interpretation*, London: SPCK, 1981.
Murray, Edward L., *Imaginative Thinking and Human Existence*, Pittsburgh, PA: Duquesne University Press, 1986.
Myers, Benjamin, *Christ the Stranger: The Theology of Rowan Williams*, Edinburgh: T&T Clark, 2012.
——, 'Rowan Williams and the politics of the empty tomb', *ABC Religion and Ethics Report*, 6 April 2012, https://www.abc.net.au/religion/rowan-williams-and-the-politics-of-the-empty-tomb/10100656, accessed 6.07.2024.
Nanay, Bence, 'Imagination and Perception', in *The Routledge Handbook of Philosophy of Imagination*, edited by Amy Kind, London: Routledge, 2016, pp. 124–34.
Newlands, George, *The Transformative Imagination: Rethinking Intercultural Theology*, Aldershot: Ashgate, 2004.
Nielsen, Niels C., Jr, 'Przywara's Philosophy of the "Analogia Entis"', *The Review of Metaphysics* 5.4 (1952), pp. 599–620, https://www.jstor.org/stable/20123292.
Oakes, Edward T., and David Moss, eds, *The Cambridge Companion to Hans Urs von Balthasar*, Cambridge: Cambridge University Press, 2004.
Oakes, Kenneth, 'The Cross and the *Analogia Entis* in Erich Przywara', in *The Analogy of Being: Invention of the Antichrist or the Wisdom of God*, edited by Thomas Joseph White, Grand Rapids, MA: William B. Eerdmans, 2011, pp. 147–71.

# BIBLIOGRAPHY

O'Connell, Robert J., *Soundings in St Augustine's Imagination*, New York: Fordham University Press, 1994.

O'Donoghue, Noel, 'A Theology of Beauty', in *The Analogy of Beauty: The Theology of Hans Urs Von Balthasar*, edited by John Riches, Edinburgh: T&T Clark, 1986, pp. 1–10.

Oliver, Simon, 'Review of *The Edge of Words*', *Religious Studies* 52.4 (2016), pp. 573–6.

Paparella, Emanuel, 'The Uniqueness of Vico's Poetic Philosophy', https://metanexus.net/uniqueness-giambattista-vicos-poetic-philosophy/, accessed 6.07.2024.

Petry, Paulo Padilla, and Fernando Hernández Hernández, 'Jacques Lacan's Conception of Desire in a Course for Fine Arts Students', *Visual Arts Research* 36.2 (2010), pp. 63–74.

Pickstock, C. J. C., 'Matter and Mattering: The Metaphysics of Rowan Williams', *Modern Theology* 31.4 (2015), pp. 599–617.

Platter, Jonathan M., 'Holiness in Excess: Between Holiness and Metaphysics in the Wake of Rowan Williams', *The Heythrop Journal* 62.5 (2021), pp. 916–27.

Polanyi, Michael, *Personal Knowledge: Towards a Post-Critical Philosophy*, London: Routledge, 1998.

———, *The Tacit Dimension*, with a new Foreword by Amartya Sen, Chicago, IL: University of Chicago Press, 2009.

Przywara, Erich, *Analogia Entis – Metaphysics: Original Structure and Universal Rhythm*, translated by John R. Betz and David Bentley Hart, Grand Rapids, MI: William B. Eerdmans, 2014.

Rausch, Thomas P., *Eschatology, Liturgy, and Christology: Toward Recovering an Eschatological Imagination*, Collegeville, MN: Liturgical Press, 2012.

Reagan, Charles E., and David Stewart, eds, *The Philosophy of Paul Ricoeur: An Anthology of His Work*, Boston, MA: Beacon Press, 1978.

Reek, Jennifer, *A Poetics of Church: Reading and Writing Sacred Spaces of Poetic Dwelling*, London: Routledge, 2017.

Resch, Dustin, 'Christ and Contemplation: Doctrine and Spirituality in the Theology of Rowan Williams', *Anglican Theological Review* 97.2 (2015), pp. 219–38.

Riches, John, ed., *The Analogy of Beauty: The Theology of Hans Urs von Balthasar*, Edinburgh: T&T Clark, 1986.

Ricoeur, Paul, *Figuring the Sacred: Religion, Narrative, and Imagination*, translated by David Pellauer, Minneapolis, MN: Fortress Press, 1995.

———, 'The Function of Fiction in Shaping Reality', in *A Ricoeur Reader: Reflection and Imagination*, edited by Mario J. Valdes, Hemel Hempstead: Harvester Wheatsheaf, 1991, pp. 117–36.

———, *Philosophical Anthropology: Writings and Lectures*, Volume 3, translated by David Pellauer, edited by Johann Michel and Jérôme Porée, Cambridge: Polity Press, 2016.

———, *The Rule of Metaphor: Multi-Disciplinary Studies in the Creation of Meaning in Language*, translated by Robert Czerny with Kathleen McLaughlin and John Costello, London: Routledge & Kegan Paul, 1977.

———, *Time and Narrative*, translated by Kathleen McLaughlin and David Pellauer, Chicago, IL: University of Chicago Press, 1984.

———, *Lectures on Ideology and Utopia*, edited and with an Introduction by G. H. Taylor, New York: Columbia University Press, 1986.

———, *From Text to Action: Essays in Hermeneutics, II*, translated by K. Blarney and J. B. Thompson, Evanston, IL: Northwestern University Press, 2008.

Rob, Fennell, ed., *Both Sides of the Wardrobe: C. S. Lewis, Theological Imagination and Everyday Discipleship*, Eugene, OR: Resource Publications, 2015.

Robinson, David C., ed., *God's Grandeur: The Arts in Imagination and Theology*, Maryknoll, NY: Orbis Books, 2007.

Roche, Mark W., 'Introduction to Hegel's Theory of Tragedy', *PhaenEx* 1.2 (2006), pp. 11–20.

Russell, Matheson, ed., *On Rowan Williams: Critical Essays*, Eugene, OR: Cascade Books, 2009.

Sartre, Jean-Paul, *The Imaginary: A Phenomenological Psychology of the Imagination*, translated by Jonathan Webber, New York: Routledge, 2003.

Scruton, Roger, *Art and Imagination: A Study in the Philosophy of Mind*, London: Routledge & Kegan Paul, 1982.

Sepper, Dennis L., 'Descartes', in *The Routledge Handbook of Philosophy of Imagination*, edited by Amy Kind, London: Routledge, 2016, pp. 27–39.

Shaviro, Steven, 'Whitehead on Causality and Perception', http://www.shaviro.com/Blog/?p=1274, accessed 27.06.2024.

Sherman, Jacob, 'Metaphysics and the Redemption of Sacrifice: On René Girard and Charles Williams', *Heythrop Journal* 51.1 (2010), pp. 45–59.

Shortt, Rupert, *Rowan Williams: An Introduction*, Harrisburg, PA: Morehouse, 2003.

———, *God's Advocates: Christian Thinkers in Conversation*, Grand Rapids, MI: William B. Eerdmans, 2005.

———, *Rowan's Rule: The Biography of the Archbishop*, revised edition, London: Hodder & Stoughton, 2014.

Smith, Jason M., 'Must We Say Anything of an "Immanent" Trinity? Schleiermacher and Rowan Williams on an "Abstruce" and "Fruitless" Doctrine', *Anglican Theological Review* 98.3 (2016), pp. 495–512.

Smith, Matthew, 'The Disincarnate Text: Ritual Poetics in Herbert, Paul, Williams, and Levinas', *Christianity and Literature* 66.3 (2017), pp. 363–84.

Soskice, Janet Martin, *Metaphor and Religious Language*, Oxford: Clarendon Press, 1985.

Spaulding, Shannon, 'Imagination through Knowledge', in *Knowledge Through Imagination*, edited by Amy Kind and Peter Kung, Oxford: Oxford University Press, 2016, pp. 207–26.

Steiner, George, *Real Presences*, Chicago, IL: University of Chicago Press, 1991.

Stokes, Dustin, 'Imagination and Creativity', in *The Routledge Handbook of Philosophy of Imagination*, edited by Amy Kind, London: Routledge, 2016, pp. 247–61.

Taylor, Charles, *Sources of the Self: The Making of the Modern Identity*, Cambridge: Cambridge University Press, 1989.

———, *A Secular Age*, Cambridge, MA: Belknap Press, 2007.

Thagard, Paul, and Cameron Shelly, 'Emotional Analogies and Analogical Inference', in *The Analogical Mind: Perspectives from Cognitive Science*, edited by D. Gentner et al., Cambridge, MA: The MIT Press, 2001, pp. 335–62.

Thiessen, Gesa E., ed., *Theological Aesthetics: A Reader*, London: SCM Press, 2004.

Thomas, R. S., *Collected Poems 1945–1990*, London: Phoenix, 1993.

Tracy, David, *The Analogical Imagination: Christian Theology and the Culture of Pluralism*, New York: Crossroad, 1981.

Trapani, John G., Jr, *Poetry, Beauty, and Contemplation: The Complete Aesthetics of Jacques Maritain*, Washington: Catholic University of America Press, 2011.

## BIBLIOGRAPHY

Vainio, Olli-Pekka, 'The Curious Case of *Analogia Entis*: How Metaphysics Affects Ecumenics?', *Studia Theologica* 69.2 (2015), pp. 171–89.

Valdés, Mario J., *A Ricoeur Reader: Reflection and Imagination*, New York: Harvester Wheatsheaf, 1991.

Van Leeuwen, Neil, 'The Imaginative Agent', in *Knowledge Through Imagination*, edited by Amy Kind and Peter Kung, Oxford: Oxford University Press, 2016, pp. 85–109.

Verene, Donald Philip, *Vico's Science of Imagination*, New York: Cornell University Press, 1991.

Vivian, Tim, 'The Unfamiliar Lord: A Meditation on Four Christ Poems by Rowan Williams', *Anglican Theological Review* 99.3 (2017), pp. 479–98.

Volpe, Medi, '"Taking Time" and "Making Sense": Rowan Williams on the Habits of Theological Imagination', *International Journal of Systematic Theology* 15.3 (2013), pp. 345–60.

Walker, Jeanne Murray, 'A Comment on the State of the Art: Poetry in 2004', *Christianity and Literature* 54.1 (2004), pp. 93–110.

Waller, Giles, '*Felix Culpa*? On Rowan Williams' *The Tragic Imagination*', *Modern Theology* 34.2 (2018), pp. 243–51.

Ward, Graham, *Unimaginable: What We Imagine and What We Can't*, London: I. B. Tauris, 2018.

Warnock, Mary, *Imagination*, London: Faber & Faber, 1976.

Watson, Gerard, 'Saint Augustine's Theory of Language', in *The Rhetoric of St. Augustine of Hippo:* De Doctrina Christiana *and the Search for a Distinctly Christian Rhetoric*, edited by Richard Leo Enos and Roger Thompson, Waco, TX: Baylor University Press, 2008, pp. 247–65.

White, Alan, R., *The Language of Imagination*, Oxford: Basil Blackwell, 1990.

White, Roger M., *Talking About God: The Concept of Analogy and the Problem of Religious Language*, Farnham: Ashgate, 2010.

White, Thomas Joseph, ed., *The Analogy of Being: Invention of the Antichrist or the Wisdom of God*, Grand Rapids, MA: William B. Eerdmans, 2011.

Zittoun, Tania, and Frédéric Cerchia, 'Imagination as Expansion of Experience', *Integrative Psychological and Behavioral Science* 47 (2013), pp. 305–24.

Zittoun, Tania, and Alex Gillespie, *Imagination in Human and Cultural Development*, London: Routledge, 2016.

Zittoun, Tania, and Vlad Glăveanu, eds, *Handbook of Imagination and Culture*, Oxford: Oxford University Press, 2018.

Žižek, Slavoj, *How to Read Lacan*, New York: W.W. Norton, 2006.

# Index

Aeschylus 27
aesthetics 28–9, 55, 168–72
*analogia entis* 4, 62, 63, 68, 203, 206, 217
analogy 62–73, 127, 161, 165, 206
annunciation 23–4
apophasis 3, 8, 10
Aquinas, Thomas 67–8, 83, 90–2, 108, 111, 123
Arabic script 176–8
Aristotle 25, 62, 66–7
art 1, 9, 28–9, 160–4, 166, 201
  *see also* aesthetics
artistic creation 163–70, 210, 218
  *see also* poiesis
Asma, Stephen 32
Augustine 88–90, 101–2, 108
  on language and divine desire 144–8, 205
Avis, Paul 48, 56

Bachelard, Gaston 49
Bailer-Jones, Daniela 66
Balthasar, Hans Urs von 72, 94–5, 160–3, 191
baptism 124
beauty 160–5
becoming 69
Bernard of Clairvaux 108
Betz, Roger 70
Black, Max 66
Body of Christ 123–4

Butler, Edward 131

Calvin 128
Castoriadis, Cornelius 38n14
celebration, theology as 9
Church
  as Body of Christ 120, 123–9, 207
  and purifying of desire 207–8
  as the Spirit's workshop 119–20
Coleridge, Samuel Taylor 29, 36, 49–50
contemplation 130, 208–9
Cox, Michael 12
creation, as a symbolic complex 145
creativity 27, 29, 33, 37, 54–5, 201–2, 209–10
  *see also* poiesis

Darwin, Charles 23
Descartes, René 25–6
desire
  Christ-focused 107
  distortions of 102
  divine 81–95, 110, 143, 161, 207
  erotic 112
  filial 110–11, 207
  human 3, 99–114, 122–3, 207
  and image of God 109
  and imagination 111–14, 119, 126

in Lacan's thought 103–4
mimetic 102–3
nuptial 111–12
transformation of 119–32, 207–8
*see also* divine desire
Diadokos of Photike vii
disaster fantasies 106
distal realm 34
divine energy 95, 101, 113, 204–5, 215
Dostoevsky, Fyodor 106–7, 183–7
dying 216–18

*ekstasis* 88, 90, 110, 131
Eliot, T. S. 201
Emmaus 4
epistemology, and imagination 25–7
*eros* 111, 141–3, 161
Eucharist 123, 127–9, 191, 208
evil 102
excess 13
of love 2–4, 91–5, 111–12, 139
of meaning 55, 147
of speech 178–93

fairy tales 60n79
faith 3, 125
fantasy 100, 104–7, 105–6, 113, 193
Farrer, Austin 84
Felin Uchaf Centre 221
fiction 30, 54, 183–5
figurative realism 56
finite and infinite 84–6, 101, 109, 161
Fraser, Giles 135n52
freedom 72
in imagination 36
Fuentes, Agustín 33

Garrett, Greg 201
Gentner, Dedre 65
Gethsemane 3, 63–5
Gillespie, Alex 34
Girard, René 102–3
Glăveanu, Vlad Petre 33, 34–5
God 9
act of creation 163
glory of 6
love of 2–4, 141–3
presence of 3, 122, 203
redirects human desire 109–10
source of finite objects 108
speaks to us 8, 9
*see also* divine desire; Trinity
Goddard, Giles 137n98
grace 70, 79, 100, 103, 108–14, 126–8, 167, 177–8, 184, 187, 201, 207–8, 219
Gregory of Nyssa 108
Griffiths, Dominic 48

Harrison, Carol 147
Hart, David Bentley 196n85
Heaney, Seamus 200
Hedley, Douglas 27
Hegel, G. W. F. 148–9, 189–90
Henriksen, Jan-Olav 116n53
Heraclitus 27
Herbert, George 200
hermeneutics 10
Higton, Mike 97n41
history 54
Hobson, Theo 135n52, 136n74
Hofstadter, Douglas 65–6, 200
holiness 209
Holy Saturday 161–2
Holy Spirit 119–20, 123–7, 132, 208
Holyoak, Keith 65, 66
Homer 27
*homo eucharisticus* 127, 202

# INDEX

hope 126–7, 181, 219
Hume, David 26

icons 100–1, 186–7
ideology 52–3
imagination 1–4, 65, 168–9,
   171–2, 198–210
 and desire 105–6, 112, 114
 and energy 153
 and language 152–3
 and secularism 23–5
 tragic 190–2, 205–6, 216–17
 transformation of 3–4, 129,
   208, 215
incarnation 145–6, 206
intelligence, of divine desire 143
intuition 72–3, 163–6
irony 151, 167, 190–3

Jesus
 as child 81–3
 crucifixion 73–4, 88, 93–4,
   103, 110, 161–2, 180, 206–7,
   221
 as Form of reality 161
 in Gethsemane 3, 63–5, 112
 as heart of creation 73, 83
 human and divine natures 83–6,
   206
 as image of God 109–11, 186
 parables 67
 resurrection 180, 191
 as Son of God 206
 transfiguration 100–1
 and transformation of human
   desire 107, 113–14
 as Word of God 83–5
John of the Cross 92–4, 108, 111,
   112
John, Gwen 180
Johnson, Mark 26–7, 32
Jones, David 166–7, 200

Kant, Immanuel 26–7, 28–9, 36
Kearney, Richard 38n15
*kenosis* 86–8, 94, 110–11, 131,
   162
Kind, Amy 25
Kingdom of God 2, 119, 209
knowledge 91, 111
 and art 168
 connatural 163–4, 172
 context 7
 of God 3
 and imagination 200
 of other people 180
 participatory 168, 210
 personal 30, 37
 poetic 163–4
 of self 104–5
Kokinov, Boicho 65
Kwasniewski, Peter 98n55

Lacan, Jacques 103–5
Lachman, Gary 24
Langer, Susanne 48
language 8, 9, 54, 141–54, 205
 about God 10, 65, 147
 descriptive/representative
   148–9
 engaging with other people
   149–50
 in fiction 183–7
 origin 45
 poetic 178–83
 symbolic 55–7, 148
 in tragedy 187–93
Lodziak, Conrad 52
Logos 50, 60n83, 205
Long, Stephen 67–8
Lossky, Vladimir 3
Lotto, Lorenzo 23
love 111–12, 204, 215
 artists' 171, 209–10
 *see also* desire

McGilchrist, Ian 24, 52, 200
MacKinnon, Donald 190
Maritain, Jacques 163–7
Martin, Michael 38n14
Mary (mother of Jesus)
  annunciation 23
  and Child (statue) 158–60
Masterman, Margaret 179
matter, and mind 143–4
Maximus the Confessor 90, 110–11, 207
meaning-making 36, 45–57
Meister Eckhardt 108
memory 201
metaphor 33, 50–2, 66, 204
Midgley, Mary 23, 24, 52
Milbank, John 165, 198, 201
mimesis 111
mission 208–9
Modell, Arnold 32–3
monastic life 129–30
moral imagination 202
Myers, Benjamin 107, 135n52
myths 52–4

nature, in Coleridge's thought 29
Nicholas of Cusa 84

O'Connor, Flannery 167
Otto, Rudolf 96n5
'Our Lady of Vladimir' (icon) 81–3

parody 193
peacemaking 130
perception 168, 176
*Philokalia* 99
Plato 27, 62
poetic intuition 163–6
poetic symbols 49–50
poetry 163–6, 178–83

*poiesis* 157–72, 176–93
Polanyi, Michael 24
prayer 125
pregnancy vii, 206
proper proportionality 68–9
Przywara, Erich 4, 68–73, 203, 206
Pseudo-Dionysius 90

reality, symbolic 29
reason 39n28, 53, 163, 166, 169, 215, 219
representation 8–10, 45
revelation 8, 55
Ricoeur, Paul 10, 30–1, 36, 49, 52–5, 58n17, 96n26
Rule of St Benedict 130

sacraments 7, 208
sacrifice 102–3
saints 208–9
Sander, Emmanuel 65–6
Sartre, Jean-Paul 30, 36
scapegoats 102–3
secularism 1, 23
self, formed by language 150–1
self-knowledge 104–5, 149, 180–1, 189–90
Serafim (saint) 121–2, 131
Shakespeare, William, tragedy 188–9
Shortt, Rupert 97n42, 219n4
silence 151
solitude 130
Soskice, Janet 56
Spaulding, Sharon 44n151
Steiner, George 23
suffering 2, 137n98
  tragic 190–1
symbolization 36, 45–57, 153
symbols 48–50, 55–7
synthesis, in imagination 36

Taylor, Charles 33–4
Thagard, Paul 66
theatre 188
Thomas, R. S. 46–8, 201
tragedy 187–92
transcendent tradition 37
 and imagination 27–31
trigger-resource-outcome model 34–5
Trinity 74–5, 86, 90–5, 110–11, 161–2, 204
truth 10, 11, 105
 and the imagination 198
 revealed by art 164

utopias 53

Van Gogh, Vincent 48
Van Leeuwen, Neil 42n109
*via negativa* 3
Vico, Giambattista 27
violence 102–3

Western culture 215
White, Roger 66–7
Whitehead, A. H. 24
Williams, Rowan
 aesthetics 160, 166, 168–72, 209–10
 aim as Archbishop 215
 and analogy 72–4, 162
 ecclesiology 126
 on imagination 11–12, 23, 152–3, 198–210
 on language 45, 143–54, 178–83, 199
 and Paul Ricoeur 10, 54–5
 poems 5, 46, 63–4, 81–2, 86–7, 120–2, 141–3, 158–60, 176–8, 216–17, 220–2
 his poetic method 11–12, 179–82, 221–2

Zittoun, Tania 33, 34–5

www.ingramcontent.com/pod-product-compliance
Lightning Source LLC
Chambersburg PA
CBHW022048290426
44109CB00014B/1024